Statistical Modeling for Management

To a number of very patient people (You know who you are), Andrea, Alex, …and all Portuguese waiters.

Graeme Hutcheson
Luiz Moutinho

Statistical Modeling for Management

Graeme D. Hutcheson
Luiz Moutinho

Los Angeles • London • New Delhi • Singapore

© Graeme D Hutcheson and Luiz Moutinho 2008

First published 2008

Apart from any fair dealing for the purposes of research or private study, or criticism or review, as permitted under the Copyright, Designs and Patents Act, 1988, this publication may be reproduced, stored or transmitted in any form, or by any means, only with the prior permission in writing of the publishers, or in the case of reprographic reproduction, in accordance with the terms of licences issued by the Copyright Licensing Agency. Enquiries concerning reproduction outside those terms should be sent to the publishers.

SAGE Publications Ltd
1 Oliver's Yard
55 City Road
London EC1Y 1SP

SAGE Publications Inc.
2455 Teller Road
Thousand Oaks, California 91320

SAGE Publications India Pvt Ltd
B 1/I 1 Mohan Cooperative Industrial Area
Mathura Road
New Delhi 110 044

SAGE Publications Asia-Pacific Pte Ltd
33 Pekin Street #02-01
Far East Square
Singapore 048763

Library of Congress Control Number: 2007931607

British Library Cataloguing in Publication data

A catalogue record for this book is available from the British Library

ISBN 978-0-7619-7011-8
ISBN 978-0-7619-7012-5 (pbk)

Typeset by C&M Digitals (P) Ltd., Chennai, India
Printed in Great Britain by The Cromwell Press Ltd, Trowbridge, Wiltshire
Printed on paper from sustainable resources

Contents

List of Tables ix
List of Figures xv
Preface xvii

1 Measurement Scales   **1**
  1.1 Continuous Data 2
    1.1.1 The underlying distribution 2
    1.1.2 Recording the data 3
    1.1.3 Applying mathematical operations 5
  1.2 Ordered Categorical Data 6
    1.2.1 The underlying distribution 6
    1.2.2 Recording the data 7
    1.2.3 Applying mathematical operations 11
  1.3 Unordered Categorical Data 13
    1.3.1 The underlying distribution 13
    1.3.2 Recording the data 13
    1.3.3 Applying mathematical operations 14
  1.4 Conclusion 15

2 Modeling Continuous Data   **17**
  2.1 The Generalized Linear Model 17
  2.2 The Ordinary Least-Squares Model 19
    2.2.1 Simple OLS regression 19
        Computing and interpreting model parameters 21
        Predicting the response variable 22
        Goodness-of-fit statistics 23
    2.2.2 Multiple OLS regression 29
        Computing and interpreting model parameters 29
        Predicting the response variable 31
        Goodness-of-fit statistics 31
  2.3 Categorical Explanatory Variables 35
  2.4 Analyzing Simple Experimental Designs for Continuous Data 36
    2.4.1 Unrelated groups design 36
        Comparing two groups using OLS regression 36

	Comparing more than two groups using OLS regression	42
	Comparing two groups using a t-test	46
	Comparing more than two groups using ANOVA	47
2.4.2	Related groups designs	47
	Comparing two groups using OLS regression	48
	Comparing more than two groups using OLS regression	53
	Comparing two groups using a t-test	54
	Comparing more than two groups using ANOVA	55
2.5	Conclusion	55

3 Modeling Dichotomous Data   57
- 3.1 The Generalized Linear Model 57
- 3.2 The Logistic Regression Model 62
  - 3.2.1 Simple logistic regression 62
    - Computing and Interpreting Model Parameters 63
    - Predicted probabilities 65
    - Goodness-of-fit statistics 66
  - 3.2.2 Multiple Logistic Regression 69
    - Computing and interpreting model parameters 71
    - Predicted probabilities 73
    - Goodness-of-fit statistics 73
  - 3.2.3 Categorical explanatory variables 76
    - Computing and interpreting model parameters 77
    - Predicted probabilities 78
    - Goodness-of-fit statistics 80
- 3.3 Analyzing Simple Experimental Designs for Dichotomous Data 82
- 3.4 Conclusion 82

4 Modeling Ordered Data   83
- 4.1 The Generalized Linear Model 83
- 4.2 The Proportional Odds Model 83
  - 4.2.1 Simple proportional odds 85
    - Checking the proportional odds assumption 86
    - Computing and interpreting model parameters 88
    - Predicted probabilities 89
    - Goodness-of-fit statistics 90
  - 4.2.2 Multiple proportional odds 93
    - Checking the proportional odds assumption 94
    - Computing and interpreting model parameters 94
    - Predicted probabilities 96
    - Goodness-of-fit statistics 97
  - 4.2.3 Categorical explanatory variables 100
- 4.3 Analyzing Simple Experimental Designs for Ordered Data 106
  - 4.3.1 Unrelated groups design 107
  - 4.3.2 Related groups design 113
- 4.4 Conclusion 119

CONTENTS

5 Modeling Unordered Data   **121**
- 5.1 The Generalized Linear Model 121
- 5.2 The Multi-nomial Logistic Regression Model 122
  - 5.2.1 Simple multi-nomial logistic regression 123
    - Computing and interpreting model parameters 123
    - Predicted probabilities 126
    - Goodness-of-fit statistics 127
  - 5.2.2 Multiple multi-nomial logistic regression including categorical variables 130
    - Computing and interpreting model parameters 131
    - Predicted probabilities 133
    - Goodness-of-fit statistics 134
- 5.3 Analyzing Simple Experimental Designs for Unordered Data 137
  - 5.3.1 Unrelated groups design 137
  - 5.3.2 Related groups design 145
- 5.4 Conclusion 152

6 Neural Networks   **153**
- 6.1 Cognitive Theory – Nodes and Links – Mental Manipulation of Data . . 153
  - 6.1.1 Roots: A parallel model of the brain 153
  - 6.1.2 Neural networks embody a process of learning 154
  - 6.1.3 Implementation of NNs 157
  - 6.1.4 The backpropagation algorithm (BP) 158
    - Details of the algorithm 161
  - 6.1.5 Basic properties of the SOM 164
  - 6.1.6 Potential benefits of the approach 167
  - 6.1.7 Business applications 167
- 6.2 Example-Applications 168
  - 6.2.1 The research model 168
  - 6.2.2 Analysis of the data 170
  - 6.2.3 Labeling of hidden nodes: male buyers 171
  - 6.2.4 Labeling of hidden nodes: female buyers 172
  - 6.2.5 Findings: male car buyers 172
  - 6.2.6 Findings: female car buyers 174
  - 6.2.7 Conclusions and implications 175

7 Approximate Algorithms for Management Problems   **177**
- 7.1 Genetic Algorithms 177
  - 7.1.1 Site location analysis using genetic algorithms 179
  - 7.1.2 Chromosome representation 180
  - 7.1.3 Fitness function 180
  - 7.1.4 Genetic operators 181
  - 7.1.5 Simple illustration 181
- 7.2 Tabu Search 182
  - 7.2.1 Example 183

	7.2.2 Application of tabu search to segmentation	183
7.3	Simulated Annealing	184
	7.3.1 Sales territory design using simulated annealing	185
	7.3.2 Information about a single SCU	186
	7.3.3 The model	187
	7.3.4 Contiguity	188
	7.3.5 Equal workload	188
	7.3.6 Equality of sales potential	188
	7.3.7 Profit	189
	7.3.8 Application of simulated annealing	190

8 Other Statistical, Mathematical and Co-pattern Modeling Techniques   191

8.1	Discriminant Analysis	191
8.2	Automatic Interaction Detection (AID)	191
8.3	Logical Type Discriminant Models: The C5 Algorithm	192
8.4	Multidimensional Scaling	198
8.5	Conjoint Analysis	199
8.6	Correspondence Analysis	200
8.7	Latent Analysis	201
8.8	Fuzzy Sets	203
8.9	Fuzzy Decision Trees	205
8.10	Artificial Intelligence	206
8.11	Expert Systems	207
	8.11.1 Method based on marketing main advantages main limitations applications	207
8.12	Fuzzy Logic and Fuzzy Expert Systems	208
8.13	Rough Set Theory	208
8.14	Variable Precision Rough Sets (VPRS)	210
	8.14.1 An overview of VPRS	210
8.15	Dempster-Shafer Theory	212
8.16	Chaos Theory	215
8.17	Data Mining	217
	8.17.1 Mining and refining data	217
	8.17.2 Siftware	218
	8.17.3 Invasion of the data snatchers	218
	8.17.4 Mining with query tools	219
8.18	Data Mining	220
	8.18.1 A computing perspective on data mining	221
	8.18.2 Data mining tools	221
	8.18.3 Try new data-mining techniques – they can overcome, augment traditional stat analysis	221

References 223

Index 231

List of Tables

1 Measurement Scales   **1**
- 1.1 Examples of interval and ratio scales 4
- 1.2 An example of categorized continuous data 5
- 1.3 Ordered categorical coding of army rank: example I 7
- 1.4 Ordered categorical coding of army rank: example II 8
- 1.5 Unordered categorical coding of army rank 8
- 1.6 Continuous variables coded as ordered categories 9
- 1.7 A continuous variable coded as ordered categorical data 10
- 1.8 Representing age using ordered categories 10
- 1.9 Mis-coding an ordered categorical variable 11
- 1.10 Highest educational attainment 12
- 1.11 Unordered categorical data: coding example I 13
- 1.12 Unordered categorical data: coding example II 14
- 1.13 Number of cars sold in a year 14

2 Modeling Continuous Data   **17**
-     **Simple OLS regression** 19
- 2.1 Data: ice cream consumption 20
- 2.2 Regression parameters 22
- 2.3 Predictions of consumption 23
- 2.4 Computing the deviance for the model "consumption = α" 25
- 2.5 Computing the deviance for the model "consumption = α + β temperature" 26
- 2.6 Assessing significance by comparing model deviances 27
- 2.7 Analysis of deviance table: the significance of variables 28
- 2.8 Estimating the significance of individual parameters using t-statistics 28
-     **Multiple OLS regression** 29
- 2.9 Regression parameters 30
- 2.10 Confidence intervals 30
- 2.11 Predictions of consumption 32

2.12	Assessing significance by comparing model deviances: individual variables	32
2.13	Assessing significance by comparing model deviances: groups of variables	33
2.14	Analysis of deviance table: the significance of variables	34
2.15	Estimating the significance of individual parameters using t-statistics	35
	Unrelated groups designs (2 groups)	36
2.16	Data: the price of whiskey (comparing 2 groups)	37
2.17	Price of whiskey: "ownership" dummy coded	39
2.18	Regression parameters	39
2.19	Confidence intervals	39
2.20	Assessing significance by comparing model deviances	41
2.21	Analysis of deviance table: the significance of variables	41
2.22	Estimating the significance of individual parameters using t-statistics	42
	Unrelated groups designs (3 groups)	42
2.23	Data: the price of whiskey (comparing three groups)	42
2.24	The indicator method of dummy coding "ownership"	43
2.25	Regression parameters	43
2.26	Confidence intervals	44
2.27	Assessing significance by comparing model deviances	45
2.28	Analysis of deviance table: the significance of variables	46
2.29	Estimating the significance of individual parameters using t-statistics	46
2.30	The two group whiskey data: t-test	47
2.31	The three group whiskey data: ANOVA	47
	Related groups designs (2 groups)	47
2.32	Data: quality ratings of stores	48
2.33	Regression parameters	49
2.34	Confidence intervals	50
2.35	Predicting the quality of the stores	51
2.36	Assessing the significance of "store" by comparing model deviances	52
2.37	Assessing the significance of "subject" by comparing model deviances	52
2.38	Analysis of deviance table: the significance of variables	52
2.39	Estimating the significance of individual parameters using t-statistics	53
	Related groups designs (3 groups)	53
2.40	Regression parameters	54
2.41	Analysis of deviance table: the significance of variables	54
2.42	The two group store data: related t-test	55
2.43	The three group store data: related ANOVA	55

LIST OF TABLES

3 Modeling Dichotomous Data — 57
- 3.1 The logit transformation — 61
- **Simple logistic regression** — 62
- 3.2 Data: example for illustrating logistic regression — 63
- 3.3 Regression parameters — 63
- 3.4 Confidence intervals — 65
- 3.5 Predicted probabilities — 66
- 3.6 Assessing significance by comparing model deviances — 68
- 3.7 Analysis of deviance table: the significance of variables — 68
- 3.8 Estimating the significance of individual parameters using the z-statistic — 69
- **Multiple logistic regression** — 69
- 3.9 Regression parameters — 72
- 3.10 Confidence intervals — 72
- 3.11 Predicted probabilities of union membership at a selection of wages and ages — 74
- 3.12 Assessing significance by comparing model deviances — 74
- 3.13 Analysis of deviance table: the significance of variables — 75
- 3.14 Estimating the significance of individual parameters using the z-statistic — 75
- **Categorical explanatory variables** — 76
- 3.15 Deviation dummy variable coding of 'occupation' — 76
- 3.16 Regression parameters — 78
- 3.17 Predicted probabilities of union membership — 79
- 3.18 Assessing significance by comparing model deviances — 80
- 3.19 Analysis of deviance table: the significance of variables — 81
- 3.20 Estimating the significance of individual parameters using the z-statistic — 81

4 Modeling Ordered Data — 83
- **Simple proportional odds** — 85
- 4.1 Data: ice cream consumption represented as ordered categories — 86
- 4.2 Test of the proportional odds assumption — 88
- 4.3 Regression parameters — 88
- 4.4 Confidence intervals — 89
- 4.5 Predicted consumption — 90
- 4.6 Assessing significance by comparing model deviances — 92
- 4.7 Analysis of deviance table: the significance of variables — 92
- 4.8 Estimating the significance of individual parameters using t-statistics — 93
- **Multiple proportional odds** — 93
- 4.9 Test of the proportional odds assumption — 94
- 4.10 Regression parameters — 96
- 4.11 Confidence intervals — 96
- 4.12 Predicted probabilities — 97

4.13	Assessing significance by comparing model deviances	98
4.14	Analysis of deviance table: the significance of variables	99
4.15	Estimating the significance of individual parameters using t-statistics	99
4.16	Comparing proportional odds and OLS regression models	100
	Categorical explanatory variables	100
4.17	Test of the proportional odds assumption	102
4.18	Regression parameters	103
4.19	Confidence intervals	103
4.20	Predicted probabilities	104
4.21	Assessing significance by comparing model deviances	105
4.22	Analysis of deviance table: the significance of variables	105
4.23	Estimating the significance of individual parameters using t-values	106
	Unrelated groups designs	107
4.24	Data: ranked price of whiskey	108
4.25	Test of the proportional odds assumption	108
4.26	Regression parameters	109
4.27	Confidence intervals	110
4.28	Predicted probabilities	110
4.29	Assessing significance by comparing model deviances	111
4.30	Estimating the significance of individual parameters using t-values (reference category for variable 'funded' = state-private partnership)	111
4.31	Estimating the significance of individual parameters using t-values (reference category for variable 'funded'= private)	112
	Related groups designs	113
4.32	Data: ranked quality ratings of stores	114
4.33	Test of the proportional odds assumption	115
4.34	Regression parameters	116
4.35	Confidence intervals	117
4.36	Predicted probabilities	118
4.37	Assessing significance by comparing model deviances	118
4.38	Analysis of deviance table: significance of variables	118
4.39	Estimating the significance of individual parameters using t-values	119

5 Modeling Unordered Data — 121

	Simple multi-nomial logistic regression	123
5.1	Data: supermarket choice	124
5.2	Regression parameters	125
5.3	Confidence intervals	126
5.4	Predicted probabilities	127
5.5	Assessing significance by comparing model deviances	128

LIST OF TABLES

5.6	Analysis of deviance table: significance of variables	128
5.7	Estimating the significance of individual parameters using Wald and z-statistics (reference supermarket = Sainsburys)	129
5.8	Estimating the significance of individual parameters using Wald and z-statistics (reference supermarket = Solo)	130
	Multiple multi-nomial logistic regression	130
5.9	Regression parameters	132
5.10	Confidence intervals	134
5.11	Predicted probabilities	134
5.12	Assessing significance by comparing model deviances	135
5.13	Analysis of deviance table: significance of variables	136
5.14	Estimating the significance of individual parameters using Wald and z-statistics	136
	Unrelated groups designs	137
5.15	Data: unordered categorical data from an unrelated groups design	139
5.16	Contingency table	139
5.17	Regression parameters	141
5.18	Confidence intervals	142
5.19	Predicted probabilities	142
5.20	Assessing significance by comparing model deviances	143
5.21	Analysis of deviance table: significance of variables	143
5.22	Estimating the significance of individual parameters using Wald and z-statistics (outcome reference category = accept)	144
5.23	Estimating the significance of individual parameters using Wald and z-statistics (outcome reference category = undecided)	144
	Related groups designs	145
5.24	Data: unordered categorical data from a related groups design	146
5.25	Regression parameters	147
5.26	Confidence intervals	148
5.27	Predicted probabilities	149
5.28	Assessing significance by comparing model deviances	149
5.29	Analysis of deviance table: significance of variables	150
5.30	Estimating the significance of individual parameters using Wald and z-statistics	151

6	**Neural Networks**	**153**
6.1	Network weights for male buyers	170
6.2	Network weights for female buyers	171
6.3	Labels given to the hidden nodes	172

7	**Approximate Algorithms for Management Problems**	**177**
8	**Other Statistical, Mathematical and Co-pattern Modeling Techniques**	**191**
	8.1 5 set of propositional rules (C5 Ra)	195
	8.2 5 set of propositional rules (C5 Rb)	196
	8.3 Classification precision	197
	8.4 Fuzzy set theory	204
	8.5 Example of a decision table	211

List of Figures

1 Measurement Scales   **1**
    1.1   The relationship the attribute, the data and the analysis   2

2 Modeling Continuous Data   **17**
    2.1   A scatterplot showing the relationship between ice cream consumption and outdoor temperature and the associated OLS regression model . .   21
    2.2   Residuals for the model "consumption = α"   24
    2.3   Residuals for the model "consumption = $\alpha + \beta$ temperature"   25
    2.4   A pictorial representation of an unrelated groups design   38
    2.5   A pictorial representation of a dependent groups design   48

3 Modeling Dichotomous Data   **57**
    3.1   Success and the experience of the sales staff   58
    3.2   The probability of success and the experience of the sales staff   59
    3.3   The log odds of success and the experience of the sales staff   60
    3.4   A logit model of the probability of success and the experience of the sales staff   62
    3.5   Union membership and wage   64
    3.6   Logistic regression model of union membership and wage   67
    3.7   Probability of being a union member and age   70
    3.8   Relationship between wage and age   71
    3.9   Probability of being a union member for different genders and occupations   77

4 Modeling Ordered Data   **83**
    4.1   Temperature and consumption level of ice cream   87
    4.2   Predicted probabilities for each group given temperature   91
    4.3   Boxplots showing relationships between each explanatory variable and the level of consumption   94
    4.4   Matrix scatterplot showing relationships between the explanatory variables   95

4.5	Level of consumption and type of advertising used	101
4.6	A pictorial representation of an unrelated groups design	108
4.7	Average ranked price of whiskey for each type of ownership	113
4.8	A pictorial representation of a dependent groups design	114
4.9	Average rated quality for each store	117

5 Modeling Unordered Data — 121

5.1	Selected supermarket and average salary	125
5.2	Selected supermarket, average salary and car use	131
5.3	Relationship between average salary and car use	132
5.4	A pictorial representation of an unrelated groups design	138
5.5	An association plot	140
5.6	A pictorial representation of a dependent groups design	145

6 Neural Networks — 153

6.1	A neural network with one hidden layer	156
6.2	The sigmoid function	160
6.3	Connections operate between all inputs and all Kohonen nodes	165
6.4	Neural network used in car buyer analysis	169

7 Approximate Algorithms for Management Problems — 177

7.1	Example of a move applied to a tree with five terminal nodes	183

8 Other Statistical, Mathematical and Co-pattern Modeling Techniques — 191

8.1	Procedural steps for correspondence analysis	201
8.2	Success and the experience of the sales staff	202
8.3	Output of logistic equation for varying r	216

Preface

This book is aimed at doctoral students and researchers working in Management and other social science subjects. It aims to provide a resource for training in basic data analysis and also provide some information about a number of more specialized techniques used in the management field. The contents have been compiled and written over a number of years during which time Graeme Hutcheson and Luiz Moutinho have been involved in teaching postgraduate students, academic staff and researchers research methods, data analysis and statistical modeling. The material presented here provides some basic notes for these courses and we are indebted to the many students who have attended our training sessions and commented on the notes and examples. Although some complex issues are addressed in later chapters, the main body of the book attempts to explain how generalized linear models can be applied to a great range of common research questions and research designs for different types of data. In particular, this material is designed to be accessible to all postgraduate students. Although an extensive statistical or mathematical knowledge is not assumed, readers might benefit from attending an introductory course on statistics, or by consulting one of the many basic statistical text books that are available.

This book can be broadly divided into two parts, one that deals with generalized linear models (GLMs) and one that deals with a number of other techniques that may be applied in management research. As the objective of the former is for teaching, these chapters are accompanied by data sets that can be analysed and the results compared to the output provided. The outputs are given in a software-neutral manner so that these can be compared to the outputs from a number of different statistical packages (in Management, SPSS is often used, although we strongly recommend the use of R, a package that is described in more detail below).

The first five chapters of the book describe how data can be classified, coded and analyzed using a number of generalized linear modeling techniques. The aim has been to provide a theoretically-consistent method for modeling continuous, ordered and unordered categorical data. The analysis of experimental data is discussed within the main chapters in a way that makes clear the links between the hypothesis tests and the regression models. Chapters 6, 7 and 8 deal with other techniques (such as neural networks and approximate algorithms) that may also be of interest to researchers in the management field.

The data that are used in this book are available for download at www.sagepub.co.uk/hutcheson_moutinho and are saved as tab-delimited text to enable them to be simply imported into a number of statistical packages and spreadsheets. The data used and where they are presented in the book are shown in the Table below.

The statistics for this book were mainly analyzed using R (see the R Development Core Team, 2007 and the R website at http://www.r-project.org/) and a number of associated packages (the most notable being the graphical user interface 'R Commander', written by John Fox, 2005). The use of R Commander, in particular, has enabled us to teach statistics to groups with little or no previous statistical experience whilst utilizing the power of the R programme. This combination of packages has proved to be so successful that and we have now adopted R as the only statistics package we use for our courses. Its ease of use along with its free download, multi-platform capabilities and extraordinary range of techniques, manuals (in many languages), examples and a generous community make it a wonderful resource for all data analysts.

Even though R may not be the easiest package to master, there are many resources available to help with analysis and graphics. Some of the resources I have found to be particularly useful have been Venables, Smith and the R Development Core Team (2002), Dalgaard (2002), Crawley (2005), Verzani (2005), Faraway (2005), Fox (2002), Venables and Ripley (2002), Murrell (2006) and Maindonald and Braun (2003).

This book was typeset by Graeme Hutcheson at Manchester University using LaTeX and a debt of gratitude is owed to Donald Knuth, the creator of TeX (Knuth, 1984), Leslie Lamport who built this into the LaTeX documentation system, and to the many contributors who freely give their time and expertise to support this package (see, for example, Grätzer (2000), Kopka and Daly (2003), Lipkin (1999) and Mittelbach et al., (2004)). Full details of the LaTeX project are available on the web at 'http://www.latex-project.org/'.

Data sets used in this book

Chapter 2	
IceCream.txt	(Table 2.1)
Whiskey2group.txt	(Table 2.16)
Whiskey3group.txt	(Table 2.23)
Quality2group.txt	(Table 2.32)
Quality3group.txt	(Table 2.32)
Chapter 3	
Union.txt	(Table 3.2)
	also available as file CPS_85_Wages from http://lib.stat.cmu.edu/datasets/
Chapter 4	
IceCreamOrdered.txt	(Table 4.1)
Whiskey3groupOrdered.txt	(Table 4.24)
Quality3groupOrdered.txt	(Table 4.32)
Chapter 5	
Stores.txt	(Table 5.1)
DecisionUnrelated.txt	Table 5.15
DecisionRelated.txt	Table 5.24

Graeme Hutcheson, Manchester University
Luiz Moutinho, Glasgow University

CHAPTER 1
Measurement Scales

In this chapter we describe ways in which data can be recorded and highlight the relationship between the actual variable being measured (the attribute) and the measurement itself (the recorded data). This distinction is an important one and forms the basis of measurement theory.

> The fundamental idea behind measurement theory is that measurements are not the same as the attribute being measured. Hence, if you want to draw conclusions about the attribute, you must take into account the nature of the correspondence between the attribute and the measurements.
>
> Sarle, 1995

The measurements made and recorded in the data do not necessarily describe the attribute accurately. This is important as the analysis and the resulting conclusions may only apply to the data even though one usually wishes to make conclusions about the attribute. Such links can only be made if the data and the attribute correspond directly. Figure 1.1 shows the relationship between the attribute, the data and the conclusions and suggests that conclusions about the attribute can only be justified if there is a direct correspondence between the attribute and the data. This is not always the case.

The ideas behind measurement theory are particularly relevant for management research as a wide variety of variables are used, many of which do not have a one-to-one correspondence between the attribute being measured and the measurement itself. The types of data commonly collected and recorded vary from physical, 'observable' information such as height, weight, heart rate, earnings, marital status, gender, and religious affiliation, to mental, essentially unobservable information, such as attitudes, stereotypes, beliefs and feelings. Although some variables are easily converted into numbers, others require some work and thought before they can be represented meaningfully.

There are many ways to categorize data and a number of different schemes have been proposed that utilize a variety of categories and sub-divisions (see, for example, Agresti and Finlay, 1997; Barford, 1985; Lindsey, 1995; Loewenthal, 2001; Rose and Sullivan, 1993; Sarle, 1995). Here we shall distinguish between just 3 scales of measurement, continuous, ordered categorical and unordered categorical. Distinguishing

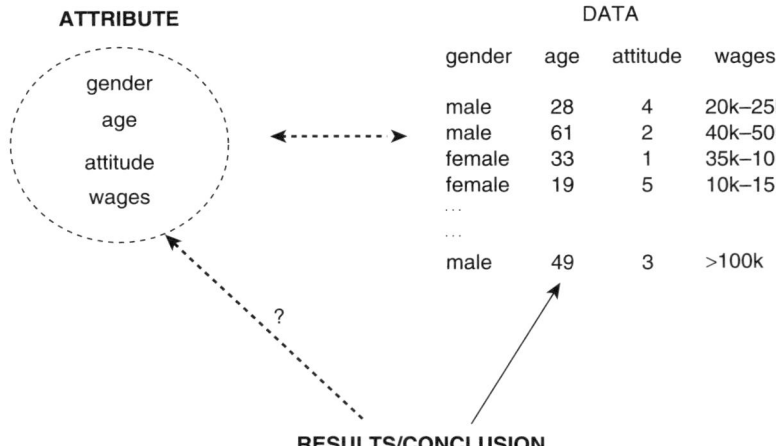

Figure 1.1 *The relationship the attribute, the data and the analysis*

between these 3 allows a wide range of statistical analyses to be applied and many of the important concepts related to modeling to be dealt with, particularly within the generalized linear modeling group of techniques. It is worth noting that assigning variables to particular scales of measurement is not always obvious as some data may be legitimately classified in a variety of ways depending on the properties of the attribute, the coding scheme used to represent this attribute, the number of observations recorded, the specific research questions being asked and the way the variable interacts with other variables in the model. The classification of data into different scales of measurement is not, therefore, an exact science. We will, however, concentrate on practical considerations by showing how variables may be profitably classified for analytical purposes.

The identification of the level of measurement used to represent a variable is important as it is this that dictates which mathematical operations can be applied to the data and ultimately the statistical analysis techniques that can be used. This is particularly important when applying generalized linear models (the subject of Chapters 2 to 5) as it is the level of measurement which identifies the analysis technique that can be applied.

1.1 Continuous Data

1.1.1 The underlying distribution

A data point (a single observation) on a continuous scale can, in theory at least, assume any value between the highest and lowest points. The only restriction on the number of values possible, is the accuracy of the measuring instrument. For example, the weight of a person can be measured fairly crudely in pounds using a set of bathroom scales, or

Continuous Data 3

measured much more accurately in grams using a professional set of medical scales. A person can, within certain limits at least, be any weight.

When describing continuous data, it is useful to distinguish 2 categories, interval and ratio, as this distinction is often made in the literature. However, for analytical purposes, the distinction between the 2 is not usually important as few statistics are applicable to only one of these scales.

Ratio scale: A ratio scale is characterized by a common and constant unit of measurement which assigns a number to all objects in the set and has a true zero point as its origin. On such a scale, the ratio of any 2 points is independent of the unit of measurement. Weight is an obvious example of a variable recorded on a ratio scale as it has a true zero (no weight) and the ratio of any 2 weights is independent of the unit of measurement. For example, if the weights of 2 different objects are determined in pounds and also in grams, we will find that the ratio of the 2 weights in pounds is identical to the ratio of the 2 weights in grams. That is, an object which is twice as heavy when measured in pounds will also be twice as heavy when measured in grams.

Interval scale: An interval scale is also characterized by a common and constant unit of measurement, but does not have a true zero point. For these data, differences are meaningful, but one cannot talk about absolute values. An obvious example of an interval scale is temperature when it is measured in Centigrade or Fahrenheit. It can be argued that a 1 degree increase in temperature from 1 to 2 degrees Centigrade is related to a 1 degree increase in temperature from 10 to 11 degrees Centigrade. The interval of the degree means something. Ratios are not meaningful, however, as 20 degrees Centigrade is not twice as hot as 10 degrees Centigrade, nor is 1 degree Centigrade infinitely hotter than 0 degrees Centigrade (the same argument applies to temperatures measured in degrees Fahrenheit[1]).

1.1.2 Recording the data

Some examples of continuous data are relatively simple to record as the information has a direct numerical representation. For example, variables recorded on continuous scales (interval and ratio) can be seen in Table 1.1 which shows average temperature differences measured in degrees Centigrade between the inside and outside of a house (interval data) and average daily gas consumption (ratio data) for 15 houses in Milton Keynes, a town in the United Kingdom.

In certain circumstances, data may also be considered to be continuous even when it is recorded using discrete categories. As a rough rule of thumb, if the data come from an underlying continuous distribution, with a relatively large number of categories and with intervals between successive ratings being at least approximately similar (see Sarle, 1995), the recorded data may be considered to be continuous, at least for

---

[1]Temperature measured on the Kelvin scale may, however, be considered to be ratio data as the Kelvin scale has a true zero.

Table 1.1 *Examples of interval and ratio scales*

Temperature difference (deg C)	Daily gas consumption (kWh)	Temperature difference (deg C)	Daily gas consumption (kWh)
10.3	69.81	15.2	81.29
11.4	82.75	15.3	99.20
11.5	81.75	15.6	86.35
12.5	80.38	16.4	110.23
13.1	85.89	16.5	106.55
13.4	75.32	17.0	85.50
13.6	69.81	17.2	90.02
15.0	78.54		

Source: The Open University (1984) *MDST242. Statistics in Society, Unit A5: Review.*
Second Edition, Milton Keynes: The Open University, Figure 2.13.
Reported in Hand et al., 1994.

some statistical purposes. For example, Mitchell, 1983, used a number of categories to record information about income. These data, shown in Table 1.2, might be profitably regarded as continuous, as there are a relatively large number of categories (12) and household income can be regarded as having an underlying continuous distribution. Although the equal-distance codes used here may be considered as continuous, the recorded data could be made to more accurately represent the underlying variable by using codes that represent the mid-points of each category (for example, rather than coding the category $10,000 – $14,999 as 4, it could be coded as $12,500 which represents the category midpoint) rather than utilizing an arbitrary number series that clearly fails to recognize the different sizes of each category. Mid-category coding is fairly straightforward but a decision has to be made about the mid-category coding for the final category '$100,000 and over', as this has no upper-limit (in this case we have decided to use a similar range as was used for the the previous category, a range of $25,000).

Although it is important for a continuous variable that has been categorized to have a relatively large numbers of categories, there are instances where one might wish to regard data as continuous even when relatively few categories have been recorded. For example, in the case of factor analysis, it is common to regard likert-type scales as continuous data (see Hutcheson and Sofroniou, 1999: 222) even though these might only be constructed from 5 categories.

It is important to note that there are no definite rules about when data collected on continuous variables should be considered as continuous and when they should be considered as categorical. The decision is dependent upon the type of data collected, the underlying distribution, the number of categories, the research questions posed and the analyses one proposes to perform.

Continuous Data

Table 1.2 *An example of categorized continuous data*

What is your total household income in 19___
from all sources before tax?

Earnings	Equal-distance code	Mid-category code
less than $5,000	☐ 1	☐ 2,500
$5,000–$7,499	☐ 2	☐ 6,250
$7,500–$9,999	☐ 3	☐ 8,750
$10,000–$14,999	☐ 4	☐ 12,500
$15,000–$19,999	☐ 5	☐ 17,500
$20,000–$24,999	☐ 6	☐ 22,500
$25,000–$29,999	☐ 7	☐ 27,500
$30,000–$39,999	☐ 8	☐ 35,000
$40,000–$49,999	☐ 9	☐ 45,000
$50,000–$74,999	☐ 10	☐ 62,500
$75,000–$99,999	☐ 11	☐ 87,500
$100,000 and over	☐ 12	☐ 112,500

Source: Mitchell, A. (1983) *The Nine American Lifestyles: Who We Are and Where We're Going.* Macmillan. Reported in Bearden et al., 1993.

1.1.3 Applying mathematical operations

Interval and ratio data allow different mathematical operations to be applied to the measurements. These data types will therefore be described separately.

Ratio data: The numbers associated with a ratio scale are 'true' numbers and can be ordered, added, subtracted, divided and multiplied. For example, 10 multiplied by 5 equals 50 (a calculation on the data) and this also applies to the variable as 10 grams (weight being measured on a ratio scale) multiplied by 5 equals 50 grams. The mathematical operations that can be applied to ratio data are shown below:

- 10 grams > 5 grams ✓
- 10 grams < 15 grams ✓
- 10 grams + 5 grams = 15 grams ✓
- 10 grams − 5 grams = 5 grams ✓
- 10 grams × 5 = 50 grams ✓
- 10 grams ÷ 5 = 2 grams ✓

Interval data: As there is no true zero with an interval scale, one cannot use multiplication or division. Although numerically, 3 multiplied by 4 equals 12, this does not hold true for the variable as 3 degrees Centigrade multiplied by 4 does not equal 12 degrees Centigrade. The mathematical operations that are not allowed on interval data are shown below:

- 10 degrees C × 5 ≠ 50 degrees C
- 10 degrees C ÷ 5 ≠ 2 degrees C

Interval data does allow a number of other mathematical operations to be applied including addition and subtraction and operations involving order. Numerically, 10 plus 5 equals 15; and this is also the case for the variable, as 10 degrees Centigrade plus 5 degrees Centigrade does equal 15 degrees Centigrade. Similarly, 20 degrees Centigrade minus 28 degrees Centigrade equals −8 degrees Centigrade. The mathematical operations allowed on interval data are shown below:

- 10 degrees C > 5 degrees C ✓
- 10 degrees C < 15 degrees C ✓

- 10 degrees C + 5 degrees C = 15 degrees C ✓
- 10 degrees C − 5 degrees C = 5 degrees C ✓

For the purposes of analysis (at least for those techniques presented in this book), interval and ratio data are considered equivalent as the same analytical techniques may be applied to both. Continuous data may be described using mean values and standard deviations, which require items in the set of data to be added (descriptions of central tendency and spread for continuous data can be found in basic statistical and methodology books). The level at which the data are recorded determines the analytical techniques that may be applied. In the case of continuous data we are able to use techniques that make use of addition and subtraction (as well as greater-than and less-than and frequency counts) and one may therefore apply OLS regression (see Chapter 2) to model such data.

1.2 Ordered Categorical Data

Although variables which have a clearly defined underlying ordered categorical distribution are quite rare, measurements are frequently gathered and coded in a way that results in ordered data. Ordered categorical data constitutes a large percentage of that used in the management field, making its coding and manipulation of particular interest.

1.2.1 The underlying distribution

Ordered categorical data is composed of a number of distinct categories which have an order. For example, a person's highest academic qualification may be a school

Ordered Categorical Data

Table 1.3 *Ordered categorical coding of army rank: example I*

Army rank	Code
Private	1
Corporal	2
Sergeant	3
Sergeant-Major	4
...	
Brigadier	35
...	
Commander-in-Chief	54

certificate, a diploma from a college, or a postgraduate degree obtained through prolonged study at a university. These qualifications represent distinct categories in that a person's highest academic achievement will be one or other of the categories, there are no in-between values. The categories also have an order, in that a school certificate is generally considered to be less advanced than a diploma and a diploma less advanced than a postgraduate degree. Other examples of ordered categorical data are seniority at work (junior manager, section head, director), judo gradings (yellow, blue and black belts) and poker hands (pairs, triples, full houses, etc.) with perhaps the classic example being found in the armed forces or police service where seniority is explicitly designated by ranks.

1.2.2 Recording the data

Ordered categorical data can be recorded from variables having underlying ordered or continuous distributions. We will deal with both types here, but will first look at ordered categorical data which is obtained from a variable having an underlying ordered categorical distribution.

From an ordered categorical distribution: The example we will use here is the classic example of army rank designated by an ordered categorical scale that runs from low to high seniority.[2] Table 1.3 depicts one of many possible coding schemes that can be used to code army rank. The numbers chosen to represent seniority (the code) merely identify relative seniority. For example, a Private is less senior than a Corporal, who is less senior than a Sergeant, who is less senior than a Brigadier. The codes themselves do not indicate the actual degree of seniority, they merely identify the position of each rank in the ordered categories. This can be demonstrated by taking the example of a Private and a Corporal. Even though a Private is recorded as 1 and a Corporal as 2, a Corporal does not necessarily have twice the level of seniority. It should also be noted that increments between items in the list may be non-standard. For example, the change in seniority between a Private (coded 1) and a Corporal (coded 2) might be quite minor, whereas the change in seniority between

---

[2] The order of seniority shown in this table is not necessarily accurate, it is provided merely for illustration.

a General (coded 53) and the Commander-in-Chief (coded 54) may be far more substantial, even though both pairs are coded using adjacent numbers. Table 1.4 depicts an alternative coding scheme for army rank that uses different codes and orders the ranks in a reverse order to that used in Table 1.3. This is, however, also a valid coding scheme as the categories are all explicitly identified and the order in the data has been maintained.

Table 1.4 *Ordered categorical coding of army rank: example II*

Army rank	Code
Private	187
Corporal	106
Sergeant	104
Sergeant-Major	98
...	
Brigadier	40
...	
Commander-in-Chief	2

Tables 1.3 and 1.4 show army rank coded as ordered data. However, once the coding of the data ceases to represent the order in the variable, the data ceases to be ordered. Table 1.5 gives an example of an ordered variable coded as unordered data. In this example, even though the variable is ordered, the data are unordered which restricts the type of analysis one can use.

Table 1.5 *Unordered categorical coding of army rank*

Army rank	Code
Private	1
Corporal	16
Sergeant	9
Sergeant-Major	98
...	
Brigadier	10
...	
Commander-in-Chief	2

From a continuous distribution: A large percentage of the ordered categorical data one encounters will be from variables which have an underlying continuous distribution (see Section 1.1) but have been coded, for what ever reason, as ordered categorical. For example, Table 1.6 shows two variables that have underlying continuous distributions, but are recorded as ordered categorical. A person's mental status may be thought

Table 1.6 *Continuous variables coded as ordered categories*

		\multicolumn{6}{c}{Socio-economic status of parents}
		1	2	3	4	5	6
Mental status	Well	64	57	57	72	36	21
	Mild symptoms	94	94	105	141	97	71
	Moderate symptoms	58	54	65	77	54	54
	Impaired functioning	46	40	60	94	78	71

Source: Agresti, A. (1989), 'Tutorial on modelling ordinal categorical response data'. *Psychological Bulletin*, 105: 290–301.

of as having an underlying continuous distribution as someone could be anywhere on a scale from "Well" through to "Impaired functioning"; there are potentially an infinite number of degrees of mental impairment between these extremes. Here the data are recorded using a 4 point ordered scale devised more for descriptive convenience than as an attempt to record the underlying distribution as accurately as possible. Similarly, socio-economic status may be thought of as having an underlying continuous distribution, but the data are recorded using 6 discrete ordered categories (1, 2, 3, 4, 5, 6). For both of these variables, there is also no direct correspondence between the codes used and what is being measured – the codes themselves merely designate ordered categories. It is also the case that the differences between categories may not be standard (i.e. the difference in socio-economic status between categories 1 and 2 might bear little relation to the difference in socio-economic status between categories 4 and 5).

Using a different scale for recording data to that which is, at least theoretically possible for the variable, is not necessarily a mistake or even undesirable – it might be that an ordered scale is the best that we can hope to obtain. For example, it might be that mental impairment is best measured on the basis of clinical judgments that are given using quite broad definitions. This simple ordered categorical scale might in fact provide the best scale of mental impairment.

Another common example of the use of ordered categories to represent continuous variables is in the measurement of attitudes, thoughts, beliefs and stereotypes, which are essentially unobservable. Attitudes and opinions are commonly assessed in management research using 5–7 point ordered scales (see, for example, Childers et al., 1985; Chonko et al., 1986; Ford et al., 1975). For demonstration purposes we will take the concept of beauty which can be thought of as a continuous variable that varies between 2 extremes (very beautiful to not at all beautiful). Although the variable "beauty" can be considered as having an underlying continuous distribution, the recorded data is likely to consist of ordered responses that distinguish between a few broad categories defined by the language we use (e.g. "beautiful", "very beautiful", "ugly"). Such data can be obtained by using a question such as that shown in Table 1.7 which uses "beautiful" and "ugly" as extremes of the same underlying attribute.

The use of the coding scheme in Table 1.7 has converted what can be considered a continuous variable into ordered categorical data. This has lost some of the information

Table 1.7 *A continuous variable coded as ordered categorical data*

How beautiful do you think the car in the picture is?

Response	Code
Very beautiful	☐ 1
Beautiful	☐ 2
Plain	☐ 3
Ugly	☐ 4
Very ugly	☐ 5

potentially available, as only 5 degrees of beauty are now indicated. Whilst it might be possible to achieve a finer discrimination of beauty by using more points on the scale, it is debatable whether people can indicate the degree to which something is beautiful to this accuracy. This 5-point scale may in fact represent the best data that can be realistically collected. Other studies that have used similar rating scales are Ohanion, 1990 and Zaichowsky, 1985, who attempted to measure the attractiveness and appeal of different products, and Leavitt, 1970 and Wells et al., 1971, who investigated emotional reactions to advertising stimuli.

Ordered categories are also commonly used to code sensitive data that could be collected as continuous, but to do so would likely lead to unacceptable amounts of missing data. For example, a direct question about age runs the risk of alienating respondents. A question such as

How old are you?   ___ years   ___ months

may elicit continuous data, but is also likely to lead to a number of missing responses. Typically, for such information, a response frame is used that makes the question less intrusive and easier to answer. For example, Mitchell, 1983 (as reported in Bearden et al., 1993) used a response frame to ask about age.

Table 1.8 *Representing age using ordered categories*

What is your current age? (Please check one box)

Age	Code	Age	Code
18–24	☐ 1	45–54	☐ 5
25–29	☐ 2	55–64	☐ 6
30–34	☐ 3	65 and over	☐ 7
35–44	☐ 4		

Source: Mitchell, A. (1983) *The Nine American Lifestyles: Who We Are and Where We're Going*. Macmillan. Reported in Bearden et al., 1993.

Ordered Categorical Data

The codes used to designate the categories in Table 1.8 (codes 1–7) are not related to the actual value of the variable and the category intervals are not standard (e.g. code 1 spans 7 years, code 2 spans 5 years, code 5 spans 10 years, and the span of code 7 is not defined). In this case, these data should be considered as ordered categorical.

Mistaking unordered categorical data for ordered: A fairly common mistake when attempting to obtain ordered categorical data is to include a 'don't know' response as part of the scale which can render a potentially ordered set of data unordered. Table 1.9 shows an example where an attempt is made to record ordered categorical data, but due to the inclusion of a 'don't know' category, the data recorded is unordered.

The use of the 'don't know' category in the middle (coded as 3) is intended to represent people who neither agree nor disagree with the statement. However, the 'don't know' response may be used by people who do not know if the company has an alcohol policy. The scale is not, therefore, an ordered categorical one and it would be incorrect to analyze these data using this assumption. The analyst must either treat them as unordered data (using categories 1, 2, 3, 4, 5), or as ordered data once the middle category has been removed (using categories 1, 2, 4, 5). Neither option is particularly attractive as the use of unordered analyses will result in the loss of some information and the use of ordered analyses on a restricted data set may discount an important section of the population and also polarizes the responses.

Table 1.9 *Mis-coding an ordered categorical variable*

The company policy on alcohol use at work should be made more stringent

Strongly agree	☐ 1
Agree	☐ 2
Don't Know	☐ 3
Disagree	☐ 4
Strongly disagree	☐ 5

1.2.3 Applying mathematical operations

The following discussion of the permissible mathematical operations that can be conducted on ordered data will be illustrated using the example data from Table 1.10. These data represent the highest academic award achieved (taken from the English education system) and should be regarded as ordered categories with higher codes representing higher academic achievement.

For these data, information about position is meaningful which allows statistics that preserve the *greater-than* and *less-than* relationships to be used. For example, in addition to knowing that the highest attainment of 12 people is a degree (code 4), we

Table 1.10 *Highest educational attainment*

Qualification	Code	Frequency
No qualifications	1	14
O level	2	52
A level	3	28
Degree	4	12
Masters	5	5
Doctorate	6	9

also know that these people have a higher qualification than those who have a code of 3 or below. We know that the highest attainment of 28 people is A level and also that these people have a lower qualification than those who obtained a code of 4 or more. With regards to order, the codes used accurately represent academic achievement. For example, numerically, 2 is greater than 1, and this also holds for educational achievement, as an O level is a higher achievement than no qualifications. Similarly, 4 is less than 5 numerically and this also holds for educational achievement as a degree is a lower achievement than a Masters. These relationships are shown clearly below:

- 2 (O level) > 1 (no qualifications)   ✓
- 4 (degree) < 5 (masters)   ✓

Mathematical procedures that add, subtract or multiply numbers assigned to the data are, however, not admissible (i.e., any mathematical operation which assumes that actual values are meaningful). Numerically, 2 plus 1 equals 3, but this does not apply to achievement, as an O level plus no qualification does not equal an A level. Similarly, although 2 multiplied by 3 equals 6, this does not hold for achievement as an O level multiplied by 3 does not equal a doctorate (coded 6). These relationships are shown clearly below:

- 2 (O level) + 1 (no qualifications) $\neq$ 3 (A level)
- 4 (degree) − 3 (A level) $\neq$ 1 (no qualifications)
- 2 (O level) × 3 $\neq$ 6 (doctorate)
- 6 (doctorate) ÷ 3 $\neq$ 2 (O level)

Ordered categorical data may be described using median values and measures of the range (descriptions of central tendency and spread for ordered data can be found in basic statistical and methodology books), statistics that make use of the greater-than and less-than operations. We are not allowed to apply the operations of addition or subtraction to these data, which means that we are unable to describe ordered data using measures of mean and standard deviation, or model ordered data using OLS regression. For these data we need to select a technique that does not violate the measurement scale and uses the greater-than and less-than operations rather than addition and subtraction. One method we may use is the proportional odds model and this is covered in detail in Chapter 4.

1.3 Unordered Categorical Data

1.3.1 The underlying distribution

Unordered categorical data consist of a number of separate categories that do not have any inherent order. For example, gender is recorded using unordered categories as a person may be, generally speaking, either male or female. Any person must fall into one or other of the categories, there are no in-between values. Unordered categorical data consisting of 2 categories are commonly referred to as dichotomous. Other examples of dichotomous unordered categorical data are success–failure, died–survived, employed–unemployed, yes–no and two-group experimental units (e.g. group A – group B). Unordered categorical data may also have more than 2 categories, as with blood group (A, B, O-negative, etc.), make of car (Ford, Nissan, BMW), residential status (owner-occupier, privately rented, council-rented), experimental group (group A, group B, group C, etc.), religious belief (Sikh, Christian, Muslim) and individual subjects that take part in a study (subject01, subject02, subject03, etc.). These data are commonly referred to as polytomous.

1.3.2 Recording the data

Unordered categorical data can be simply recorded using the category labels. For example, entering the data as male–female, succeed–fail, yes–no, etc. Unordered categorical variables may also be represented using numbers, which can cause some confusion. For example, Table 1.11 shows how a polytomous unordered categorical variable indicating make of car may be represented numerically using the numbers 1 to 6.[3]

Table 1.11 *Unordered categorical data: coding example I*

Which make of car is your main family transport?	Code
Ford	☐ 1
Nissan	☐ 2
BMW	☐ 3
Jaguar	☐ 4
Alfa Romeo	☐ 5
Ferrari	☐ 6

The categories used to indicate the make of car that provides the main family transport in Table 1.11 are separate and the codes have no inherent order (the numbers themselves are essentially arbitrary). So long as each category is represented by a unique identifier, any numbers may be used to represent the cars. For example, the coding scheme used in Table 1.12 is just as valid, even though it is unusual.

---

[3] Representing such variables as numbers is very common and may actually be required by the statistical analysis package.

Table 1.12 *Unordered categorical data: coding example II*

Which make of car is your main family transport?	Code
Ferrari	☐ −1
Ford	☐ 0
Alfa Romeo	☐ 36
Nissan	☐ 4.2
Jaguar	☐ −298
BMW	☐ 0.04

It should be noted that there are many examples where it is usual for an unordered categorical variable to be coded using a numeric system. The identification of individual subjects or cases in a related-groups design is often achieved through numerical identification (for example, 300 subjects can be identified using the codes 1 to 300). Although such a coding scheme is numeric, the actual variable is not. The numbers merely identify different subjects; there is no inherent order to the data. If mistakes are not to be made, it is important that the type of data is identified and taken into account during analysis (that is, we do not apply operations meant for numerical variables on codes used to identify categorical variables).

1.3.3 Applying mathematical operations

Table 1.13 shows the number of cars sold in a year by a particular company. Six different models of car are included in the data along with a simple numeric code indicating the make of car and a measure of frequency.

Table 1.13 *Number of cars sold in a year*

Make of Car	Code	Number sold
Ford	1	46
BMW	2	21
Jaguar	3	32
Nissan	4	54
Ferrari	5	12
Alfa Romeo	6	19

If we had used a numeric code to identify the make of car (as is required by some statistical packages), we need to be careful when interpreting any statistics based on this code. Although numerically, 1 is less than 4, and 1 plus 2 does equal 3, such mathematical operations cannot be applied to the codes used to represent the make of car. It is clear that when dealing with the make of car, 1 (a Ford) is not less than

Conclusion

4 (a Nissan) and 1 (a Ford) plus 2 (a BMW) does not equal 3 (a Jaguar). There is no direct correspondence between the make of car and the coding scheme. As the numeric codes used to represent the make of car are more or less arbitrary, mathematical operations that require an ordered or a measured scale cannot be computed. For example, greater-than and less-than relationships do not hold, nor does addition, subtraction, multiplication and division. These are clearly shown below.

- Ford (1) $\not<$ Nissan (4)
- Alfa Romeo (6) $\not>$ Jaguar (3)
- Ford (1) + BMW (2) $\neq$ Jaguar (3)
- Ferrari (5) − Jaguar (3) $\neq$ BMW (2)
- BMW (2) × 3 $\neq$ Alfa Romeo (6)
- Alfa Romeo (6) ÷ 2 $\neq$ Jaguar (3)

Unordered categorical data may be described using frequency counts (the most frequent category, the mode) but not measures that require the use of the greater-than or less-than relationships, or addition and subtraction. For the analysis of unordered categorical data a technique needs to be used that does not violate the measurement scale. One method we may use is the multi-nomial logistic regression model or, for binary categories, a logistic regression. These techniques are covered in detail in Chapters 3 and 5).

1.4 Conclusion

This chapter was designed to show that the way data are coded is important. In particular, it is crucial for an analyst to realize the relationship between the attribute and the measurements themselves. The level of measurement of data is particularly important as it is this that dictates which statistical analysis techniques may be used. In this book, the analysis of continuous data is dealt with through the use of ordinary least squares regression, ordered categorical data through the proportional odds model and unordered categorical data through the multi-nomial logistic regression model. In order to apply these techniques appropriately and fully appreciate their advantages and limitations, students must be familiar with the measurement scales of the variables that they are modeling. Indeed, measurement theory is crucial to the whole endeavour of data analysis and its importance has been summed up by Sarle, in the final section of his paper:

> Measurement theory encourages people to think about the meaning of their data. It encourages critical assessment of the assumptions behind the analysis. It encourages responsible real-world data analysis.
>
> Sarle, 1995

CHAPTER 2
Modeling Continuous Data

This chapter introduces the ordinary least-squares regression model which can be used to model continuous variables. We cover the theory behind the technique, the interpretation of the parameters and confidence intervals and also the computation and interpretation of the model-fit statistics. We also show how categorical variables can be included and how the technique can be applied to the analysis of simple experimental data.

OLS regression is a particularly important technique not only because it provides a method of modeling continuous data, but also as it is central to understanding the wider application of the generalized linear model to other types of data. The techniques described in this chapter mostly apply to the other regression techniques covered in this book (logistic regression, proportional odds and multi-nomial logistic regression models) and forms the basis of the explanations given for all these techniques.

2.1 The Generalized Linear Model

This chapter introduces generalized linear models (GLMs) and shows how they can be used to model continuous, ordered and unordered data (the three basic scales of data described in Chapter 1). The object is to provide a coherent introduction to data modeling rather than provide a comprehensive coverage of all techniques under the GLM umbrella. GLMs enable descriptive and predictive models to be built that are sufficiently general to be applicable to much social science data. They can be used to model data collected from survey and experimental studies and can replace many of the more traditional hypothesis tests that are still in common use. Of particular importance is the unified theoretical framework that the method offers, as this enables certain "economies of scale" to be realized that allow a whole range of data to be analyzed using similar techniques.

The use of the techniques will be described using a modeling procedure whereby a particular variable can be modeled (or predicted) using information about other variables. For example,

Variable Y *may be predicted by* Variable X_1 *and* Variable X_2.

Variable Y (the variable that is being modeled – the *response variable*) could be wage, educational attainment, test score, share price, a binary category indicating success and failure, university chosen or religious affiliation. Variables X_1 and X_2 (the variables used to predict Y – the *explanatory variables*) could be age, average school grade, gender, nationality, race, attractiveness, weight, attitude to innovation or treatment group. In short, variables Y, X_1 and X_2 can be recorded on any of the scales described in Chapter 1. Using the concrete example of a particular company's share price, the relationship above can be written as:

Share Price *may be predicted by* output *and* market confidence.

From the relationship above one can deduce that share price may be determined by the company's output and the confidence shown in the market the company operates in. This is not likely to be a perfect relationship as a number of other variables not represented in the model will also influence share price (such as government policy and exchange rates). In general, for the model above, high output and high market confidence is likely to be associated with a relatively high share price (although this might not always be the case). The model can be said to consist of 3 components, the response variable, Y, the explanatory variables, X_1 and X_2 and a function that links the 2. These 3 components form the basis of the Generalized Linear Model where they are commonly referred to as the random component, the systematic component and the link function.

- **The random component:**

  the probability distribution assumed to underlie the response variable.

- **The systematic component:**

  the fixed structure of the explanatory variables, usually characterized by a linear function ($\alpha + \beta_1 x_1 + \beta_2 x_2 + \beta_3 x_3 + ... + \beta_k x_k$).

- **The link function:**

  the function that maps the systematic component onto the random component. This function can be one of *identity* for normally distributed random components, or one of a number of non-linear links when the random component is not normally distributed.

The GLM can be summarized as:

$$\text{Random component} \xrightarrow{\text{Link Function}} \text{Systematic component}$$

with a concrete example being:

$$\text{Share price} \xrightarrow{\text{Link Function}} \text{Output } and \text{ Market confidence}$$

The probability distribution assumed to underlie the random component is a function of the data. For example, when the response variable is continuous, a normal distribution may be used, whereas a binomial distribution may be used when the response variable is dichotomous. The link function is also dependent on the scale in which the response variable is recorded. For example, for a normally-distributed response variable, the relationship between the random and systematic components is one of identity (=), where the random component actually equals the systematic component. For a binomially distributed response variable, the relationship between the random and systematic components is the log odds, or logit.

This chapter introduces the generalized linear models using ordinary least-squares regression, a technique that can be used to model a continuous response variable. In later chapters this technique is generalized to the prediction of binary and multi-category ordered and unordered response variables. The introduction to GLMs provided here has been very concise and only provided a basic description of the theory behind the technique. There are, however, a number of books and articles that deal with this topic in some depth, and interested readers are advised to consult one or more of these references (for example, Agresti, 1996; Collett, 2003; Dobson, 2002; Draper and Smith, 1998; Fahrmeir and Tutz, 2001; Gill, 2001; Hoffmann, 2004; Hutcheson and Sofroniou, 1999; Lindsey, 1995, 1997; McCullagh and Nelder, 1989; McCulloch and Searle, 2001; Nelder and Wedderburn, 1972).

2.2 The Ordinary Least-Squares Model

A continuous response variable can be modeled using ordinary least-squares regression (OLS regression), one of the GLM modeling techniques. We will describe the theory and application of the technique in relation to a simple data set and build from a simple to a multi-variable model that includes categorical explanatory variables. The data that are to be used here to illustrate the technique are from Koteswara, 1970 (reported in Hand et al., 1994) who presents data collected over 30 4-week periods from March 18th 1951 to July 11th 1953.[1] The data show ice cream consumption (pints per capita), the price of ice cream (in dollars per pint), the weekly family income (in dollars) and the mean outdoor temperature (in degrees Fahrenheit). These data are shown in Table 2.1.

2.2.1 Simple OLS regression

Simple OLS regression refers to the case where there is a continuous response variable and a single explanatory variable. For example, ice cream consumption (measured on a continuous scale) may be predicted, at least to some extent, by mean outdoor temperature. As the response variable is continuous, an identity link (=) is used to link the random and systematic components of the model. At a very basic level, the relationship between the two variables can be represented as:

Ice cream consumption *may be predicted by* outdoor temperature

---

[1] These data are used as they are easy to understand and provide a good basis for demonstration.

Table 2.1 *Data: ice cream consumption*

Ice cream consumption	Price	Family income	Temperature
.386	.270	78	41
.374	.282	79	56
.393	.277	81	63
.425	.280	80	68
.406	.272	76	69
.344	.262	78	65
.327	.275	82	61
.288	.267	79	47
.269	.265	76	32
.256	.277	79	24
.286	.282	82	28
.298	.270	85	26
.329	.272	86	32
.318	.287	83	40
.381	.277	84	55
.381	.287	82	63
.470	.280	80	72
.443	.277	78	72
.386	.277	84	67
.342	.277	86	60
.319	.292	85	44
.307	.287	87	40
.284	.277	94	32
.326	.285	92	27
.309	.282	95	28
.359	.265	96	33
.376	.265	94	41
.416	.265	96	52
.437	.268	91	64
.548	.260	90	71

Source: Koteswara, 1970.

This is a very simplified view of ice cream consumption and merely states that consumption may be affected by outdoor temperature. There are clearly many more variables that are likely to play a role in the amount of ice cream sold, but these are not included in this example. The non-represented information could have been included in the model as an error term, but for simplicity, this term has not been made explicit.[2] Generally, one would expect ice cream consumption to increase as outdoor temperature increases and this is precisely what we observe in the scatterplot of the

---
[2] In any case, the regression model does not explicitly include the amount of error in the regression equation. This information is provided in the model-fit statistics.

The Ordinary Least-Squares Model

2 variables shown in Figure 2.1. Furthermore, it would appear that the relationship between the 2 variables can be approximated by a straight line.

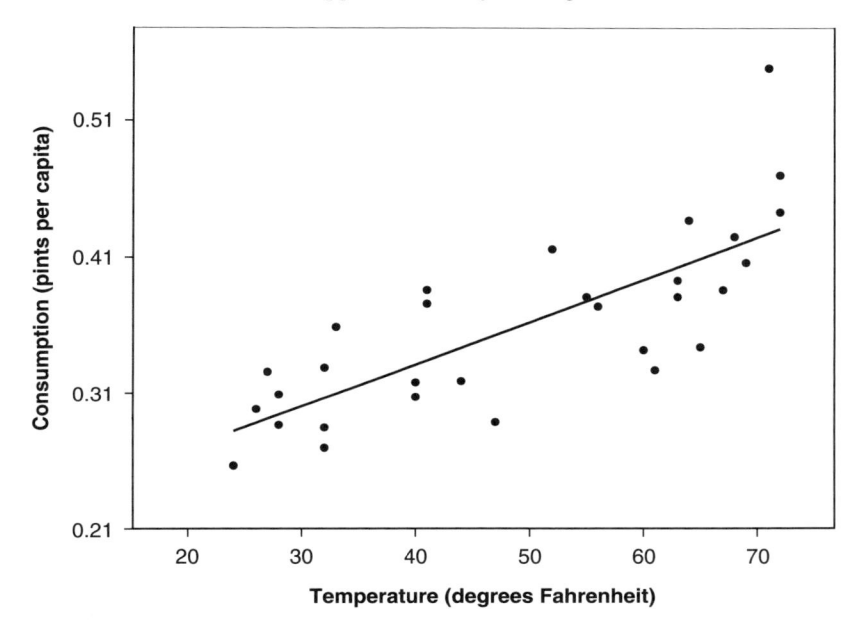

Figure 2.1 *A scatterplot showing the relationship between ice cream consumption and outdoor temperature and the associated OLS regression model*

The equation of a straight line is "$Y = \alpha + \beta x$", which represents the relationship between the 2 variables in the current example. The straight-line regression model of consumption is therefore:

$$\text{consumption} = \alpha + \beta \text{ temperature} \qquad (2.1)$$

Computing and interpreting model parameters: The relationship between the response variable (consumption) and the explanatory variable (temperature) may be represented by a straight line and can therefore be given in the form "$Y = \alpha + \beta x$". This linear model is derived using an algorithm that minimizes the sum of the squares of the distances from each data point to the line (hence it is known as the least-squares technique) producing a line of best-fit (the straight line drawn on the graph in Figure 2.1). Readily available statistical software can compute the model parameters for the model "consumption = $\alpha + \beta$ temperature" and these are shown in Table 2.2. From the estimates provided in this table, one can obtain the intercept (α) and the regression coefficient for temperature (β) to get the equation of the line of best-fit, which is

$$\text{consumption} = 0.207 + (0.003 * \text{temperature}). \qquad (2.2)$$

Table 2.2 *Regression parameters*

	Estimate	Standard error
(Intercept)	0.207	0.0247
Temperature	0.003	0.0005

Model: consumption = $\alpha + \beta$ temperature

The estimate for the variable "temperature" indicates that for each unit increase in temperature, per capita consumption of ice cream is expected to increase by 0.003 pints. This increase in ice cream consumption is the average increase one would expect.[3]

It is useful to also determine the limits within which one might expect consumption to change given a unit increase in temperature (i.e., how accurate the β parameter is). These limits are known as confidence intervals and may be calculated using Equation 2.3.

$$\text{Large sample 95\% confidence interval for } \beta = \hat{\beta} \pm 1.96(\text{s.e. } \hat{\beta}) \qquad (2.3)$$

where $\hat{\beta}$ indicates that β is estimated from the data.

For the model above,

$$\text{Large sample 95\% confidence interval for } \beta = 0.003 \pm (1.96 \times 0.0005)$$
$$= 0.002, \ 0.004$$

In 95% of cases, the expected increase in per capita consumption of ice cream for each degree rise in temperature is between 0.002 and 0.004 pints per capita. In other words, for a unit increase in temperature (a one degree rise) in 95% of cases one would expect consumption to increase by at least 0.002 pints per capita but not more than 0.004 pints per capita. As both of these confidence intervals predict an increase in the consumption of ice cream, we can conclude that at the 95% 2-tailed level of significance, "temperature" does have a significant affect on the response variable (this is confirmed in the next section when the model-fit statistics are discussed).

Predicting the response variable: From the model provided above in Equation 2.2, it is a simple matter to obtain predictions for the response variable at any given value of temperature (provided that it is within the range of observations recorded during the study). For example, when the temperature is 50 degrees Fahrenheit, ice cream consumption is predicted to be

$$\text{consumption} = 0.207 + (0.003 * 50)$$
$$= 0.357$$

---

[3] The estimate for the intercept is not all that informative in this case as it just indicates the consumption when the temperature is zero (as we do not know if a linear model holds for temperatures this low), interpreting this value is often futile.

The Ordinary Least-Squares Model

which can be confirmed by looking at the graph of the regression model in Figure 2.1. It is an easy matter to compute these predictions using software. Table 2.3 shows predicted probabilities of ice cream consumption for a number of different temperatures computed using the R statistical package. From the predicted values in the table, it is easy to see that the predicted consumption increases with temperature.

Table 2.3 *Predictions of consumption*

Temperature	Predicted consumption
41	0.334
56	0.381
63	0.403
68	0.418
69	0.421
65	0.409
61	0.396
47	0.353
32	0.306
24	0.281
28	0.294

Model: consumption = 0.207 + (0.003 * temperature)

Goodness-of-fit statistics: In addition to the model parameters and confidence intervals, it is useful to have an indication of how well the model fits the data. For this we need to compute some model-fit statistics. How well the model fits the data can be determined by comparing the observed scores (the data) with those predicted from the model. The difference between these 2 values (the deviation or residual, as they are sometimes called) provides an indication of how well the model predicts each data point. Adding up the deviances for all the data points after they have been squared (in order to remove any negative values) provides a measure of how much the data deviates from the model overall. The sum of all the squared residuals is known as the residual sum of squares (RSS) and essentially provides a measure of model-fit. A poorly fitting model will deviate markedly from the data and will consequently have a relatively large RSS, whereas a good-fitting model will not deviate markedly from the data and will consequently have a relatively small RSS (a perfectly fitting model will have an RSS equal to zero, as there will be no deviation). The RSS statistic therefore provides a measure of model-fit and can be used to determine the significance of individual and groups of parameters for a regression model. This statistic is also known as the *deviance* and is discussed in depth by Agresti, 1996 (pages 96–7).

A "model" computed for a single continuous response variable, Y, has the form "$Y = \alpha$", where α is equal to the mean value (if the only information you have about a continuous variable is the variable itself, the best prediction you can make about its value is the mean value). The residuals for such a model are simply the difference between each data point and the mean of the distribution (the predicted value from the model, designated as $\bar{x}$). The deviance in the model can be computed by adding up all of the squared residuals for each data point as defined in Equation 2.4 and illustrated for the variable consumption in Figure 2.2.

$$\text{deviance} = (x_1 - \bar{x})^2 + (x_2 - \bar{x})^2 + \ldots + (x_k - \bar{x})^2 \tag{2.4}$$

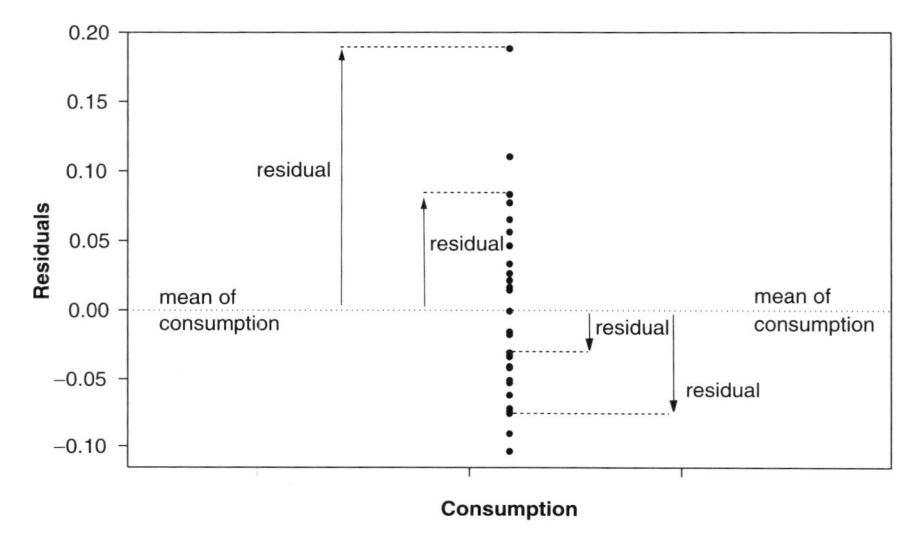

Figure 2.2 *Residuals for the model "consumption = α"*

Table 2.4 shows the residuals and squared residuals for each consumption data point. These residuals have been calculated by simply subtracting the mean value of consumption (0.3594) from each of the observed values ($x_i - \bar{x}$). Adding up all of the squared residuals provides the deviance for the model "consumption = α", which is calculated as 0.1255.

The deviance can also be derived for models that include one or more explanatory variables. Figure 2.3 gives a visual representation of how the residuals are calculated for the simple regression model "consumption = α + β temperature". The residuals are calculated as the distances from each data point to the regression line (rather than to the average value) and these are clearly shown in the diagram. For a comprehensive illustration of modeling relationships and determining residual scores for simple regression models, see Miles and Shevlin (2001). Table 2.5 shows the residuals and squared residuals for each consumption data point.[4] Adding up all of the squared residuals provides the deviance for the model "consumption = α + β temperature", which is calculated as 0.0500.

The deviance is an important statistic as it enables the contribution made by an explanatory variable to the prediction of a response variable to be determined. If by adding a variable to the model, the deviance is greatly reduced, the added variable can

---
[4]These have been computed using commonly available software.

The Ordinary Least-Squares Model

Table 2.4 *Computing the deviance for the model "consumption = α"*

Consumption	Residual	Residual squared	Consumption	Residual	Residual squared
0.39	0.0266	0.0007	0.38	0.0216	0.0005
0.37	0.0146	0.0002	0.47	0.1106	0.0122
0.39	0.0336	0.0011	0.44	0.0836	0.0070
0.42	0.0656	0.0043	0.39	0.0266	0.0007
0.41	0.0466	0.0022	0.34	−0.0174	0.0003
0.34	−0.0154	0.0002	0.32	−0.0404	0.0016
0.33	−0.0324	0.0011	0.31	−0.0524	0.0027
0.29	−0.0714	0.0051	0.28	−0.0754	0.0057
0.27	−0.0904	0.0082	0.33	−0.0334	0.0011
0.26	−0.1034	0.0107	0.31	−0.0504	0.0025
0.29	−0.0734	0.0054	0.36	−0.0004	0.0000
0.30	−0.0614	0.0038	0.38	0.0166	0.0003
0.33	−0.0304	0.0009	0.42	0.0566	0.0032
0.32	−0.0414	0.0017	0.44	0.0776	0.0060
0.38	0.0216	0.0005	0.55	0.1886	0.0356

Model: consumption = α
deviance = $\sum \text{residual}^2 = 0.1255$

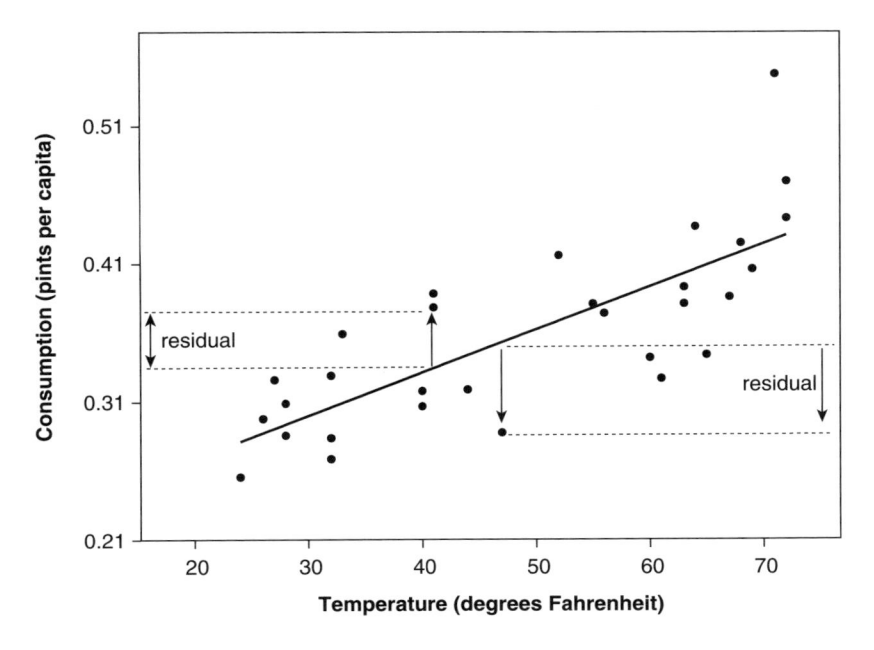

Figure 2.3 *Residuals for the model "consumption = $\alpha + \beta$ temperature"*

Table 2.5 *Computing the deviance for the model "consumption = α+β temperature"*

Consumption	Residual	Residual squared	Consumption	Residual	Residual squared
0.39	0.0517	0.0027	0.38	−0.0216	0.0005
0.37	−0.0069	0.0000	0.47	0.0394	0.0016
0.39	−0.0096	0.0001	0.44	0.0124	0.0002
0.42	0.0068	0.0000	0.39	−0.0291	0.0008
0.41	−0.0153	0.0002	0.34	−0.0513	0.0026
0.34	−0.0648	0.0042	0.32	−0.0246	0.0006
0.33	−0.0694	0.0048	0.31	−0.0242	0.0006
0.29	−0.0649	0.0042	0.28	−0.0223	0.0005
0.27	−0.0373	0.0014	0.33	0.0352	0.0012
0.26	−0.0254	0.0006	0.31	0.0151	0.0002
0.29	−0.0079	0.0001	0.36	0.0496	0.0025
0.30	0.0103	0.0001	0.38	0.0417	0.0017
0.33	0.0227	0.0005	0.42	0.0476	0.0023
0.32	−0.0132	0.0002	0.44	0.0313	0.0010
0.38	0.0032	0.0000	0.55	0.1205	0.0145

Model: consumption = α + β temperature
deviance = $\sum \text{residual}^2 = 0.0500$

be said to have had a large effect. If, on the other hand, the deviance is not greatly reduced, the added variable can be said to have had a small effect. The change in the deviance that results from the explanatory variable being added to the model is used to determine the significance of that variable's effect. To assess the effect that a variable has on the model, one simply compares the deviance statistics before and after the variable has been added. For a simple OLS regression model, the effect of the explanatory variable can be assessed by comparing the RSS statistic for the full regression model with that for the null model (see Equation 2.5).

$$\text{RSS}_{\text{diff}} = (\text{RSS}_0) - (\text{RSS}_1) \tag{2.5}$$

where RSS_0 refers to the null model $Y = \alpha$,
and RSS_1 refers to the model $Y = \alpha + \beta x$.

For the example above, the effect that temperature has on ice cream consumption can be ascertained by comparing the deviance in the null model "consumption = α", with the deviance in the model "consumption = α + β temperature". The only difference between these 2 models is that one includes temperature and the other does not. The difference in RSS between the models will therefore illustrate the effect of temperature. Commonly available statistical software provides these statistics for simple OLS regression models and these are shown in Table 2.6.

For our example of ice cream consumption, the addition of the explanatory variable "temperature" into the model results in a change in deviance of 0.0755 (RSS_{diff}). The

The Ordinary Least-Squares Model

Table 2.6 *Assessing significance by comparing model deviances*

Model	RSS	df	RSS$_{diff}$	F-value	P-value
consumption = α	0.1255	29	0.0755	42.28	4.8e−07
consumption = $\alpha + \beta$ temperature	0.0500	28			

RSS represents the deviance in the model
RSS$_{diff}$ is the difference in deviance between the two models
F-statistic = 42.28 on 1 and 28 degrees of freedom

significance of this can be determined by calculating an F-statistic using Equation 2.6. In this equation, 2 nested models are compared, a larger model designated as $p+q$ (the model "consumption = $\alpha + \beta$ temperature") and a nested model designated as p (the model "consumption = α"). It is important that the models are nested as one cannot compare deviance statistics for un-nested models (eg., "$Y = \alpha$ + temperature" and "$Y = \alpha$ + price"). Only nested models can be compared as this allows an evaluation of the change in deviance that results from the addition of the explanatory variable.

$$F_{(df_p - df_{p+q}), df_{p+q}} = \frac{RSS_p - RSS_{p+q}}{(df_p - df_{p+q})(RSS_{p+q}/df_{p+q})} \quad (2.6)$$

where p represents the smaller (null) model, consumption = α,
$p + q$ represents the larger model consumption = $\alpha + \beta$ temperature,
and df are the degrees-of-freedom for the designated model.

Substituting the values from Table 2.6 into Equation 2.6, it is simple to obtain an F-statistic that enables us to evaluate the significance of adding a variable into the model. In this case, the significance of adding "outdoor temperature" into the model is calculated as:

$$F_{(29-28), 28} = \frac{0.1255 - 0.0500}{(29 - 28)(0.0500/28)}$$

$$F_{1, 28} = 42.28$$

An F value of 42.28 on 1 and 28 degrees of freedom is highly significant (P = 0.000000479, or, as it is commonly given, 4.8e−07) and suggests that outdoor temperature is significantly related to ice cream consumption. This information does not need to be computed manually as it is commonly provided by software in an analysis of deviance table (see Table 2.7). Although this table is redundant for this model (as the information has already been provided above), it is included here to illustrate the typical presentation of results from software.

The significance of individual parameters in the model can also be estimated using a t-statistic which is simply the estimate divided by the standard error. The t-statistic for "temperature" is therefore 0.003/.0004, which is 6.502 (this is the estimate from software, which uses many more decimal places than have been reported here). This

Table 2.7 *Analysis of deviance table: the significance of variables*

	Sum Sq	df	F-value	P-value
coefficient				
temperature	0.0755	1	42.28	4.8e−07
residuals	0.0500			

Model: consumption $= \alpha + \beta$ temperature

value is then tested for significance using a 2-tailed test with $n - k - 1$ degrees of freedom (where n is the number of cases and k is the number of parameters excluding the constant, which, for this example is 28). The t-statistic and associated significance level is shown in Table 2.8 below. For simple OLS regression models, the t-statistic is directly comparable to the F-statistic reported in Tables 2.6 and 2.7 (in fact $\sqrt{F} = t$; $\sqrt{42.28} = 6.502$).

Table 2.8 *Estimating the significance of individual parameters using t-statistics*

	Estimate	Standard error	T-value	P-value
(intercept)	0.207	0.0247	8.375	4.1e−09
temperature	0.003	0.0005	6.502	4.8e−07

Model: consumption = $\alpha + \beta$ temperature

In addition to the model-fit statistics, the R^2 statistic is also commonly quoted and provides a measure that indicates the percentage of variation in the response variable that is "explained" by the model. R^2 is defined as:

$$R^2 = \frac{\text{RSS due to regression}}{\text{Total RSS, corrected for mean} \bar{Y}} \qquad (2.7)$$

From the results in Table 2.6, R^2 can be calculated using the deviance measure for the regression divided by the total deviance. The total deviance is that associated with the null model (consumption $= \alpha$), and is equal to 0.1255. The deviance due to the regression is the difference between the null model and the full model (consumption $= \alpha + \beta$ temperature) and is equal to $0.1255 - 0.0500$, or 0.0755 (RSS$_{\text{diff}}$). Using these figures, R^2 can be computed.

$$R^2 = \frac{0.0755}{0.1255}$$
$$= 0.60$$

In this case one can say that 60% of the variability in the response variable is accounted for by the explanatory variable. Although R^2 is widely used, it has a tendency to increase as the slope of the regression line increases and is not, therefore, a completely

The Ordinary Least-Squares Model

unbiased measure (see Barrett, 1974).[5] One solution to this problem is to calculate an *adjusted* R^2 statistic (R_a^2) which takes into account the number of terms entered into the model and does not necessarily increase as more terms are added. Adjusted R^2 can be derived using equation 2.8.

$$R_a^2 = R^2 - \frac{k(1-R^2)}{n-k-1} \tag{2.8}$$

where R^2 is the coefficient of multiple determination,
n is the number of cases used to construct the model,
and k is the number of terms in the model (not including the constant).

The R^2 and R_a^2 statistics do not provide an indication of significance and are therefore of most use as descriptive statistics providing an idea of the strength of the linear relationship between the response and explanatory variables. Draper & Smith (1981, page 92) conclude that these measures "might be useful as an initial gross indicator, but that is all". Given that neither statistic provides a "perfect" measure of model fit, this book will use the more widely adopted R^2 statistic when describing model fits.

To conclude this section, one can say on the basis of the simple regression model, that outdoor temperature appears to be related to ice cream consumption. As outdoor temperature increases, consumption tends to also increase. This relationship is highly significant. However, this is a very simple model and one would need to investigate other variables that might have an effect on consumption before an accurate determination of the effect of temperature can be made. A more detailed investigation into ice cream consumption is shown in Section 2.2.2 where a multiple OLS regression model is described.

2.2.2 Multiple OLS regression

OLS regression can easily be adapted to include a number of explanatory variables. For example, ice cream consumption is likely to be affected by a number of variables in addition to outdoor temperature. Table 2.1 shows data on two other variables that might be important in predicting ice cream consumption (price and family income). Ice cream consumption may be predicted using all 3 explanatory variables, a model of which is shown below.

> Ice cream consumption *may be predicted by* outdoor temperature *and* price *and* family income.

Computing and interpreting model parameters: Multiple explanatory variables are represented as a linear function in much the same way as a single variable. The

---

[5]Indeed, R^2 will **always** increase as variables are added to the model.

additional variables are simply added to the model (the model is thus said to be additive). For the example above, the model will look like:

$$\text{consumption} = \alpha + \beta_1 \text{ outdoor temperature} + \\ \beta_2 \text{ price} + \beta_3 \text{ family income} \quad (2.9)$$

Ice cream consumption can be predicted, at least to some extent, by taking into account the outdoor temperature, the price of the ice cream and family income. For simplicity, only the "main effects" (i.e. the effect of each variable on its own) are included in the model described below. Any interactions there may be between the explanatory variables are not taken into account. Table 2.9 provides the parameters for the multiple OLS regression model in Equation 2.9.

Table 2.9 *Regression parameters*

	Estimate	Standard error
(intercept)	0.197	0.270
Price	−1.044	0.834
Family income	0.003	0.001
Temperature	0.003	0.000

The regression parameters for each of the explanatory variables represent the average change in ice cream consumption that is expected to result from a change of one unit in that explanatory variable *when all other variables are held constant*. For example, for each unit rise in price, consumption decreases by an average of 1.044 pints per capita.[6] Similarly, for each unit increase in temperature, consumption increases by an average of 0.003 pints per capita. These partial regression coefficients identify the effect that each explanatory variable has on consumption independent of other variables in the model (that is, it identifies the unique contribution made by the explanatory variable in determining consumption).

As with simple OLS regression, confidence intervals for the β parameters can be easily computed using software (see Equation 2.3 for the method of computation). The 95% confidence intervals are shown in Table 2.10 below. From the table, we can

Table 2.10 *Confidence intervals*

	2.5%	50%	97.5%
Price	−2.759	−1.044	0.671
Family income	0.001	0.003	0.006
Temperature	0.003	0.003	0.004

---

[6]One should be aware that a unit change in price is a very large change. For the data collected, price in fact only fluctuates between .260 to .292.

The Ordinary Least-Squares Model

see that in 95% of cases, the expected increase in per capita consumption of ice cream for each degree rise in temperature is between 0.003 and 0.004 pints per capita (to 3 decimal places). In other words, for a unit increase in temperature (a one degree rise) in 95% of cases one would expect consumption to increase by at least 0.003 pints per capita but not more than 0.004 pints per capita. As both of these confidence intervals predict an increase in the consumption of ice cream, we can conclude that at the 95% 2-tailed level of significance, "temperature" does have a significant effect on the response variable in the model shown in Equation 2.9 (this is confirmed in the next section when the model-fit statistics are discussed). The variable "price" shows 95% confidence intervals that predict both a decrease (-2.759) and an increase (0.671) in ice cream consumption for a unit increase in price. As these intervals include 0, the variable "price" in this model does not appear to be significant (this is confirmed in the next section when the model-fit statistics are discussed).

Predicting the response variable: As with the simple OLS regression model, it is a simple matter to obtain predictions for the response variable at any given values of the explanatories. From the estimates provided in Table 2.9, one can obtain the intercept (α) and the regression coefficients for each of the explanatory variables. Substituting these values into Equation 2.9:

$$\text{consumption} = 0.197 + (-1.044 \times \text{price}) + \\ (0.003 \times \text{income}) + (0.003 \times \text{temperature})$$

Given a certain price, income and temperature (provided that these are within the range of observations recorded during the study), one can predict the amount of ice cream that will be consumed. For example, when the price is 0.280, income is 85 and temperature is 50 degrees Fahrenheit, ice cream consumption is predicted to be

$$\text{consumption} = 0.197 + (-1.044 \times 0.280) + (0.003 \times 85) + (0.003 \times 50) \\ = 0.310$$

Table 2.11 shows predicted probabilities of ice cream consumption for a number of different incomes, prices and temperatures computed using the R statistical package.

Goodness-of-fit statistics: Similar to simple OLS regression, the significance of individual and groups of variables in a multiple OLS regression model can be calculated by comparing the deviance statistics (RSS) for nested models. The general form for comparing nested models is given as:

$$\text{RSS}_{\text{diff}} = (\text{RSS}_p) - (\text{RSS}_{p+q}) \tag{2.10}$$

where RSS is the measure of deviance,
p is the smaller, nested model,
and $p + q$ is the larger model.

Table 2.11 *Predictions of consumption*

Income	Price	Temperature	Predicted consumption
78	0.270	41	0.315
79	0.282	56	0.358
81	0.277	63	0.394
80	0.280	68	0.405
94	0.265	41	0.373
96	0.265	52	0.418
91	0.268	64	0.440
90	0.260	71	0.469

Model : consumption $= 0.197 + (-1.044 \times \text{price}) + (0.003 \times \text{income}) + (0.003 \times \text{temperature})$

Although these statistics are provided by software (for example, in an analysis of deviance table similar to the one shown below), it is useful to look at how these statistics are calculated and this is shown in Table 2.12 which displays the deviance measures for a number of models along with some specific comparisons and the corresponding F and P values.

Table 2.12 *Assessing significance by comparing model deviances: individual variables*

	RSS	df	RSS$_{\text{diff}}$	F-value	P-value
Determining the effect of price					
consumption $= \alpha + \beta_1$ price $+ \beta_2$ income $+ \beta_3$ temp.	0.035	26	0.002	1.567	0.222
consumption $= \alpha + \beta_2$ income $+ \beta_3$ temp.	0.037	27			
Determining the effect of family income					
consumption $= \alpha + \beta_1$ price $+ \beta_2$ income $+ \beta_3$ temp.	0.035	26	0.011	7.973	0.009
consumption $= \alpha + \beta_1$ price $+ \beta_2$ temp.	0.046	27			
Determining the effect of outdoor temperature					
consumption $= \alpha + \beta_1$ price $+ \beta_2$ income $+ \beta_3$ temp.	0.035	26	0.082	60.252	3.1e−08
consumption $= \alpha + \beta_1$ price $+ \beta_2$ income.	0.117	27			

The significance of each change in deviance (RSS$_{\text{diff}}$) is obtained by computing an F-statistic. Equation 2.11 shows the general form of the equation used to derive F.

$$F_{(df_p-df_{p+q}),df_{p+q}} = \frac{\text{RSS}_p - \text{RSS}_{p+q}}{(df_p-df_{p+q})(\text{RSS}_{p+q}/df_{p+q})} \tag{2.11}$$

where p represents the smaller model,
$p + q$ represents the larger model,
and df are the degrees-of-freedom for the designated model.

Substituting numbers into the equation, one can work out the effect that any particular variable, or group of variables, has. For example, the significance of adding the variable "price" to the model "consumption $= \alpha + \beta_1$ outdoor temperature $+\beta_3$ family income" can be calculated as:

$$F_{(27-26),26} = \frac{0.002126}{(27-26)(0.035273/26)}$$
$$F_{1,26} = 1.567091$$

which is the same value as that provided for the variable "price" in Table 2.12. The F-value of 1.567 on 1 and 26 degrees of freedom is not significant (P=0.222). The significance of multiple variables can also be computed by comparing nested models. Table 2.13 shows how the contribution made by multiple variables may be obtained. The deviance measure for a number of models is provided along with

Table 2.13 *Assessing significance by comparing model deviances: groups of variables*

Model	RSS	df	RSS$_{\text{diff}}$	F-value	P-value
Determining the effect of all three variables					
consumption $= \alpha + \beta_1$ price $+$ β_2 income $+ \beta_3$ temp.	0.035	26	0.090	22.175	2.5e−07
consumption $= \alpha$	0.126	29			
Determining the effect of two variables (price and temperature)					
consumption $= \alpha + \beta_1$ price $+$ β_2 income $+ \beta_3$ temp.	0.035	26	0.090	33.156	7.0e−08
consumption $= \alpha + \beta$ income	0.125	28			

the difference in deviances between 2 selected model comparisons and the corresponding F and P values. The significance of all 3 variables can be computed by comparing the null model with the full model. The corresponding F-statistic can be calculated as:

$$F_{(29-26),26} = \frac{0.090251}{(29-26)(0.035273/26)}$$

$$F_{3,26} = 22.17490$$

which is the same value as that provided in Table 2.13. The F-value of 22.17490 on 3 and 26 degrees of freedom is highly significant (P = 2.5e − 07). Using an identical procedure, the significance of the combined effect of price and temperature on the full model can also be derived. The change in deviance of 0.0899 is highly significant as $F_{2,26} = 33.156, p = 7.0e - 08$. The information on model-fit for individual parameters does not need to be computed manually as it is commonly provided by software in an analysis of deviance table (see Table 2.14).

Table 2.14 *Analysis of deviance table: the significance of variables*

	Sum Sq	df	F-value	P-value
coefficient				
income	0.011	1	7.973	0.009
price	0.002	1	1.567	0.222
temperature	0.082	1	60.252	3.1e−08
residuals	0.035	26		

Model: consumption = $\alpha + \beta_1$ income + β_2 price + β_3 temperature

The significance of individual parameters in the model can also be estimated using a t-statistic which is simply the estimate divided by the standard error. The t-statistic for "temperature" in the model "consumption = $\alpha + \beta_1$ income + β_2 price + β_3 temperature" is 0.0034584/.0004455, which is 7.762. This value is then tested for significance using a 2-tailed test with $n - k - 1$ degrees of freedom (where n is the number of cases and k is the number of parameters excluding the constant, which, for this example is 26). The t-statistics and associated significance levels are shown in Table 2.15 below. For single parameter variables (i.e., not categorical), the t-statistics are directly comparable to the F-statistics reported in Tables 2.12 and 2.14 (in fact $\sqrt{F} = t$).

From the results in Tables 2.12 and 2.13, R^2 can be calculated for each model by dividing the deviance measure for the regression by the total deviance. For the model "consumption = $\alpha + \beta_1$ price + β_2 income", the deviance due to the regression (the variables price and income) is the difference between the deviance for the null model "consumption = α" (0.126; see Table 2.13) and the deviance for the model "consumption = $\alpha + \beta_1$ price + β_2 income " (0.117; see Table 2.12). The value of R^2 for this model is calculated as:

$$R^2 = \frac{0.126 - 0.117}{0.126}$$

$$= 0.071$$

Table 2.15 *Estimating the significance of individual parameters using t-statistics*

	Estimate	Standard error	T-value	P-value
(Intercept)	0.197	0.270	0.730	0.472
Income	0.003	0.001	2.824	0.009
Price	1.044	0.834	−1.252	0.222
Temperature	0.003	0.000	7.762	3.1e−08

Model: consumption $= \alpha + \beta_1$ income $+ \beta_2$ price $+ \beta_3$ temperature

In this case one can say that 7.1% of the variability in the response variable is accounted for by the explanatory variables price and income. A model that includes all 3 explanatory variables has an R^2 value of $(0.126 - 0.035)/0.126$, which equals 0.72. We can say that altogether, the 3 explanatory variables account for about 72% of the variance in consumption. It is a simple matter to compute R^2 for the other models presented in the tables and we leave the reader to compute these by hand or by the use of statistical software.

To conclude this section, one can say that 72% of the variability in ice cream consumption is accounted for by the 3 variables price, family income and temperature. From Table 2.15, outdoor temperature is seen to have the most significant effect on consumption ($t_{26} = 7.762$), followed by income ($t_{26} = 2.824$) and then price ($t_{26} = -1.252$). It should be noted, however, that these relationships are only likely to hold within the range of the collected data. Price, for example, has a marginal effect on consumption ($p > 0.01$) compared to the other variables included in the model, but its effect would be likely to change markedly if it were to be increased by, say, a factor of 100. What we can conclude is that within the price range investigated in this study, fluctuations in price only had a marginal effect on consumption. Also, the effect of family income is significant, but 1 would advise caution when interpreting this figure as, presumably, consumption would not increase indefinitely with family income as there is likely to be an upper limit on the amount of ice cream an individual can consume.

2.3 Categorical Explanatory Variables

It is relatively simple to include categorical explanatory variables into an OLS regression model if these variables are appropriately coded. A categorical variable may be entered into the model as a series of individual comparisons that can be evaluated individually or collectively (i.e. for a categorical variable representing industry sector; a number of individual sub-categories such as banking, construction and tourism can be compared with respect to their relationship with the response variable as well as the overall relationship between the variable "industry sector" and the response).

The individual comparisons made within the categorical variable depend on the way in which the variable has been coded. Two different methods of coding are dealt with in this book, one which compares categories with a specific reference category (indicator coding) and one that compares categories with the average of all categories (deviation coding). These 2 coding schemes are dealt with in detail in the sections on analyzing simple experimental designs and also in Chapters 3, 4, and 5, where their use is applied to models of ordered and unordered categorical response variables. Detailed descriptions and further information about coding categorical variables can be found in Crawley, 2005, Fox, 2002, Hutcheson and Sofroniou, 1999, and Miles and Shevlin, 2001.

2.4 Analyzing Simple Experimental Designs for Continuous Data

The analysis of grouped data assessed on a continuous response variable has traditionally been conducted through the use of a technique known as Analysis of Variance (ANOVA). This analytical technique is applied to experimental data and provides a way of determining whether the average scores of groups differ significantly. Regression, on the other hand, is most often applied to data obtained from correlational or non-experimental research. These separate analytical traditions have encouraged the mistaken belief that regression and ANOVA are fundamentally different types of statistical analysis. In this section we will demonstrate that grouped data can be analyzed using regression methods and that ANOVA is in fact a special case of regression analysis. For a more detailed explanation of the relationship between ANOVA and regression, see Rutherford, 2001.

The following discussion will describe the analysis of experimental data using OLS regression and the more traditional hypothesis tests. The analysis of unrelated and related groups will be dealt with for designs that have 2 or more experimental conditions. In order to emphasize the similarities between the analysis of experimental and correlational data, the methods and structure of the analyses below will closely follow those that have already been discussed for simple and multiple OLS regression models.

2.4.1 Unrelated groups design

With an unrelated groups design, the cases in the groups are independent of one another. That is, different cases have been chosen for each group (e.g. a random sample of 40 people are exposed to condition 1 and a different random sample of 40 people are exposed to condition 2). There is no relationship between the members of the 2 groups.

Comparing two groups using OLS regression: The problem of comparing groups can be couched in terms of the modeling techniques already discussed earlier in this chapter. Namely, a variable can be predicted to some extent using information about another variable. In this case a continuous variable (test score, wage, weight, IQ, etc.) can be predicted to some extent using information about group membership (teaching method used, gender, ethic origin, etc.). To use the regression model terminology, test score *can be predicted by* teaching method

reading ability *can be predicted by* gender

volume of sales *can be predicted by* location of store.

For these examples, we are aiming to model a continuous response variable using a categorical explanatory variable. The data set we are to use to demonstrate this can

Table 2.16 *Data: the price of whiskey (comparing 2 groups)*

State owned	Privately owned
4.65	4.82
4.55	5.29
4.11	4.89
4.15	4.95
4.20	4.55
4.55	4.90
3.80	5.25
4.00	5.30
4.19	4.29
4.75	4.85

Source: Chance, 1991. Reported in Hand et al., 1994.

be found on page 318 of Hand et al., (1994). It shows the price charged for whiskey by state-owned and privately-owned companies. The research hypothesis is of the form

price of whiskey *can be predicted by* type of ownership.

A pictorial representation of this design is shown in Figure 2.4 below and shows that the 20 companies are unrelated to one another across the 2 groups (state-owned and privately-owned). The aim of the analysis is to see if type of ownership is related to the price of whiskey.[7] The regression equation is of the form

$$\text{price of whiskey} = \alpha + \beta \text{ ownership}.$$

The variable "ownership" is an unordered categorical variable and needs to be appropriately coded before it can be entered into the model. One coding method that can be used is to "dummy code" each category using the numbers 0 and 1 to indicate the presence or absence of the attribute. For example, the 2 category variable "ownership" can be represented using 2 dummy codes, one indicating private-ownership and the other state-ownership. If we use this coding scheme, the data will look like it does in Table 2.17. Due to multicollinearity (see Hutcheson and Sofroniou, 1999), it is not possible to put both dummy codes into the model at the same time as one of

---

[7]It should be noted that this will not provide any **causal** evidence as to the link, as the groups are not randomly selected and other factors may therefore play a role in determining price.

38   Modeling Continuous Data

	State-owned	Privately-owned
Company	1	11
Company	2	12
Company	3	13
Company	4	14
	...	...
Company	10	20

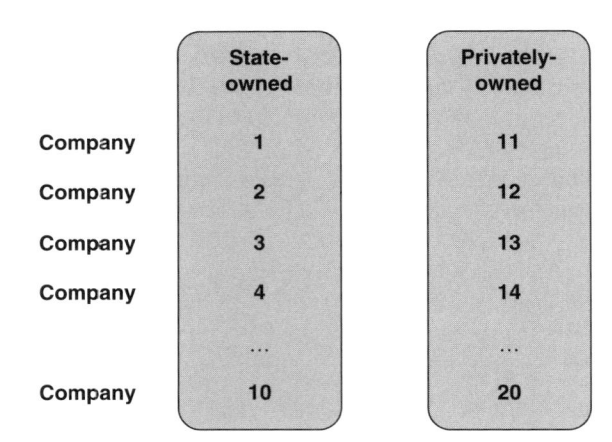

Figure 2.4 *A pictorial representation of an unrelated groups design*

them will be redundant. One of the dummy codes is therefore omitted and becomes the reference category, that is, it is the category that provides the comparison. For example, if the dummy code "state" is entered into the regression model, "private" will be the comparison category. If the dummy code "private" is entered into the model, "state" will be the comparison category.

Dummy codes are typically constructed automatically by software. Although there are a number of ways in which the codes can be constructed (enabling different contrasts to be made) we will use the indicator method here using 0 and 1 which provides comparisons with a reference category (commonly known as treatment contrasts). Later on (in Chapter 3, when we deal with modeling dichotomous data using logistic regression) another coding method is introduced, deviation coding, that enables comparisons to be made with the average of all categories as opposed to a single reference category. The use of the treatment contrasts is made explicit in the regression output by the inclusion of the "T" identifier before the parameter description. Table 2.18 shows the model parameters that have been calculated using standard regression software.

In Table 2.18, the parameter "ownership (T.private)" shows the category privately-funded" compared to "state-funded". The "T" identifier indicates that it is a treatment contrast and "private" indicates that this category is the one that is compared to the reference. The interpretation of the parameter estimate for this dummy variable is very similar to that for a continuous variable. A unit increase in the explanatory variable represents going from "state-owned" (coded as 0) to "privately-owned" (coded as 1) and therefore results in comparing one category with the other. The estimate of 0.614, indicates that a privately-owned company on average charges 0.614 units more than a state-owned company.

It is useful to also compute the confidence intervals for the regression coefficient (see Equation 2.3). Table 2.19 shows these intervals for the parameter "ownership (T.private)". In 95% of cases, we would expect the difference in the price of whiskey

Analyzing Simple Experimental Designs for Continuous Data

Table 2.17 *Price of whiskey: "ownership" dummy coded*

| Price | Ownership | |
	State	Private
4.65	1	0
4.55	1	0
4.11	1	0
4.15	1	0
4.20	1	0
4.55	1	0
3.80	1	0
4.00	1	0
4.19	1	0
4.75	1	0
4.82	0	1
5.29	0	1
4.89	0	1
4.95	0	1
4.55	0	1
4.90	0	1
5.25	0	1
5.30	0	1
4.29	0	1
4.85	0	1

Table 2.18 *Regression parameters*

	Estimate	Standard error
(Intercept)	4.295	0.100
Ownership (T.private)	0.614	0.142

Model: price = $\alpha + \beta$ ownership
Ownership reference category = state-owned

between privately-owned and state-owned companies to be between 0.316 and 0.912. Of particular interest here is that both estimates predict that privately-owned companies charge more for whiskey which suggests that this relationship is significant to the 0.05 level (this is confirmed when the model-fit statistics are investigated).

Table 2.19 *Confidence intervals*

	2.5%	50%	97.5%
Ownership (T.private)	0.316	0.614	0.912

Using the parameters in Table 2.18, the regression equation can be written as

$$\text{price of whiskey} = 4.295 + (0.614 * \text{ownership}).$$

It is simple to use this model to make predictions about the price of whiskey for the different types of company. For example, the price of whiskey produced in a state-owned company (where ownership is designated as 0) can be calculated as

$$\text{price of whiskey: state-owned company} = 4.295 + (0.614 * 0)$$
$$= 4.295$$

whereas the price of whiskey produced in a privately-owned company (where ownership is designated as 1) can be calculated as

$$\text{price of whiskey: privately-owned company} = 4.295 + (0.614 * 1)$$
$$= 4.909.$$

These values can also be derived using simple descriptive statistics, as the predicted prices of the whiskey produced by state-owned and privately-owned companies are simply the mean values.

Similar to the OLS regression models described so far, model-fit statistics can be obtained by comparing the deviances (the RSS statistics) of nested models. For example, in order to assess the significance of the variable "ownership", one needs to compare the two models:

$$\text{whiskey price} = \alpha$$
$$\text{whiskey price} = \alpha + \beta \text{ ownership (T.private)}.$$

The deviance in the null model "whiskey price $= \alpha$" is equal to 3.695 (computed using commonly available software) and for the model "whiskey price $= \alpha + \beta$ ownership (T.private)" the deviance is equal to 1.810 (see Table 2.20). The reduction in deviance between the two models (1.885) indicates the effect that ownership has on the price of whiskey. The significance of this reduction in deviance can be calculated using the F-test, shown in Equation 2.12.

$$F_{(df_{\text{null}}-df_{\text{model}}), df_{\text{model}}} = \frac{\text{RSS}_{\text{null}} - \text{RSS}_{\text{model}}}{(df_{\text{null}}-df_{\text{model}})(\text{RSS}_{\text{model}}/df_{\text{model}})} \quad (2.12)$$

where "null" indicates the model $Y = \alpha$,
"model" indicates the model $Y = \alpha + \beta x$,
RSS is the residual sum of squares for the designated model,
and df is the degrees of freedom for the designated model.

For the model of whiskey price, the value of F is

$$F_{19-18,18} = \frac{3.6953 - 1.8103}{(19 - 18)(1.8103/18)}$$
$$F_{1,18} = 18.742$$

Analyzing Simple Experimental Designs for Continuous Data

Table 2.20 *Assessing significance by comparing model deviances*

Model	RSS	df	RSS$_{diff}$	F-value	P-value
Price = α	3.670	19	1.885	18.742	4.0e−04
Price = $\alpha + \beta$ ownership	1.810	18			

RSS represents the deviance in the model
RSS$_{diff}$ is the difference in deviance between the two models
F-statistic = 18.74 on 1 and 18 degrees of freedom

which is significant (p = 4.0e−04). The results are summarized in Table 2.20 below.

The information on model-fit for individual parameters does not need to be computed manually as it is commonly provided by software in an analysis of deviance table (see Table 2.21). Although this table is redundant for this example as the information on RSS has already been provided, it is included here as it is commonly output by software.

Table 2.21 *Analysis of deviance table: the significance of variables*

	Sum Sq	df	F-value	P-value
Coefficient				
Ownership	1.885	1	18.742	4.0e−04
Residuals	1.810	18		

Model: price = $\alpha + \beta_1$ ownership

The significance of individual parameters in the model can also be estimated using a t-statistic which is simply the estimate divided by the standard error. The t-statistic for "ownership" is therefore 0.614/0.142, which is 4.329 (this is the estimate from software, which uses many more decimal places than have been reported here). This value is then tested for significance using a 2-tailed test with $n-k-1$ degrees of freedom (where n is the number of cases and k is the number of parameters excluding the constant, which, for this example is 18). The t-statistic and associated significance level is shown in Table 2.22 below. The t-statistic for a dichotomous explanatory variable is directly comparable to the F-statistic reported in Tables 2.20 and 2.21 (in fact $\sqrt{F} = t$; $\sqrt{18.742} = 4.329$).

On this evidence it would appear that whiskey produced by privately-owned companies is more expensive than that produced by state-owned companies. This is significant at the .0005 level. When interpreting these results it is, however, important to realize that the relationship between the two variables cannot be considered as causal. It might well be that the private sector does charge more for its whiskey, but it could also be that state-owned companies tend to operate in city areas where strong competition keeps prices down. The difference in prices may therefore be due to location and not just ownership.

Table 2.22 *Estimating the significance of individual parameters using t-statistics*

	Estimate	Standard error	t-value	P-value
(Intercept)	4.295	0.100	42.827	
Ownership (T.private)	0.614	0.142	4.329	4.0e−04

Model: whiskey price $= \alpha + \beta$ ownwership

Comparing more than two groups using OLS regression: Using the technique of regression, it is possible to compare more than 2 groups. This is demonstrated by adding another group to the data used above (these data are hypothetical and are added merely to provide a third group comparison) and is shown below in Table 2.23.

Table 2.23 *Data: the price of whiskey (comparing three groups)*

State–owned	Privately–owned	State–private partnership*
4.65	4.82	4.72
4.55	5.29	4.90
4.11	4.89	4.04
4.15	4.95	4.98
4.20	4.55	4.37
4.55	4.90	5.12
3.80	5.25	4.98
4.00	5.30	4.79
4.19	4.29	4.42
4.75	4.85	4.80

* hypothetical data

For these data, the research hypothesis is of the form

price of whiskey *can be predicted by* ownership.

The data to be modeled (the response variable) is price, which can be considered to be a continuous variable. Ownership is the explanatory variable and takes one of 3 values (state-owned, privately-owned, or a state-private partnership). In order to include a multi-category explanatory variable in the regression model, ownership is dummy coded into 2 dichotomous variables. For simplicity, we will use the indicator coding method shown in Table 2.24 where the 3 category variable "ownership" is represented as 2 separate dummy variables, each indicating the presence or absence of a particular category. For example, dummy variable 1 records whether or not the company is privately-owned, whilst dummy variable 2 records whether or not the company is owned by a state–private partnership.[8]

---

[8]For a full description of indicator coding, please refer to Hutcheson and Sofroniou, 1999.

Analyzing Simple Experimental Designs for Continuous Data

Table 2.24 *The indicator method of dummy coding "ownership"*

Original variable	Dummy variables 1	2
State	0	0
Private	1	0
State–private	0	1

You will note that although there are 3 categories of ownership, there are only 2 dummy variables. In general, if we have j categories, a maximum of $j-1$ dummy variables can be entered into a model. The dummy variable which is omitted is called the reference category and is the category against which other dummy variables are compared (so long as all $j-1$ dummy variables are included in the model). It should be noted that the choice of reference category is often quite arbitrary, although sometimes there will be reasons that a particular reference category is chosen. For example, when comparing a number of treatments for a particular illness, it might make sense to compare each with the standard treatment currently used to treat the disease (see Hardy, 1993, for a more in-depth discussion of reference category choice). After coding "ownership" using indicator coding (treatment contrasts) with state-owned as the reference category, the regression model is of the form:

$$\text{price of whiskey} = \alpha + \beta_1 \text{ ownership (T.private)} + \beta_2 \text{ ownership (T.partnership)}.$$

The single variable "ownership" is therefore represented by 2 parameters which are shown in Table 2.25; "ownership (T.private)" compares privately-owned companies to state-owned and shows that whiskey from privately-owned companies is, on average, 0.614 units more expensive than for state-owned companies. Similarly, whiskey from a state-private partnership is, on average, 0.417 units more expensive than for state-owned companies.

Table 2.25 *Regression parameters*

	Estimate	Standard error
(Intercept)	4.295	0.102
Ownership(T.private)	0.614	0.145
Ownership(T.partnership)	0.417	0.145

Model: price = $\alpha + \beta_1$ ownership (T.private) + β_2 ownership (T.partnership)

Ownership reference category: state-owned

As with other OLS regression models, confidence intervals for the regression coefficients can be easily calculated (see Table 2.26). In 95% of cases, we would expect the difference in the price of whiskey between privately-owned and state-owned companies to be between 0.317 and 0.911 and that between a partnership and state-owned to be between 0.120 and 0.714. Of particular interest here is that as all estimates predict an increase in price privately-owned and state–private partnership are both significantly different to state-owned companies at the 0.05 level (this is confirmed when the model-fit statistics are investigated).

Table 2.26 *Confidence intervals*

	2.5%	50%	97.5%
Ownership (T.private)	0.317	0.614	0.911
Ownership (T.partnership)	0.120	0.417	0.714

The regression equation for this model is

$$\text{price of whiskey} = 4.295 + (0.614 * \text{ownership (T.private)}) + (0.417 * \text{ownership (T.partnership)})$$

which allows predictions to be made for each of the three different types of ownership.

$$\text{price of whiskey: state-owned company} = 4.295 + (0.614 * 0) + (0.417 * 0)$$
$$= 4.295$$

$$\text{price of whiskey: privately-owned company} = 4.295 + (0.614 * 1) + (0.417 * 0)$$
$$= 4.909$$

$$\text{price of whiskey: state–private partnership} = 4.295 + (0.614 * 0) + (0.417 * 1)$$
$$= 4.712$$

These values can also be derived using simple descriptive statistics, as the predicted prices of the whiskey produced by state-owned companies, privately-owned companies and state-private partnerships is simply the mean values for these groups.

Similar to the OLS regression models described so far, model-fit statistics can be obtained by comparing the deviances (the RSS statistics) of nested models. Using these statistics, the significance of individual parameters (e.g., ownership (T.private)) and variables (ownership) can be obtained. Deviance statistics for the model of whiskey price are shown in Table 2.27. From this table we can see that adding the 2 parameters that constitute the variable "ownership" to the model "whiskey price = α" reduces the deviance by 1.966. This reduction in deviance equates to an F-value of 9.398 (see Equation 2.11), which is tested for significance at 2 and 27 degrees of freedom (2 parameters difference between the models and n-k-1, where n is the number of cases and k the number of parameters in the larger model excluding the intercept).

Analyzing Simple Experimental Designs for Continuous Data

Similarly, the significance of a single category can also be computed by comparing the deviances of nested models. For example, the significance of the privately-owned companies compared to state-owned (i.e., comparing 2 categories from within the variable "ownership") can be obtained by comparing the deviances for the 2 nested models:

whiskey price $= \alpha + \beta_1$ ownership (T.private) $+ \beta_2$ ownership (T.partnership)
whiskey price $= \alpha + \beta$ ownership (T.partnership)

If we remove the information about private ownership (contained in the parameter "ownership (T.private)" the deviance is reduced by 1.884, which is significant at the .0005 level ($F_{1,27} = 18.025, p = 0.0002$). Privately-owned companies therefore charge significantly more than state-owned companies.

Table 2.27 *Assessing significance by comparing model deviances*

Model	RSS	df	RSS$_{diff}$	F-value	P-value
Determining the overall effect of ownership					
Price $= \alpha$	4.789	29	1.966	9.398	7.9e-04
Price $= \alpha + \beta_1$ own (T.private) $+ \beta_2$ own (T.partner)	2.824	27			
Determining the effect of privately-owned					
Price $= \alpha + \beta$ own (T.partner)	4.708	28	1.884	18.025	0.0002
Price $= \alpha + \beta_1$ own (T.private) $+ \beta_2$ own (T.partner)	2.824	27			
Determining the effect of state–private partnership					
Price $= \alpha + \beta$ own (T.private)	3.693	28	0.869	8.314	0.0076
Price $= \alpha + \beta_1$ own (T.private) $+ \beta_2$ own (T.partner)	2.824	27			

RSS represents the deviance in the model
RSS$_{diff}$ is the difference in deviance between the two models
Ownership reference category: state-owned

By changing the reference category, different group comparisons may be obtained. For example, to obtain a comparison between privately-owned and state–private partnership, one could designate either of these as the reference category and then recalculate the model. If we do this, different comparisons are made between the categorical variable categories, but all model-fit statistics will remain the same.

The information on model-fit is commonly provided by software in an analysis of deviance table (see Table 2.28). This table shows the significance of the variable "ownership" and is derived using the RSS statistics discussed above.

Table 2.28 *Analysis of deviance table: the significance of variables*

	Sum Sq	df	F-value	P-value
Coefficient				
Ownership	1.966	2	9.398	7.9e−04
Residuals	2.824	27		

Model: price $= \alpha + \beta_1$ ownership

The signifiance of individual parameters in the model can be estimated using a t-statistic which is simply the estimate divided by the standard error. The t-statistic for "ownership (T.private)" is therefore 0.6140/0.1446, which is 4.246. This value is then tested for significance using a 2-tailed test with $n-k-1$ degrees of freedom (where n is the number of cases and k is the number of parameters excluding the constant, which, for this example is 27). The t-statistic and associated significance level is shown in Table 2.29 below. The t-statistics for these parameters are directly comparable to the F-statistics reported in Table 2.27 (in fact $\sqrt{F} = t$; for example, $\sqrt{8.314} = 2.883$, allowing for rounding error).

Table 2.29 *Estimating the significance of individual parameters using t-statistics*

	Estimate	Standard error	T-value	P-value
(Intercept)	4.295	0.102	42.000	0.000
Ownership (T.private)	0.614	0.145	4.246	0.000
Ownership (T.partnership)	0.417	0.145	2.883	0.008

Model: price $= \alpha + \beta_1$ ownership(1) $+ \beta_2$ ownership(2)

Reference category: state-owned

From these analyses, it is clear that there is a relationship between the price of whiskey and the type of company ownership. Compared to state-owned companies, privately-owned companies and state–private partnerships tend to charge more for their whiskey. Both these results are significant to the 0.01 level. As this was a correlational study, little can be concluded as to whether this is a causal relationship or not.

Comparing two groups using a t-test: The same analysis as was conducted in Section 2.4.1 can be obtained using an unrelated t-test. This test can be conducted using a number of packages and is detailed in numerous introductory statistics books and manuals and will not, therefore, be explained in detail here. The results obtained from a typical statistical software package are reproduced in Table 2.30 to provide a comparison with the regression analyses already described.

Table 2.30 *The two-group whiskey data: t-test*

	Mean	df	t	P-value
Group 1: state-owned	4.295	18	4.329	0.0004
Group 2: privately-owned	4.909			

We can see that the analysis obtained using the unrelated t-test (t = 4.329) is identical to that obtained using OLS regression (see Table 2.22).

Comparing more than two groups using ANOVA: The same analysis as was conducted in Section 2.4.1 can be obtained using a one-way ANOVA. This test can be conducted using a number of packages and is detailed in numerous introductory statistics books and manuals and will not, therefore, be explained in detail here. The output from an ANOVA computation is shown in Table 2.31 below.

Table 2.31 *The three-group whiskey data: ANOVA*

	df	Sum of squares	Mean squares	F-value	p-Value
Ownership	2	1.966	0.983	9.398	0.0008
Residuals	27	2.824	0.105		

We can see that the analysis obtained using the one-way ANOVA (F = 9.398) is identical to that obtained using OLS regression (see Table 2.27). The overall group effect of type of ownership is significantly linearly related to the price of whiskey.

2.4.2 Related groups designs

With a related groups design, the cases in the groups are the same (repeated measures) or they are matched (matched groups). That is, the same case (or pair of cases) takes part in each phase of the experiment (e.g. 40 people are exposed to condition 1 and then the same 40 people are exposed to condition 2). The analysis of a related groups design is the same as for an unrelated groups design apart from the inclusion of the additional information about subject.

The data set used to illustrate the related groups analyses is hypothetical and shows the overall rating of quality for a number of stores. Ten subjects were asked to rate the quality of different stores using a large number of criteria (quality of goods, services, staff, store atmosphere, etc.). The data shown are the average scores for each store. These data (which are considered to be continuous) are shown in Table 2.32 with the design of the study illustrated pictorially in Figure 2.5.

Table 2.32 *Data: quality ratings of stores*

Subject	Store A	Store B	Store C
1	3.8	3.2	3.1
2	4.0	2.4	3.7
3	4.1	4.2	3.9
4	4.1	3.2	3.9
5	4.1	3.3	4.0
6	4.1	3.9	3.9
7	4.2	3.8	4.3
8	4.5	3.8	4.4
9	4.5	3.9	4.7
10	4.6	3.9	4.3

Comparing two groups using OLS regression: For this demonstration, as we are interested in a 2-group comparison, only data from stores A and B will be considered. The research hypothesis is of the form:

Quality *can be predicted by* store

The aim of the analysis is to see if quality ratings are related to the store. That is, does the overall rating of quality differ between stores A and B. The data to be modeled (the response variable) is quality, which can be considered to be a continuous variable making OLS regression an appropriate analytical technique. The store evaluated is the explanatory variable and takes one of 2 values (store A or store B). It is not appropriate to analyse the data in the same way as the unrelated groups design above, as there is likely to be a correlation between the measurements. Some subjects may be harder to please than others and may give stores lower ratings because of this. A store's rating will therefore depend not only on factors related to the store, but will also depend on factors related to the subject. We are thus interested not only in the

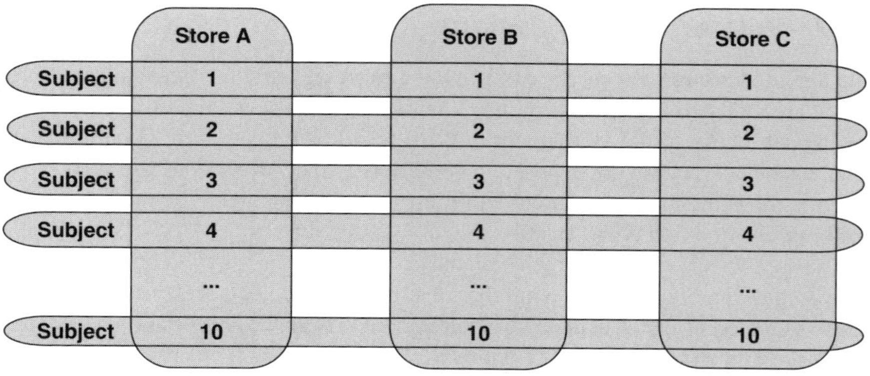

Figure 2.5 *A pictorial representation of a dependent groups design*

differences between the groups (store A and store B) but also in the difference between each subject's ratings for the stores. Taking into account the coding of the unordered categorical data into $j-1$ comparisons (for the variables "store" and "subject"), the regression model is of the form:

$$\text{quality} = \alpha + \beta_1 \text{storeB} + \beta_2 \text{subject2} + \beta_3 \text{subject3} + \beta_4 \text{subject4}$$
$$+ \beta_5 \text{subject5} + \beta_6 \text{subject6} + \beta_7 \text{subject7} + \beta_8 \text{subject8}$$
$$+ \beta_9 \text{subject9} + \beta_{10} \text{subject10}.$$

where store A and subject1 are the reference categories. Table 2.33 shows the parameters for this model with the variable "store" dummy coded using the indicator coding method with Store A designated as the reference category (hence the parameter identifier "T.storeB" indicating a treatment comparison of store B compared to the reference category). The variable "subject" is also dummy coded using the indicator method with subject 1 designated as the reference category (hence the "subject[T.2]" parameter indicating treatment comparisons of each identified subject to the reference category, subject 1).

Table 2.33 *Regression parameters*

	Estimate	Standard error
(Intercept)	3.820	0.236
Store[T.B]	−0.640	0.142
Subject[T.2]	−0.300	0.318
Subject[T.3]	0.650	0.318
Subject[T.4]	0.150	0.318
Subject[T.5]	0.200	0.318
Subject[T.6]	0.500	0.318
Subject[T.7]	0.500	0.318
Subject[T.8]	0.650	0.318
Subject[T.9]	0.700	0.318
Subject[T.10]	0.750	0.318

Model: quality = $\alpha + \beta_1$ store + β_{2-10} subject
Store reference category: store A
Subject reference category: subject 1

The output in Table 2.33 may look quite confusing as there are now many parameters in the model. We are, however, not particularly interested in the parameters associated with the variable "subject" as these are included to control for the repeated measurements. Controlling for "subject" enables us to evaluate the relationship between "store" and "quality" independent of "subject". The parameter of interest here is the one associated with the variable "store". For a unit increase in store (i.e. comparing "store B" to the reference category "store A"), quality decreases by 0.64. Store B, therefore appears to be rated as having a lower quality than store A.

It is useful to also compute the confidence intervals for the regression coefficients, and these are shown in Table 2.34. The confidence intervals are interpreted in a similar way to the models discussed previously in this chapter. For example, in 95% of cases, one would expect the quality ratings for store B to be between 0.962 and 0.318 lower than for store A. As both of these predict a decrease, the difference between stores A and B looks to be significant at the 95% level (this is confirmed when the model-fit statistics are investigated later in this chapter). Confidence intervals are also provided for the subjects, but as these are not of any real interest (the research hypothesis is related to the differences between the stores and not between subjects), they will not be discussed here.

Table 2.34 *Confidence intervals*

	2.5%	50%	97.5%
(Intercept)	3.286	3.820	4.354
Store[T.B]	−0.962	−0.640	−0.318
Subject[T.2]	−1.020	−0.300	0.420
Subject[T.3]	−0.070	0.650	1.370
Subject[T.4]	−0.570	0.150	0.870
Subject[T.5]	−0.520	0.200	0.920
Subject[T.6]	−0.220	0.500	1.220
Subject[T.7]	−0.220	0.500	1.220
Subject[T.8]	−0.070	0.650	1.370
Subject[T.9]	−0.020	0.700	1.420
Subject[T.10]	0.030	0.750	1.470

Model: quality = $\alpha + \beta_1$ store $+ \beta_{2-10}$ subject

Once the model parameters have been obtained, it is a simple matter to compute predictions from the model. Substituting the model parameters shown in Table 2.33, the regression equation is

$$\begin{aligned}\text{quality} = \ & 3.82 + (-0.64 * \text{store B}) + (-0.30 * \text{sub2}) + (0.65 * \text{sub3}) \\ & + (0.15 * \text{sub4}) + (0.20 * \text{sub5}) + (0.50 * \text{sub6}) \\ & + (0.50 * \text{sub7}) + (0.65 * \text{sub8}) + (0.70 * \text{sub9}) \\ & + (0.75 * \text{sub10}).\end{aligned}$$

This model can be used to obtain the predicted quality ratings for each subject for each store. Table 2.35 shows these predictions which have been computed using software. The predicted ratings show the predictions from the model. The predicted ratings of quality for the stores is different for each subject. If we average the store ratings across all the subjects we get a rating of 4.20 for store A and a rating of 3.56 for store B. The difference between these 2 represents the differences between the stores, which is equivalent to 0.64 (4.20 − 3.56); the regression parameter for store[T.B] in Table 2.33.

Table 2.35 *Predicting the quality of the stores*

Store	Subject	Predicted rating of quality
A	1	3.82
A	2	3.52
A	3	4.47
A	4	3.97
A	5	4.02
A	6	4.32
A	7	4.32
A	8	4.47
A	9	4.52
A	10	4.57
B	1	3.18
B	2	2.88
B	3	3.83
B	4	3.33
B	5	3.38
B	6	3.68
B	7	3.68
B	8	3.83
B	9	3.88
B	10	3.93

Model: quality = $\alpha + \beta_1$ store + β_{2-10} subject

Similar to the OLS regression models described so far, model-fit statistics can be obtained by comparing the deviances (the RSS statistics) of nested models. For example, in order to assess the significance of the variable "store", one needs to compare the deviances of the 2 models:

$$\text{quality} = \alpha + \beta_{1-9} \text{ subject}$$
$$\text{quality} = \alpha + \beta_1 \text{ store} + \beta_{2-10} \text{ subject}$$

The deviance in the model "quality = $\alpha + \beta_{1-9}$ subject" is equal to 2.960 and for the model "quality = $\alpha + \beta_1$ store + β_{2-10} subject" the deviance is equal to 0.912. The difference in deviance between the 2 models is 2.048 and indicates the effect of the variable "store" on "quality" after "subject" has been accounted for. The significance of this change in deviance can be calculated using the F-test, shown in Equation 2.11. These results are summarized in Table 2.36 below.

By comparing the deviances of nested models, it is also possible to calculate the significance of the subject variable. To do this, one simply compares the deviances for the 2 nested models shown in Table 2.37 below (one model includes the variable "subject" whilst the other does not). Removing subject from the model increases the deviance by 2.212, which is not a significant increase. Subject, is therefore not significant for this model.

Table 2.36 *Assessing the significance of "store" by comparing model deviances*

Model	RSS	df	RSS$_{diff}$	F-value	P-value
Quality = $\alpha + \beta_1$ store + β_{2-10} subject	0.912	9			
			2.048	20.211	0.001
Quality = $\alpha + \beta_{1-9}$ subject	2.960	10			

RSS represents the deviance in the model.
RSS$_{diff}$ is the difference in deviance between the two models.

The information on model-fit for individual parameters does not need to be computed manually as it is commonly provided by software in an analysis of deviance table (see Table 2.38). Although this table is redundant for this example as the information on RSS has already been provided, it is included here as it is commonly output by software.

The significance of individual parameters in the model can be estimated using a t-statistic which is simply the estimate divided by the standard error. The t-statistic for "store(T.B)" is therefore $-0.640/0.142$, which is -4.507 (using more decimal places, the actual value of t is -4.496, a value provided by software in Table 2.39). This value is then tested for significance using a 2-tailed test with $n - k - 1$ degrees of freedom (where n is the number of cases and k is the number of parameters excluding the constant, which, for this example is 9). The t-statistics and associated significance level for all parameters are clearly shown in the table.

Table 2.37 *Assessing the significance of "subject" by comparing model deviances*

Model	RSS	df	RSS$_{diff}$	F-value	P-value
Quality = $\alpha + \beta_1$ store + β_{2-10} subject	0.912	9			
			2.212	2.425	0.102
Quality = $\alpha + \beta_1$ store	3.124	18			

RSS represents the deviance in the model.
RSS$_{diff}$ is the difference in deviance between the two models.

Table 2.38 *Analysis of deviance table: the significance of variables*

	Sum sq	df	F-value	P-value
Coefficient				
Subject	2.212	9	2.425	0.102
Store	2.048	1	20.210	0.001
Residuals	0.912	9		

Model: quality = $\alpha + \beta_1$ store + β_{2-10} subject

Table 2.39 *Estimating the significance of individual parameters using t-statistics*

	Estimate	Standard error	T-value	P-value
(Intercept)	3.820	0.236	16.181	$5.8e-08$
Store[T.B]	−0.640	0.142	−4.496	0.002
Subject[T.2]	−0.300	0.318	−0.942	0.371
Subject[T.3]	0.650	0.318	2.042	0.072
Subject[T.4]	0.150	0.318	0.471	0.649
Subject[T.5]	0.200	0.318	0.628	0.545
Subject[T.6]	0.500	0.318	1.571	0.151
Subject[T.7]	0.500	0.318	1.571	0.151
Subject[T.8]	0.650	0.318	2.042	0.072
Subject[T.9]	0.700	0.318	2.199	0.055
Subject[T.10]	0.750	0.318	2.356	0.043

Model: quality = $\alpha + \beta_1$ store + β_{2-10} subject
Store reference category: store A
Subject reference category: subject 1

On this evidence it would appear that stores A and B are rated differently with respect to quality. Store A is rated significantly higher than store B. Subject was not significantly related to quality and was included in the model to control for the repeated measurements.

Comparing more than two groups using OLS regression: Using the regression technique, it is easy to extend the analysis of related groups designs to cases where there are more than 2 groups. The interpretation of parameters for more than 2 groups and the inclusion of the subject variable to take account of the repeated measurements in the design of the study, have already been discussed in previous sections and will not, therefore, be dealt with in any detail here. What is presented is a minimal set of analyses that show the relationship between all 3 stores and ratings of quality for a related groups design.

Using the data shown in Table 2.32, all 3 stores can be compared. The response variable, "quality", is continuous which makes OLS regression a suitable analytical technique with the variables "store" and "subject" dummy coded. Table 2.40 shows the parameter estimates and t-statistics for the model of quality using all three stores.

The regression parameters in Table 2.40 are interpreted in much the same way as they were for the model with just 2 stores. Stores B and C have lower quality ratings compared to store A (0.640 and 0.180 lower, respectively) whilst taking account of subject. The significance of these parameters is provided by the t-statistics, which show that store B is significantly different to store A, but store C is not significantly different from store A. The major difference between the stores appears to be between stores A and B. A number of individual subjects are different from the reference subject, but this finding is not of any particular importance to our research question.

Table 2.40 *Regression parameters*

	Estimate	Standard error	T-value	P-value
(Intercept)	3.640	0.181	20.108	0.000
Store[T.B]	−0.640	0.128	−5.000	0.000
Store[T.C]	−0.180	0.128	−1.406	0.177
Subject[T.2]	0.000	0.234	0.000	1.000
Subject[T.3]	0.700	0.234	2.995	0.008
Subject[T.4]	0.367	0.234	1.569	0.134
Subject[T.5]	0.433	0.234	1.854	0.080
Subject[T.6]	0.600	0.234	2.567	0.019
Subject[T.7]	0.733	0.234	3.138	0.006
Subject[T.8]	0.867	0.234	3.708	0.002
Subject[T.9]	1.000	0.234	4.279	0.001
Subject[T.10]	0.900	0.234	3.851	0.001

Quality $= \alpha + \beta_{1-2}$ store $+ \beta_{3-11}$ subject
Store reference category: store A
Subject reference category: subject 1

An analysis of deviance table is also useful for assessing the overall relationship between the explanatory variables and ratings of quality (see Table 2.41). We can see from this table that the variable "store" is significantly related to rated quality. Subject is also significantly related to rated quality (this result is, however, not of any particular interest).

Table 2.41 *Analysis of deviance table: the significance of variables*

	Sum Sq	df	F-value	P-value
Coefficient				
Subject	3.405	9	4.618	$2.8e-03$
Store	2.179	2	13.297	$2.8e-04$
Residuals	1.475	18		

Model: quality $= \alpha + \beta_1$ store $+ \beta_{2-10}$ subject

Comparing two groups using a t-test: The same analysis as was conducted in Section 2.4.2 can be obtained using a related t-test. This test can be conducted using a number of packages and is detailed in numerous introductory statistics books and manuals and will not, therefore, be explained in detail here. The results obtained from a typical statistical software package are reproduced in in Table 2.42 to provide a comparison with the regression analyses already described.

We can see that the analysis obtained using the related t-test (t = 4.496) is identical to that obtained using OLS regression (see Tables 2.33 and 2.36) and is interpreted in exactly the same way.

Conclusion

Table 2.42 *The two-group store data: related t-test*

	Mean	df	t	P-value
Store A	4.20	9	4.496	0.0015
Store B	3.56			

Comparing more than two groups using ANOVA: The same analysis as was conducted in Section 2.4.2 can be obtained using an ANOVA. This test can be conducted using a number of packages and is detailed in numerous introductory statistics books and manuals and will not, therefore, be explained in detail here. The output from an ANOVA computation is shown in Table 2.43 below.

Table 2.43 *The three-group store data: related ANOVA*

	df	Sum of squares	Mean squares	F-value	p-value
Store	2	2.179	1.089	13.297	0.0003
Subject	9	3.405	0.378	4.618	0.0028
Residuals	18	1.475	0.082		

We can see that the analysis obtained using the ANOVA is identical to that obtained using OLS regression (see Table 2.41) and is interpreted in an identical way.

2.5 Conclusion

In this chapter, OLS regression has been used to model continuous response variables using continuous and grouped explanatory variables. Detailed descriptions have been provided about the interpretation of the regression coefficients and model-fit statistics and the equivalence of the regression technique to the more traditional hypothesis tests has been made explicit. The t-tests and ANOVAs can be regarded as special cases of the more general technique of OLS regression.

The advantages of the regression technique is that it allows data to be analyzed and interpreted under the generalized linear modeling (GLM) umbrella. Analyzing data in this way enables complex models to be built up that include different types of explanatory variables taking into account design constraints (repeated measures designs, for example). The use of GLM methods is particularly powerful when compared to the standard hypothesis tests as it allows one to apply similar techniques to other types of response variable. We will find in the following chapters how to generalize the use of OLS regression to ordered and unordered categorical data.

CHAPTER 3
Modeling Dichotomous Data

Binary categorical variables are quite common in management research and can indicate, for example, whether someone will make a purchase or not or whether a certain course of action has been a success. To model a binary response variable, one can use the generalized linear modeling technique of logistic regression. This chapter introduces logistic regression, explains the theory behind the technique and the interpretation of the model parameters and model-fit statistics for models containing single and multiple explanatory variables.

Logistic regression is a particularly important technique not only because it provides a method of modeling binary data, but also as it is central to understanding the wider application of the generalized linear model to multi-category ordered and unordered data. The techniques of proportional odds modeling and multi-nomial logistic regression, which are discussed in subsequent chapters and allow multi-category ordered and unordered response variables to be modeled, can be seen as extensions to the basic logistic regression model that is the subject of this chapter.

3.1 The Generalized Linear Model

In Chapter 2, we showed how a linear model (OLS regression) can be used to model a continuous response variable. In this chapter we show how this analysis technique can be generalized to enable a binary response variable to be modeled. In order to demonstrate this, a hypothetical example is used showing whether or not a sale is achieved given the years of experience of a sales team. The response variable is a binary classification of success (successful or unsuccessful for each sales enquiry made) and the explanatory variable is a continuous variable representing years of service of the sales team. This model of 'success' can be represented as:

Success *may be predicted by* the experience of the sales team

In general, we may expect that the more experience a sales team has, the greater the probability there is of a sale being made (although this is not the only factor likely to affect the outcome). The scatterplot in Figure 3.1 which shows the raw data plotted suggests that this is the case for these data as successful outcomes do appear to be associated with a greater degree of experience.

The relationship between success and experience is not, however, that easy to discern from Figure 3.1 which depicts the raw data. The relationship can be more clearly shown when the **probability of success** at different levels of experience is plotted against the experience of the sales team rather than the actual binary outcome of each case.[1] This is shown in Figure 3.2 which clearly shows that this probability increases with the experience of the sales team (in the graph, the individual cases are shown using unfilled circles and the overall probability of success for given levels of experience are shown using filled circles).

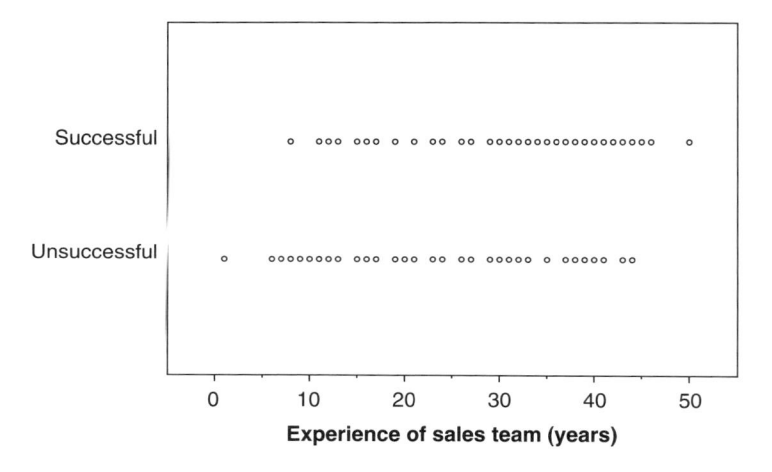

Figure 3.1 *Success and the experience of the sales staff*

From Figure 3.2, it can also be seen that the relationship between the probability of success and experience is not linear. The OLS regression model shown in the graph does not provide a particularly close fit to the probability data (the filled circles). Most importantly, the probability data are constrained between 0 and 1, but the model is not (the OLS regression model is the straight line model shown on the graph, 'success = $\alpha + \beta$ experience'). At values of experience below 15 years, the OLS regression model underestimates the probability of success (as the value of probability cannot go below zero, the model actually provides invalid predictions for probability) whilst it overestimates the probability for values of experience above 40 years (again, the model predicts invalid values, as probabilities cannot assume values greater than 1). Looking at the pattern made by the solid circles (i.e., the probability of success data), the relationship between the probability of success and the number of years of experience would appear to be S-shaped (sigmoid) rather than linear. If this is the case, then clearly the linear OLS regression model 'success = $\alpha + \beta$ experience' does not provide an

---

[1] To obtain this graph, 'experience' was represented as a number of equally-sized categories and the probability of success calculated for each category from the data.

The Generalized Linear Model

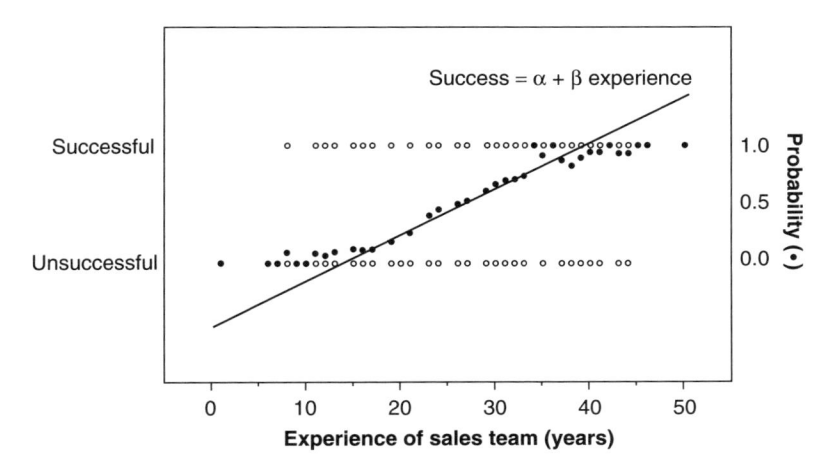

Figure 3.2 *The probability of success and the experience of the sales staff*

accurate representation of the relationship between the probability of obtaining a particular response and the explanatory variable and is not, therefore, appropriate to use to model these data.[2]

It is, however, still possible to apply a linear model to these data if the relationship between the probability measure of response and the explanatory variables can be represented as a straight line. The discussion of the generalized linear model in Chapter 2 indicated that for a binomially-distributed response variable, the relationship between the random and systematic components of the model is the log odds, or logit. This model is shown in Equation 3.1:

$$\text{logit}[\text{Pr}(Y=1)] = \alpha + \beta_1 X_1 + \beta_2 X_2 + \ldots + \beta_k X_k \quad (3.1)$$

where Pr(Y=1), refers to the probability of the response variable equalling 1 (which corresponds to one of the categories), and X_1 to X_k are the explanatory variables. For the above example, the relationship between success and experience can be represented as:

$$\text{logit}[\text{Pr}(\text{success})] = \alpha + \beta \text{ experience}$$

The log odds of the probability of success may be predicted, at least to some extent, by the linear model '$\alpha + \beta$ experience'. As we will see, this is a linear model (similar to the OLS regression models discussed in Chapter 2) as each unit increase in 'experience' predicts a standard change (β) in the value of the response variable (in this case, logit[Pr(success)]). Figure 3.3 shows the log odds of the probability of success plotted against experience. Of particular interest here is the fact that the values

---

[2]Or, in fact, any measure of probability derived from a binary response variable.

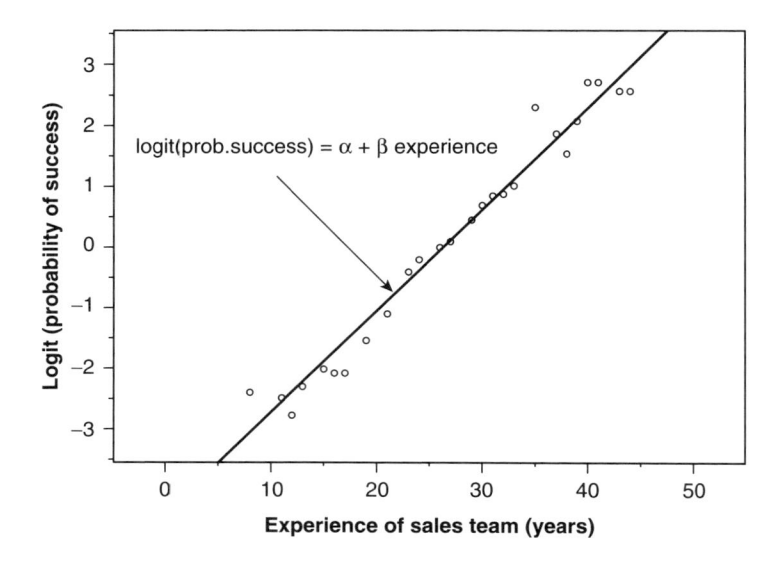

Figure 3.3 *The log odds of success and the experience of the sales staff*

of the response variable are not now constrained between 0 and 1, and a linear model (the model 'logit[Pr(success)] = $\alpha + \beta$ experience') now more closely represents the relationship. In essence, the logit transformation of the original response variable data has transformed the S-shaped relationship suggested in Figure 3.2 into a linear relationship between the random and systematic components of the model.

The parameters for the model shown in Figure 3.3 now relate to the log odds (the logit) of success, rather than the probability of success. Although this manipulation makes it possible to fit a linear model, logits are not particularly easy to interpret. This is not much of a problem, however, as once the model has been fit, it is easy to transform the logit scale back to a probability scale by using the inverse of the log odds transformation. Basically, logit scores have been used so that a linear model of the response variable can be fitted and in order to interpret the model more easily, the logit model may be transformed back into probability scores, or into odds. A probability value, Pr(x), may be transformed into a logit using the equation

$$\log \frac{\Pr(x)}{1 - \Pr(x)} = \text{logit}(x) \qquad (3.2)$$

and a logit value, logit(x), may be transformed into a probability using the equation

$$\frac{e^{\text{logit}(x)}}{1 + e^{\text{logit}(x)}} = \Pr(x). \qquad (3.3)$$

For the above example, it is a simple matter to convert probabilities of success into logit scores and also to convert logit scores of success back into probabilities.

For example, if the model predicts a logit score of 1.72, the probability associated with this is $e^{1.72}/(1+e^{1.72})$, which equates to a probability of 5.585/6.585, or 0.848. A logit score of 1.72 is equivalent to a probability of success of 0.848. Similarly, if we wished to know the logit value associated with a probability of 0.5, this can simply be computed as $\log[0.5/(1-0.5)]$, which equals $\log(1)$ or 0.00. From Figure 3.3 we can see that a 50% success rate is associated with an experience level of about 27 years (this is the experience level associated with a logit score of 0, which is equivalent to a success rate of 50%). Table 3.1 demonstrates a number of probabilities being converted into logits and a number of logits being converted into probabilities. Also provided is the odds, which is more easily interpreted than the log odds and is, as we will see, commonly used to describe the relationship between the explanatory and response variables.

Table 3.1 *The logit transformation*

Probability → logit

Probability x	Odds $x/(1-x)$	Log odds $\log[x/(1-x)]$
0.1	0.11	−2.20
0.5	1.00	0.00
0.9	9.00	2.20

Logit → probability

Log odds x	Odds e^x	Probability $e^x/[1+e^x]$
−3.00	0.05	0.05
0.00	1.00	0.50
3.00	20.09	0.95

Using the logit → probability transformation, it is a simple matter to transform the linear logit model shown in Figure 3.3 to the non-linear model of probability suggested in Figure 3.2 (this non-linear model can be imagined by connecting the filled dots on the graph with a line). When this is done, the linear model changes into a non-linear S-shaped model that more accurately reflects the relationship between the response and explanatory variables. Figure 3.4 shows the logit model depicted on the original probability scale.[3]

By using a logit transformation, therefore, one can model a binary response variable using a linear model. The use of logits enables the basic linear model to be generalized to non-linear relationships (particularly those related to categorical data) and is particularly important as the technique can be extended to enable multi-category ordered and unordered response variables to be modeled (see Chapters 4 and 5).

---

[3]This S-shaped model is simply achieved by predicting values of the response variable from the model and then plotting these against values of the explanatory variable. The curved line on the graph is the linear logit model that has been transformed back into a probability.

Figure 3.4 *A logit model of the probability of success and the experience of the sales staff*

3.2 The Logistic Regression Model

The logistic regression model will be illustrated using data taken from the Current Population Survey (CPS). These data are used to supplement census information between census years and are available in the public domain from the CPS_85_Wages link on the Statlib datasets archive at http://lib.stat.cmu.edu/datasets/ (see Berndt, 1991). These data consist of a random sample of 534 persons from the CPS, with information on a number of characteristics of the workers including wage (dollars per hour), age (in years), gender, occupation (management, sales, clerical, service, professional, other) and union membership (yes, no). The variables used from this data set are shown below in Table 3.2 along with some of the data.

The aim of the regression models we are to use in this chapter are to predict the likelihood that someone is a union member (this variable is a simple binary classification of membership indicating whether or not an individual is a member of the union). It is important to note that the models presented here are merely for illustration and should not be assumed to constitute well thought out models of union membership.

3.2.1 Simple logistic regression

Simple logistic regression refers to the case where there is a dichotomous response variable and a single explanatory variable. As the response variable is dichotomous, a logit link is used to link the random and systematic components of the model. The relationship we are to model here is the one between union membership and wage. Using the logit model, this relationship is represented as:

$$\text{logit}[\Pr(\text{union member})] = \alpha + \beta \text{ wage} \qquad (3.4)$$

The Logistic Regression Model

Table 3.2 *Data: example for illustrating logistic regression*

Case no.	Union membership	Age	Wage	Gender	Occupation
1	no	35	5.10	female	other
2	no	57	4.95	female	other
3	no	19	6.67	male	other
4	no	22	4.00	male	other
5	no	35	7.50	male	other
↓					
530	no	29	11.36	male	professional
531	no	51	6.10	female	professional
532	yes	48	23.25	female	professional
533	yes	31	19.88	male	professional
534	no	55	15.38	male	professional

This is a very simplified model and merely states that the probability someone is a union member may be related to the amount they earn. There are clearly many more variables that are likely to play a role in union membership, but these are not included in this example. The scatterplot in Figure 3.5 shows the raw data (unfilled circles) and the probabilities of union membership for a number of categories of wage (filled circles) and suggests that the probability of union membership increases as wage levels increase. This does not, however, appear to be a particularly strong relationship and it is unclear from the graph whether or not it is significant.

Computing and interpreting model parameters: The model parameters for the simple logistic regression model discussed above (see Equation 3.4) were computed using software[4] and are shown in Table 3.3 below. From this table we can derive the

Table 3.3 *Regression parameters*

	Estimate	Standard error	Odds ratio
(Intercept)	−2.207	0.233	
Wage	0.072	0.020	1.075

Model: $\text{logit}[\Pr(\text{union member})] = \alpha + \beta \text{ wage}$

intercept (α) and the regression coefficient (β) for the model. The model of union membership is therefore

$$\text{logit}[\Pr(\text{union member})] = -2.207 + (0.072 \times \text{wage})$$

---
[4]The software package used here is R (R Development Core Team, 2007).

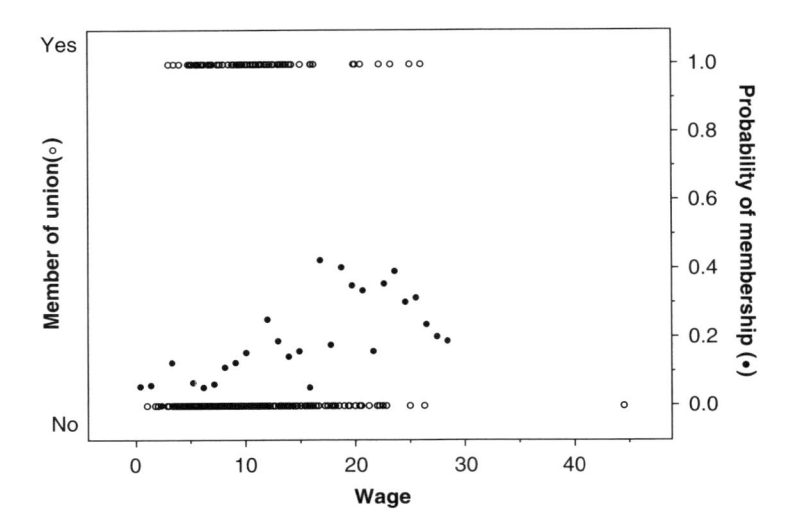

Figure 3.5 *Union membership and wage*

and is interpreted in the following way. As wage increases by 1 dollar per hour (a unit increase in wage), logit[Pr(union member)] increases by 0.072. This is almost identical to the way in which the parameters for an OLS regression model are interpreted. The only difference here is that the parameters now relate to the log odds of the probability of being a union member, rather than the actual value of the response variable. Log odds are, however, difficult to interpret as we do not commonly think in these terms. A more useful statistic to work with is the odds, which in this case are 1.075 ($e^{0.072}$). For each unit increase in wage, the odds of being a member of the union increase from 1 to 1.075 (a 7.5% increase). Higher earners are therefore more likely to be members of the union.

It is useful to also determine the limits within which one might expect the probability of being a union member to change given a unit change in wage. In order to answer this question, 95% confidence intervals may be calculated using Equation 3.5.

$$\text{confidence intervals for } \beta = \hat{\beta} \pm 1.96(\text{ASE}) \tag{3.5}$$

This equation is very similar to that shown for the confidence intervals of the parameters in OLS regression, except that the standard errors estimated for logistic regression are asymptotic standard errors (see Hutcheson and Sofroniou, 1999, for an explanation of this). Table 3.4 shows the 95% 2-tailed confidence intervals for the regression parameters provided in Table 3.3. From the table we can see that in 95% of cases a unit change in 'wage' is associated with a change in logit[Pr(union member)] of between 0.032 and 0.111, with the odds expected to change from 1.033 (i.e., $e^{0.032}$) to 1.118 (i.e., $e^{0.111}$). For each unit increase in 'wage', the odds of being a member of the union can be expected to increase by at least 3.3% (1.033 times the previous value) and at most 11.8% (1.118 times the previous value). As both of these confidence intervals predict an increase in the odds ratio we can conclude that at the 95% 2-tailed level

The Logistic Regression Model

of significance, 'wage' does have a significant affect on the response variable (this is confirmed in the next section when the model-fit statistics are discussed).

Table 3.4 *Confidence intervals*

	β Coefficient	ASE	95% CIs for β Lower	95% CIs for β Upper	95% CIs for e^β Lower	95% CIs for e^β Upper
Wage	0.072	0.020	0.032	0.111	1.033	1.118
(Constant)	−2.207	0.233				

Logit[Pr(union member)] = −2.207 + 0.072 wage

Predicted probabilities: Predictions can be provided for logistic regression models in much the same way as they were for the OLS regression models discussed in Chapter 2, and can be computed for any given value of the explanatory variable (one must be careful, however, not to use values of the explanatory variable that are outside the range of observed values). For a given value of wage, the log odds, odds and probability of someone being a member of the union can be easily calculated. For example, when wage equals 5 dollars per hour, the probability of being a union member is 0.136 compared to a probability of 0.662 when wages are 40 dollars per hour. These calculations are shown below:

wages of $5 per hour

log odds[Pr(union member)] $= \alpha + \beta x$
$= -2.207 + (0.072*5)$
$= -1.847$

odds[Pr(union member)] $= e^{\alpha+\beta x}$
$= e^{-1.847}$
$= 0.158$

Pr(union member) $= e^{\alpha+\beta x}/(1 + e^{\alpha+\beta x})$
$= 0.158/(1+0.158)$
$= 0.136$

wages of $40 per hour

log odds[Pr(union member)] $= \alpha + \beta x$
$= -2.207 + (0.072*40)$
$= 0.673$

odds[Pr(union member)] $= e^{\alpha+\beta x}$
$= e^{0.673}$
$= 1.960$

Pr(union member) $= e^{\alpha+\beta x}/(1 + e^{\alpha+\beta x})$
$= 1.960/(1+1.960)$
$= 0.662$.

It is an easy matter to compute these predictions using software. Table 3.5 shows predicted probabilities of union membership for a number of different wages computed using the R statistical package. Although not shown here, it is possible to also determine the confidence intervals for the predictions of the response variable (see Sofroniou and Hutcheson, 2002, for details about this).

Table 3.5 *Predicted probabilities*

Wage	Predicted probability of union membership
4.00	0.128
4.45	0.132
4.95	0.136
5.10	0.137
6.67	0.151
7.50	0.159
13.07	0.219
19.47	0.308

Logit[Pr(union member)] $= -2.207 + 0.072$ wage

From Table 3.5 we can see that the probability of being a union member increases as the variable 'wage' increases. It is useful to depict this model graphically. Figure 3.6 shows the logistic regression model for union membership given wage.[5] The non-linear nature of the model can be clearly seen in the curvature of the fitted line and also shows that the higher values of wage are associated with a higher probability of being a union member.

Goodness-of-fit statistics: In addition to the model parameters, it is useful to have an indication of how well the model fits the data. For this we need to compute some model-fit statistics. There are, however, a number of aspects to assessing the model-fit. These can be utilized to assess the entire model (all the variables considered together), individual variables and individual categories within variables. There are a number of statistics that can be used to estimate significance and those used depend, to a large extent, on the software package being used. This chapter will utilize statistics based on the deviance measure ($-2LL$) to estimate the whole model and individual variables, but will also use the z-statistic to estimate the effect of individual variables and categories within explanatory variables when the variable is categorical. Although it is possible to use statistics based on the deviance measure to estimate the significance of individual categories within variables, this is not particularly easy to achieve in software[6] and is

---

[5] This graph has been produced by simply plotting the predicted probabilities shown in Table 3.5 against the explanatory variable.

[6] The computation of $-2LL$ statistics for the individual categories of a variable often involves manually re-coding the data and then manually comparing nested models (see Hutcheson and Sofroniou, 1999, for a full description of this).

The Logistic Regression Model

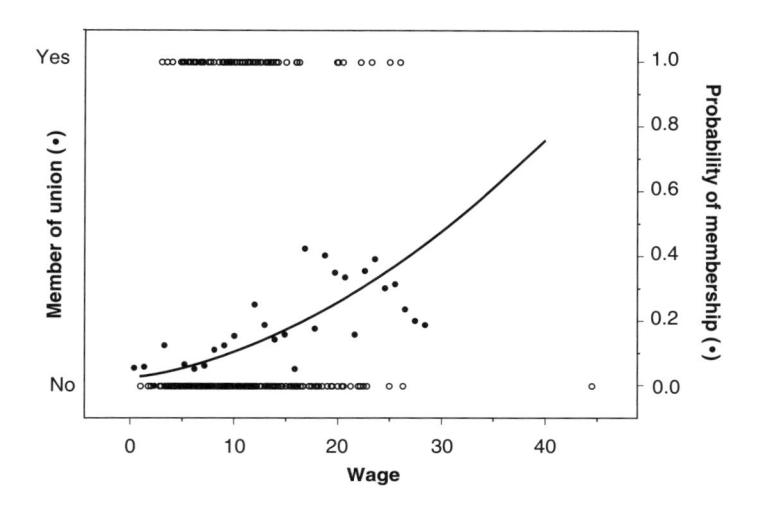

Figure 3.6 *Logistic regression model of union membership and wage*

therefore often estimated using z-statistics. As this technique is commonly utilized in software, this technique will also be used in this discussion

For a logistic regression model, model fit can be determined by comparing measures of deviance for nested models. The log-likelihood statistic provides a measure of deviance for a logistic regression model (that is, a measure of the difference between the observed values and those predicted from the model) and can be used as a goodness-of-fit statistic. This measure of deviance broadly corresponds to the RSS statistic, which is a measure of deviance for an OLS regression model (see Ryan, 1997: 267). The log-likelihood statistic is usually quoted as -2 times the log-likelihood ($-2LL$) as this has approximately a χ^2 distribution, thus enabling significance to be evaluated. The interpretation of $-2LL$ is quite straightforward – the smaller its value, the better the model fit (a $-2LL$ score equal to 0 indicates a perfect model where there is no deviance).

Similar to OLS regression, the effect of a particular explanatory variable may be computed by comparing the deviance between nested models (one model including the explanatory variable and the other not) and evaluating significance using the chi-square distribution with the number of degrees of freedom equal to the difference in the number of terms between the 2 models. For a simple logistic regression model, the effect of the explanatory variable can be assessed by comparing the $-2LL$ statistic for the full regression model with that for the null model (see Equation 3.6).

$$-2LL_{\text{diff}} = (-2LL_0) - (-2LL_1) \tag{3.6}$$

where $-2LL_0$ refers to the null model logit$[\Pr(Y = 1)] = \alpha$,

and $-2LL_1$ refers to the model logit$[\Pr(Y = 1)] = \alpha + \beta x$.

For the model 'logit[Pr(union member)] $= \alpha + \beta$ wage', the deviance statistics for the null and regression models and the significance of the change in deviance

Table 3.6 *Assessing significance by comparing model deviances*

Model	Deviance (−2LL)	df	−2LL$_{\text{diff}}$	df$_{\text{diff}}$	P-value
Logit[Pr(Y = 1)] = α	503.084	533	12.584	1	0.0004
Logit[Pr(Y = 1)] = $\alpha + \beta$ wage	490.500	532			

−2LL$_{\text{diff}}$ is the difference in deviance between the two models

Chi-square statistic = 12.584 on 1 degree of freedom

(−2LL$_{\text{diff}}$) are shown in Table 3.6. From this table we can see that adding the variable 'wage' to the model decreases the deviance from 503.084 to 490.500, a decrease of 12.584. This change in deviance is tested at 1 degree of freedom using the χ^2 statistic and is found to be significant (0.0004). We can therefore say that the variable 'wage' significantly reduces the deviance in union membership and the 2 variables are significantly related. This information is commonly provided by software in an analysis of deviance table. Although this table is redundant for this model (as the information has already been provided above), an analysis of deviance table is useful for multiple regression models and for models that include categorical explanatory variables and is included here for completeness.

Table 3.7 *Analysis of deviance table: the significance of variables*

	−2LL	df	P-value
Coefficient			
Wage	12.584	1	0.0004

Model: logit[Pr(union member)] = $\alpha + \beta$ wage

In addition to those statistics based on −2LL, the significance of the explanatory variable can be estimated using a z-statistic. The z-statistic is simply the estimates divided by the standard error which can be easily tested for significance. The z-statistic for wage is therefore 0.072/0.020, which is 3.577 (this is the estimate from software, which uses many more decimal place than have been reported here). This value is then tested for significance using a 2-tailed test. Using the z-statistic, we find that wage is still significantly related to union membership.

In addition to the significance of individual variables, it is also useful to have an idea of the percentage of variation in the response variable that is 'explained' by the model. In OLS regression, this information is provided by the R^2 statistic, however, this should not be used in logistic regression as it can produce misleading results (see Ryan, 1997, for a detailed explanation of this). A number of alternative measures similar to the R^2 statistic have, however, been proposed for logistic regression models including those by Cox and Snell (1989), (see also, Cox and Wermuth, 1992) and Nagelkerk (1991). These statistics are commonly known as pseudo R Square measures and can be computed using a number of statistical packages. For the model 'logit[Pr(union

The Logistic Regression Model

Table 3.8 *Estimating the significance of individual parameters using the z-statistic*

	Estimate	Standard error	z statistic	P-value
(Intercept)	−2.207	0.233		
Wage	0.072	0.020	3.577	0.0003

Model: logit[Pr(union member)] = $\alpha + \beta$ wage

member)] = $\alpha + \beta$ wage' Cox & Snell R Square = 0.023 and Nagelkerke R Square = 0.038. These statistics indicate that, although 'wage' is significant, it does not explain much of the variation in union membership (as we would expect from Figure 3.5). This is, however, to be expected, as there are many factors other than wage likely to influence union membership.[7]

To conclude the simple logistic regression analysis; the wage of an individual does appear to be significantly related to union membership ($\chi^2 = 12.584$, df = 1, p = 0.0004), although this relationship explains relatively little of the variation in the response variable (pseudo R square measures are in the region of 0.05). The relationship is positive, with higher wages associated with higher probabilities of union membership. It should be noted, however, that as this was not an experimental study, this association should not be interpreted as causal. It is easy to hypothesize factors other than wage that might be responsible for the relationship, including length of service (higher wages tend to be earned by older employees who have had more opportunity to join the union), changing attitudes to union membership (unions may have been more active in the past), or the type of job available in the company (the company may, for example, be moving away from manufacturing, which traditionally has a higher level of union participation).

3.2.2 Multiple Logistic Regression

In the section above it was found that wage is positively related to union membership ($\chi^2 = 12.584$ on 1 degree of freedom, $p = 0.0004$). It is possible, however, that this effect is due, at least in part, to the age of the employees (amongst other things). Older employees will tend to earn more due to their experience and length of service and may also be more likely to be union members as they have had more opportunity to join a union and might also have been working at times when unions were more active than they are today. It would be useful, therefore, to include age when modeling union membership. This can be simply achieved by including 'age' as an explanatory variable in the model.

Union membership *may be predicted by* wage *and* age.

---

[7] It should be noted that, similar to the OLS regression R^2 statistic, pseudo R^2 statistics should be used with caution and advisably only used as a supplementary statistic.

The logistic regression equation for multiple explanatory variables is similar to the case where there is just one explanatory variable except that more than one variable is entered into the model. Including the variable 'age' gives the logistic regression model

$$\text{logit}[\text{Pr(union member)}] = \alpha + \beta_1 \text{wage} + \beta_2 \text{age} \qquad (3.7)$$

which is a very simplified model and merely states that the probability someone is a union member may be related to the amount they earn and their age. It is useful at this point to investigate the relationship between age and union membership. Although we could do this using a simple logistic regression model, we will just illustrate the relationship simply using a graph. Figure 3.7 shows a scatterplot illustrating the relationship between the age of the employee and the probability that they are a member of the union. This graph has been obtained by categorizing the ages into groups and then calculating the probability that the members of these groups are union members.

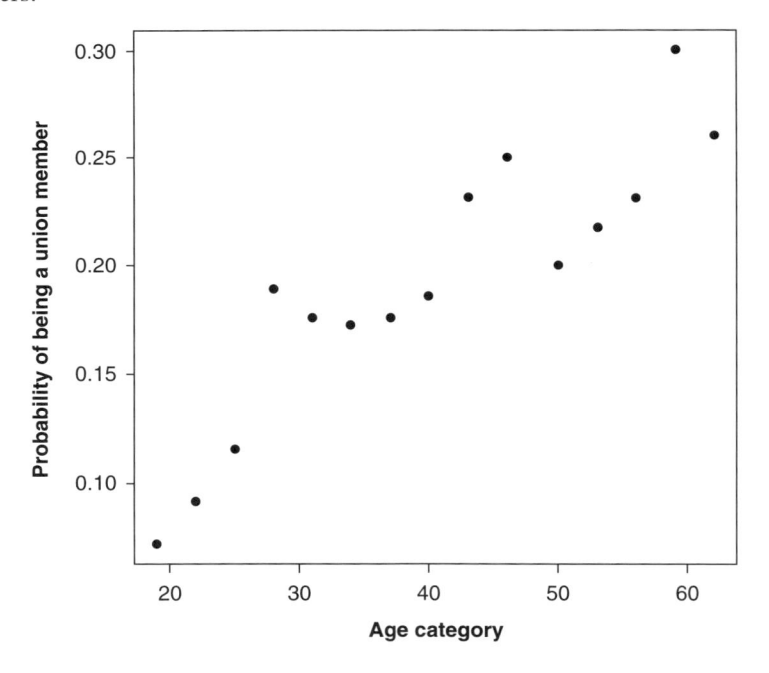

Figure 3.7 *Probability of being a union member and age*

Figure 3.7 suggests that the probability of being a union member appears to increase with age. Union membership may therefore be related to the age of the employee. It is also important to look at the relationship between the explanatory variables 'age' and 'wage', as a strong relationship between these variables will prove problematic when interpreting the regression coefficients. The variables 'age' and 'wage' are significantly related as shown by an OLS regression model ($F_{1,532} = 17.2$, $\text{Pr} = 3.917e - 05$), although the relationship does not account for much of the variance as Adjusted R^2 is

The Logistic Regression Model

only 0.0295, which suggests that only about 3% of the variation in wage can be accounted for by the variable 'age'. This weak relationship can be seen in Figure 3.8, which shows a scatterplot for these 2 variables along with the linear regression and lowess best-fit lines. From these graphs it looks as though the variables 'wage' and 'age' are both likely to be related to union membership and as there is no strong relationship between them, their regression parameters in a multiple regression model should provide a good indication of their effect on the response variable. It is useful to now look at the effect of both variables together using a multiple logistic regression model.

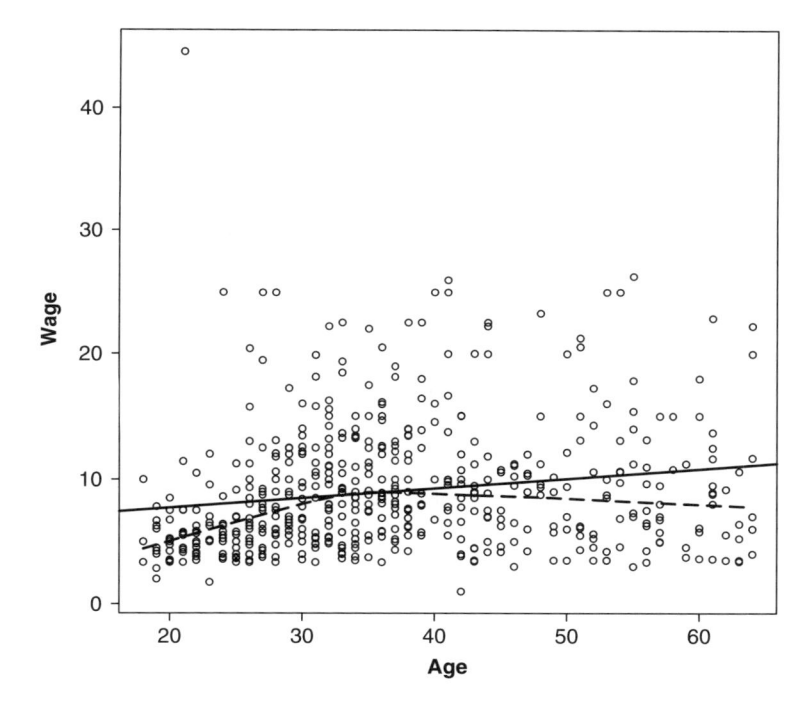

Figure 3.8 *Relationship between wage and age*

Computing and interpreting model parameters: Table 3.9 shows the parameters for the multiple logistic regression model shown in Equation 3.7. The logistic regression model for union membership is therefore,

$$\text{logit}[\Pr(\text{union member})] = -2.976 + (0.065 \times \text{wage}) + (0.022 \times \text{age})$$

These model parameters are interpreted in much the same way as they are for multiple OLS regression. The only difference is that the estimates now relate to the log odds. For each unit increase in wage (i.e. as wages increase by one dollar per hour) when age is held constant, the log odds of the probability of being a member of the union increase by 0.065. This corresponds to an odds ratio of 1.067 ($e^{0.065}$);

Table 3.9 *Regression parameters*

	Estimate	Standard error	Odds ratio
(Intercept)	−2.976	0.427	
Wage	0.065	0.020	1.067
Age	0.022	0.010	1.022

Model: logit[Pr(union member)] = $\alpha + \beta_1$wage $+ \beta_2$age

so, for each unit increase in wage, the odds of being a union member increase by 6.7%. Even after taking age into account, higher paid employees are more likely to be members of the union. Similarly, for each unit increase in age (i.e. as age increases by one year) when wage is held constant, the log odds of the probability of being a member of the union increase by 0.022. This corresponds to an odds ratio of 1.022 ($e^{0.022}$); so, for each unit increase in age, the odds of being a union member increase by 2.2%. Even after taking wage into account, older employees are more likely to be members of the union. From these results it looks as though older and more highly paid employees are more likely to be members of the union. As predicted from Figure 3.8, the addition of the variable 'age' to the model has not affected the parameters for 'wage' much (as 'wage' and 'age' are not strongly related). The parameter for 'wage' has changed from 0.072 in the simple model to 0.065 in the multiple model, a change of 0.007.

As with simple logistic regression, confidence intervals can be easily computed for the regression parameters using Equation 3.5. Table 3.10 shows the 95% 2-tailed confidence intervals for the regression parameters provided in Table 3.9. From the table we can see that in 95% of cases a unit change in 'wage' whilst 'age' is kept constant, is associated with a change in logit[Pr(union member)] of between 0.026 and 0.105, with the odds expected to change from 1.026 (i.e., $e^{0.026}$) to 1.111 (i.e., $e^{0.105}$). For each unit increase in 'wage', whilst controlling for 'age', the odds of being a member of the union can be expected to increase by at least 2.6% and at most 11.1%. As both of these confidence intervals predict an increase in the odds ratio we can conclude that at the 95% 2-tailed level of significance, 'wage' does have a significant affect on the response variable even when controlling for 'age' (this is confirmed in the next section when the model-fit statistics are discussed).

Table 3.10 *Confidence intervals*

	β Coefficient	ASE	95% CIs for β Lower	95% CIs for β Upper	95% CIs for e^β Lower	95% CIs for e^β Upper
Wage	0.065	0.020	0.026	0.105	1.026	1.111
Age	0.022	0.010	0.003	0.041	1.003	1.042
(Constant)	−2.976	0.427				

Logit[Pr(union member)] $= -2.976 + (0.065 \times \text{wage}) + (0.022 \times \text{age})$

The Logistic Regression Model

Predicted probabilities: Once the logistic regression model has been derived, the log odds, odds and probability of someone being a member of the union can be easily calculated for any combination of age and wage (although, as before, one needs to be careful when predicting values outside of the range of the recorded data). For example, when wage = 5 dollars per hour and age is equal to 40, the log odds of someone being a member of the union are -1.771, which corresponds to an odds ratio of 0.170 and a probability of 0.145. The calculations showing this are shown below.

$$\begin{aligned}
\log \text{odds}[\Pr(\text{union member})] &= \alpha + \beta_1 x_1 + \beta_2 x_2 \\
&= -2.976 + (0.065 \times \text{wage}) + (0.022 \times \text{age}) \\
&= -2.976 + (0.065 \times 5) + (0.022 \times 40) \\
&= -1.771
\end{aligned}$$

$$\begin{aligned}
\text{odds}[\Pr(\text{union member})] &= e^{\alpha + \beta_1 x_1 + \beta_2 x_2} \\
&= e^{-1.771} \\
&= 0.170
\end{aligned}$$

$$\begin{aligned}
\Pr(\text{union member}) &= e^{\alpha + \beta_1 x_1 + \beta_2 x_2} / (1 + e^{\alpha + \beta_1 x_1 + \beta_2 x_2}) \\
&= 0.170 / (1 + 0.170) \\
&= 0.145
\end{aligned}$$

It is an easy matter to compute these predictions using software. Table 3.11 shows predicted probabilities of union membership for a number of different wages and ages computed using the R statistical package. Although not shown here, it is possible to also determine the confidence intervals for the predictions of the response variable (see Sofroniou and Hutcheson, 2002).

Goodness-of-fit statistics: The significance of individual and groups of variables in a logistic regression model can be calculated by comparing the $-2LL$ statistics for nested models. The general form for comparing nested models is given as:

$$-2LL_{\text{diff}} = (-2LL_p) - (-2LL_{p+q}) \tag{3.8}$$

where $-2LL$ is -2 times the log likelihood (a measure of deviance),
p is the smaller, nested model,
and $p + q$ is the larger model.

By comparing different models one can calculate the effect that individual variables, groups of variables, or all of the explanatory variables have on the response variable. For example, the effect of all explanatories can be assessed by comparing the deviances of the two nested models.

$$\text{logit}[\Pr(\text{union member})] = \alpha + \beta_1 \text{wage} + \beta_2 \text{age}$$
$$\text{logit}[\Pr(\text{union member})] = \alpha.$$

Table 3.11 *Predicted probabilities of union membership at a selection of wages and ages*

Wage	Age	Predicted probability of union membership
5.10	35	0.133
4.95	57	0.197
6.67	19	0.107
4.00	22	0.097
7.50	35	0.152
13.07	28	0.181
4.45	43	0.149
19.47	27	0.247

Logit[Pr(union member)] = −2.976 + (0.065 × wage) + (0.022 × age)

Similarly, the effect of the single parameter representing age can be assessed by comparing the deviances of the two nested models.

$$\text{logit}[\text{Pr(union member)}] = \alpha + \beta_1 \text{wage} + \beta_2 \text{age}$$
$$\text{logit}[\text{Pr(union member)}] = \alpha + \beta_1 \text{wage}.$$

Table 3.12 shows the −2LL statistics associated with a number of nested models and the significance of the differences in these scores. The difference in −2LL when age and wage are both removed from the model is equal to 17.560. This statistic approximates to a chi-square distribution and is tested for significance with 2 degrees of freedom (the nested models differ by two parameters). This is significant at the 0.0005 level. When a single parameter is removed from the model, the difference

Table 3.12 *Assessing significance by comparing model deviances*

	−2LL	df	−2LL$_{\text{diff}}$	df$_{\text{diff}}$	P-value
The overall effect of wage and age					
Logit(p) = α	503.084	533	17.560	2	0.0002
Logit(p) = $\alpha + \beta_1$wage + $\beta_2$age	485.524	531			
The effect of wage					
Logit(p) = $\alpha + \beta_1$ age	495.665	532	10.141	1	0.0015
Logit(p) = $\alpha + \beta_1$wage + $\beta_2$age	485.524	531			
The effect of age					
Logit(p) = $\alpha + \beta_1$ wage	490.500	532	4.976	1	0.0257
Logit(p) = $\alpha + \beta_1$wage + $\beta_2$age	485.524	531			

The Logistic Regression Model

in $-2LL$ is tested at 1 degree of freedom. The variable 'wage' is significant at the 0.005 level, and the variable 'age' is significant at the 0.05 level. This information is commonly provided by software in an analysis of deviance table similar to that shown in Table 3.13.

Table 3.13 *Analysis of deviance table: the significance of variables*

	$-2LL$	df	P-value
Coefficient			
Wage	10.141	1	0.001
Age	4.976	1	0.026

Model: logit[Pr(union member)] = $\alpha + \beta_1$ wage + β_2 age

In addition to those statistics based on $-2LL$, the significance of the explanatory variable can be estimated using a z-statistic. The z-statistic is simply the estimates divided by the standard error which can be easily tested for significance. The z-statistic for wage is therefore $0.065/0.020$, which is 3.239. This value is then tested for significance using a 2-tailed test. Using the z-statistic, we find that wage is still significantly related to union membership.

Table 3.14 *Estimating the significance of individual parameters using the z-statistic*

	Estimate	Standard error	z statistic	P-value
(Intercept)	-2.976	0.427		
Wage	0.065	0.020	3.239	0.0012
Age	0.022	0.010	2.249	0.0245

Model: logit[Pr(union member)] = $\alpha + \beta$ wage

Although the variables wage and age are significantly related to union membership, these variables do not explain much of the variation in the response variable. This is illustrated by the pseudo R square statistics which show that for the full model, Cox and Snell R Square equals .032 and Nagelkerke R Square equals .053. It appears that only about 5% of the variability in union membership can be explained by age and wage.

To conclude the multiple logistic regression analysis; the wage level and age of an individual does appear to be significantly related to union membership when considered together ($\chi^2 = 17.560$, df $= 2$, p $= 0.0002$). The individual explanatory variables are also significantly related to union membership (for wage, $\chi^2 = 10.141$, df $= 1$, p $= 0.0015$, and for age $\chi^2 = 4.976$, df $= 1$, p $= 0.0257$). Although this relationship is significant, it only explains relatively little of the variation in the response variable (pseudo R square measures are in the region of 0.05). The relationships are positive, with higher wages and ages associated with higher probabilities of union membership. Similar to the simple logistic regression model already discussed, these associations should not be interpreted as causal.

3.2.3 Categorical explanatory variables

As with OLS regression, it is relatively simple to include categorical explanatory variables into the model once they have been appropriately coded. Chapter 2 demonstrated how a categorical variable can be included in an OLS regression model using the indicator coding method (providing treatment contrasts) where each of the groups are compared to a reference category. Many other dummy coding methods are available including one which compares each group to the average of all groups. This technique is known as deviation coding (providing sum contrasts) and its application to the variable 'occupation' is shown in Table 3.15 (see Hutcheson and Sofroniou, 1999, for a full description of deviation coding).

Table 3.15 *Deviation dummy variable coding of 'occupation'*

Occupation	Dummy variables					
	1	2	3	4	5	6
Management	1	0	0	0	0	0
Sales	0	1	0	0	0	0
Clerical	0	0	1	0	0	0
Service	0	0	0	1	0	0
Professional	0	0	0	0	1	0
Other	−1	−1	−1	−1	−1	−1

As with indicator coding, the categorical variable is represented as a series of dummy variables. A maximum of $j-1$ dummy variables can be entered into a model. Using the coding in Table 3.15, the reference category is 'other' and the analysis will not produce any parameters for this category. In order to illustrate the use of categorical data in a logistic regression analysis, 2 categorical variables, gender and occupation, will be added to the analysis conducted above. For illustration purposes, gender is dummy coded using the indicator method (treatment contrasts) whilst occupation is coded using the deviation method (sum contrasts). When interpreting the regression parameters, the dummy variable representing gender is compared to the reference category whereas occupation is compared to the average of all categories. The regression model is of the form:

$$\text{logit}[\text{Pr}(\text{union member})] = \alpha + \beta_1 \text{wage} + \beta_2 \text{age} + \beta_3 \text{gender} + \beta_{4-8} \text{occupation} \quad (3.9)$$

You will note from Equation 3.9, that the variable 'occupation' has 5 regression coefficients associated with it. This is because it has 6 categories and only $j-1$ categories are able to enter into the equation. Before we compute a regression model, it is useful to look at how gender and occupation relate to union membership and also look at the relationship between gender and occupation. Figure 3.9 shows this information in the form of a clustered bar chart and illustrates some interesting relationships in the data. There appears to be a relationship between occupation and the probability of being a union member as there are clear differences between the occupations. There also may be some relationship between gender and union membership as females generally are less likely to be union members apart from those employed in a professional role. It is also interesting to note the relationship between gender and occupation as there are very few female union members who are employed in management and sales roles even though females are well represented in these occupations. On the evidence provided in the graph, one might expect occupation to be a highly significant predictor of union membership and perhaps gender (albeit at a reduced level). With these preliminary analyses in mind, it is useful to investigate the effect of all variables on union membership using a multiple logistic regression model.

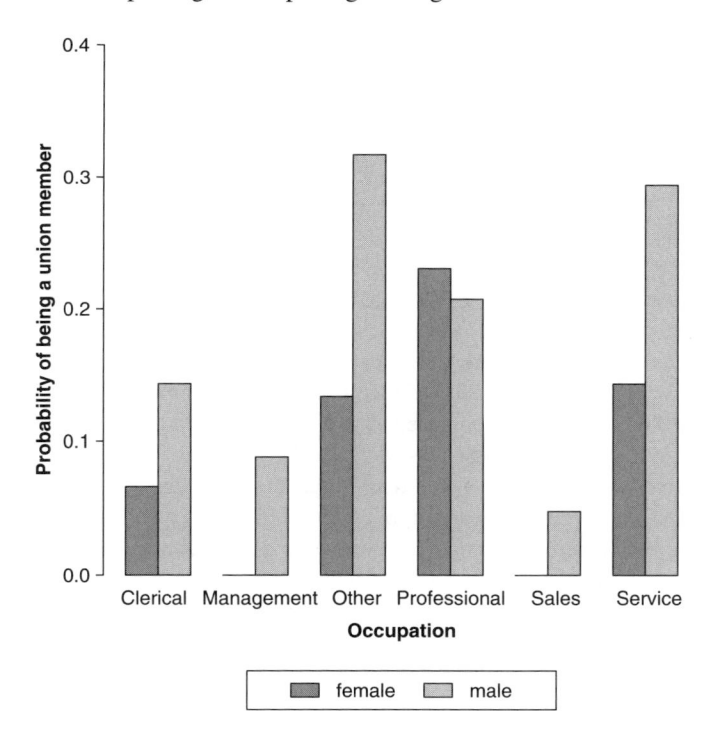

Figure 3.9 *Probability of being a union member for different genders and occupations*

Computing and interpreting model parameters: One parameter is calculated for each of the continuous variables 'age' and 'wage', one parameter compares males with females (indicator coding), and 5 parameters compare $j - 1$ categories of occupation with the average of all occupation categories (deviation coding). These are shown in Table 3.16 below.[8]

---

[8] Many statistical packages automatically code categorical explanatory variables into dummy categories. These analyses have been computed using R, which allows categorical variables to be automatically dummy coded using a variety of methods to provide treatment and sum contrasts.

Table 3.16 *Regression parameters*

	Estimate	Standard error	Odds ratio
(Intercept)	−4.475	0.566	0.011
Wage	0.088	0.025	1.091
Age	0.030	0.010	1.030
Gender			
gender[T.male]	0.614	0.287	1.847
Occupation			
Occupation[S.management]	−1.370	0.570	0.254
Occupation[S.sales]	−1.588	0.870	0.204
Occupation[S.clerical]	0.095	0.394	1.099
Occupation[S.service]	1.074	0.333	2.927
Occupation[S.professional]	0.615	0.305	1.850

Model: logit[Pr(union member)] = $\alpha + \beta_1$wage + $\beta_2$age + $\beta_3$gender + $\beta_{(4-8)}$occupation

For each unit increase in wage (i.e. as wages increase by one dollar per hour) when age, gender and occupation are held constant, the log odds of the probability of being a member of the union increase by 0.088. This corresponds to an odds ratio of 1.091 ($e^{0.088}$); so, for each unit increase in wage, the odds of being a union member increase by 0.091, or nearly 10%. Even after taking age, gender and occupation into account, higher paid employees are more likely to be members of the union. Looking at the parameters for gender, the log odds of the probability of being a member of the union increases by 0.614 for males compared to females. This corresponds to an odds ratio of 1.847; so males are 1.847 times as likely as females to be members of the union. The occupation variable is interpreted in much the same way except the deviation coding method makes the comparison between each dummy code and the average of all categories. For example, compared to the average of all occupations, those in the management field are less likely to be members of a union (an odds ratio of 0.254, which makes them only 0.25 times as likely to be a member when compared to the average of all employees), whilst those in the service profession are more likely (an odds ratio of 2.927 which makes them nearly 3 times as likely to be members of the union compared to the average of all employees).[9]

Predicted probabilities: Using the parameters from Table 3.16 above, it is a simple matter to provide predictions for the probability of someone being a member of the union. These can be computed from the logistic regression model for union membership:

$$\text{logit}[\Pr(\text{union member})] = -4.475 + (0.088 \times \text{wage}) + (0.030 \times \text{age}) + $$
$$(0.614 \times \text{male}) - (1.370 \times \text{management}) - (1.588 \times \text{sales}) +$$
$$(0.095 \times \text{clerical} + (1.074 \times \text{service}) + (0.615 \times \text{professional}) \qquad (3.10)$$

---

[9] The parameters for females and the 'other' profession (the reference categories used above) can be computed relatively easily by changing the reference category and re-running the analysis (consult the software manual for your statistical package to discover the best way to achieve this).

The Logistic Regression Model

The categorical variables are coded according to a 0 and 1 coding scheme (the presence or absence of that attribute). For example, for a male who is in management, male = 1 and management = 1, with all other occupations coded as 0, whereas a female in sales has male = 0, sales = 1 and all other occupations coded as 0. It is a simple matter to compute the probability of being a union member for any combination of values for the explanatory values. For example, for a 40-year-old female clerical worker earning 5 dollars per hour, the log odds of her being a member of the union can be calculated by substituting the values for the explanatory variables into Equation 3.10. This calculation is shown below:

$$\text{logit}[\Pr(\text{union member})] = -4.475 + (0.088 \times 5) + (0.030 \times 40) +$$
$$(0.614 \times 0) - (1.370 \times 0) - (1.588 \times 0) +$$
$$(0.095 \times 1) + (1.074 \times 0) + (0.615 \times 0)$$

and results in log odds value equal to -2.74. The associated odds and probability statistics can be easily computed from the log odds.[10] Similarly, for a 60-year-old male service industry worker earning 12 dollars per hour, the log odds of him being a member of the union are:

$$\text{logit}[\Pr(\text{Union member})] = -4.475 + (0.088 \times 12) + (0.030 \times 60) +$$
$$(0.614 \times 1) - (1.370 \times 0) - (1.588 \times 0) +$$
$$(0.095 \times 0) + (1.074 \times 1) + (0.615 \times 0)$$

which equals 0.069 (with an associated odds ratio of 1.072 and a probability of 0.517). Predictions from a multiple logistic regression model with categorical data are easily obtainable from software and Table 3.17 shows predictions for a selection of values of the explanatory variables.

Table 3.17 *Predicted probabilities of union membership*

Wage	Age	Gender	Ooccupation	Predicted probability of union membership
5.10	35	female	other	0.140
11.84	44	male	management	0.053
3.80	22	female	sales	0.006
11.11	32	male	clerical	0.136
10.00	44	female	clerical	0.100
4.35	51	female	service	0.181
3.50	63	male	service	0.352
24.98	41	male	professional	0.539
4.35	21	female	professional	0.054

---

[10] In this case, the odds are 0.065 ($e^{-2.74}$) and the probability is $0.061 (0.065/(1 + 0.065))$.

Goodness-of-fit statistics: In addition to the model parameters, confidence intervals and predictions, it is useful to have an indication of how well the model fits the data and how significantly each explanatory variable is related to the response. As with the logistic regression models discussed above, significances may be estimated using statistics based on the deviance ($-2LL$) and on z-statistics. In this section, the significance of the variables is to be estimated using statistics based on the measure of deviance, and the significances associated with comparing categories of the explanatory variables is to be estimated using z-statistics.

For a multiple logistic regression model, the effect of individual or groups of explanatory variables can be assessed by comparing the $-2LL$ statistics for 2 nested models (see Equation 3.8). The resulting statistic is tested for significance using the chi-square distribution with the number of degrees of freedom equal to the difference in the number of terms between the 2 models. Table 3.18 shows the deviance statistics associated with a number of models and the significances associated with all variables considered together and gender and occupation individually.

Table 3.18 *Assessing significance by comparing model deviances*

	$-2LL$	df	$-2LL_{diff}$	df_{diff}	P-value
The effect of all variables					
Logit[Pr(union member)] = α	503.084	533			
Logit[Pr(union member)] = α + $\beta_1$wage + $\beta_2$age + $\beta_3$gender + $\beta_{(4-8)}$occupation	437.815	525	65.270	8	4.3e $-$ 11
The effect of gender					
Logit[Pr(union member)] = α + $\beta_1$wage + $\beta_2$age + $\beta_{(4-8)}$occupation	442.523	526			
Logit[Pr(union member)] = α + $\beta_1$wage + $\beta_2$age + $\beta_3$gender + $\beta_{(4-8)}$occupation	437.815	525	4.708	1	0.030
The effect of occupation					
Logit[Pr(union member)] = α + $\beta_1$wage + $\beta_2$age + $\beta_3$gender	474.336	530			
Logit[Pr(union member)] = α + $\beta_1$wage + $\beta_2$age + $\beta_3$gender + $\beta_{(4-8)}$occupation	437.815	525	36.521	5	7.5e-07

From Table 3.18 we can see that in our model occupation is strongly related to union membership with gender also related, but at a less significant level. Information about the significance of each individual explanatory variable is also typically displayed

The Logistic Regression Model

in statistical packages in an analysis of deviance table similar to the one shown in Table 3.19.

Table 3.19 *Analysis of deviance table: the significance of variables*

	−2LL	df	p-value
Coefficients			
Wage	11.788	1	0.0006
Age	8.301	1	0.0040
Gender	4.708	1	0.030
Occupation	36.521	5	7.47e−07

Model: logit[Pr(union member)] = $\alpha + \beta_1$wage + $\beta_2$age + $\beta_3$gender + β_{4-8}occupation

In addition to those statistics based on −2LL, the significance of individual categories of the explanatory variables can be estimated using z-statistics. The z-statistic is simply the estimate divided by the standard error and is tested for significance using a 2-tailed test (i.e., Pr(>|z|)). Table 3.20 shows the z-statistics and the associated level of significance for each parameter in the model for union membership.

Table 3.20 *Estimating the significance of individual parameters using the z-statistic*

	Estimate	Standard error	z statistic	P-value
(Intercept)	−4.475	0.566	−7.904	2.7e−15
Wage	0.088	0.025	3.477	5.1e−04
Age	0.030	0.010	2.886	0.004
Gender[T.male]	0.614	0.287	2.142	0.032
Occupation[S.clerical]	0.095	0.394	0.241	0.810
Occupation[S.management]	−1.370	0.570	−2.402	0.016
Occupation[S.other]	1.174	0.282	4.163	3.1e−05
Occupation[S.professional]	0.615	0.305	2.015	0.044
Occupation[S.sales]	−1.588	0.870	−1.825	0.068

Model: logit[Pr(union member)] = $\alpha + \beta_1$wage + $\beta_2$age + $\beta_3$gender + β_{4-8}occupation

From Table 3.20, we can see that the occupation variable has been coded using the deviation method (indicated by the S character (sum comparison) before the category label) which compares the identified category with the average of all categories. For example, clerical workers are not significantly different in their union membership from the average of all workers in the study ($z = 0.241$, $p = 0.810$), whereas those employed in 'other' profession are ($z = 4.163$, $p = 3.1e - 05$).

To conclude the multiple logistic regression analysis, the wage level, age, gender and occupation of an individual when considered together are significantly related to union membership ($\chi^2 = 65.27, df = 8, p = 4.3e - 11$). All individual explanatory variables are significantly related to union membership with type of occupation being the most significant. Higher wages and ages are associated with higher probabilities of union membership. Males are more likely to be members and type of occupation also has a significant relationship.

3.3 Analyzing Simple Experimental Designs for Dichotomous Data

Chapter 2 showed how the inclusion of categorical explanatory variables in a regression model enabled the experimental group designs to be analyzed using GLMs. The techniques discussed there can be equally applied to binary response variables and logistic regression used to analyze independent and dependent group experimental designs. The analysis of these designs for dichotomous data will not be discussed here as they are covered in detail using the more general technique of multi-nomial logistic regression, which can be used to analyze a dichotomous response variable as well as one that is multi-category. For an experimental design where the outcome is dichotomous, one should apply the multi-nomial logistic regression technique described in Chapter 5.

3.4 Conclusion

In this chapter, logistic regression has been used to model binary response variables using continuous and categorical explanatory variables. The use of the logit transformation has been described in detail particularly with reference to the application of linear models to categorical data. Detailed descriptions have been provided about the interpretation of the regression coefficients and model-fit statistics and the similarities between these statistics and those used in OLS regression.

Logistic regression and the use of logits is particularly important as it provides a basis for modeling multi-category ordered and unordered response variables. These models are dealt with in Chapters 4 and 5.

CHAPTER 4
Modeling Ordered Data

This chapter introduces the proportional odds model, which can be used to model ordered categorical response variables. The chapter covers the theory behind the technique and the interpretation of the parameters and the model-fit statistics. It also shows how it can be used to analyze data from simple experimental studies when the response variable is ordered categorical.

There are a number of other methods available that can be used to model ordered categorical data including linear-by-linear models and continuation ratio logits. These techniques are covered in detail by Hutcheson and Sofroniou (1999) including the analysis of an example data set and will not, therefore be described in any detail here. We will, however, discuss the use of the proportional odds model, which is an extension of the logistic regression model for binary data and is, perhaps, the most widely used technique applied to model ordered data.

4.1 The Generalized Linear Model

In previous chapters we have seen how generalized linear models can be used to model continuous data using the technique of OLS regression and model binary data using logistic regression. In this chapter we will demonstrate how the GLM framework (more particularly, the logit model) can be extended to predict ordered categorical data. These data provide some challenge for analysis as the numbers used to represent the categories impart meaning only about order and not about actual magnitude. It is not appropriate, therefore, to use a technique that makes use of the numeric functions that should only be applied to continuous data (plus, minus, etc., see Chapter 1). If one is to model ordered categorical data appropriately, a technique needs to be applied that takes account of the order but is invariant to the particular coding method used (that is, all legitimate coding methods used to represent the data should provide the same results).

4.2 The Proportional Odds Model

The proportional odds model can most simply be understood as an extension of logistic regression. This technique allows one to model ordered data by analyzing it as a number of dichotomies. A binary logistic regression model compares one dichotomy (for example, passed–failed, died–survived, etc.) whereas the proportional odds model compares a number of dichotomies by arranging the ordered data into a series of binary comparisons. For example, a 4-category ordered variable Y (coded using j categories, 1, 2, 3, 4) can be represented as 3 binary comparisons.

binary comparison 1:	1	compared to	2, 3, 4
binary comparison 2:	1, 2	compared to	3, 4
binary comparison 3:	1, 2, 3	compared to	4

Using this method of categorizing the data enables the order in the data to be accounted for as comparisons are being made between higher and lower levels of the variable ($Y > j$ and $Y \leq j$). It is easy to see that this method takes into account the order in the data, but is invariant of the actual codes used to designate Y as long as the order is represented appropriately. For example, if the variable Y was coded using 0, 2, 9, 38 as opposed to 1, 2, 3, 4, exactly the same series of binary comparisons would be made.

binary comparison 1:	0	compared to	2, 9, 38
binary comparison 2:	0, 2	compared to	9, 38
binary comparison 3:	0, 2, 9	compared to	38

Each binary comparison can be viewed as a separate logistic regression model; that is, as a logit model using the log odds. To model a 4-category ordered response variable, 3 regression models need to be equated which are of the form (assuming that the response variable has been coded 1, 2, 3, 4):

binary comparison 1: $\text{logit}[\Pr(Y > 1)] = \alpha + \beta_1 X_1 + \beta_2 X_2 + \ldots + \beta_k X_k$

binary comparison 2: $\text{logit}[\Pr(Y > 2)] = \alpha + \beta_1 X_1 + \beta_2 X_2 + \ldots + \beta_k X_k$

binary comparison 3: $\text{logit}[\Pr(Y > 3)] = \alpha + \beta_1 X_1 + \beta_2 X_2 + \ldots + \beta_k X_k$

The models above provide three estimates for the effect that each explanatory variable has on the response. It is, however, easier (and more useful) to interpret a single parameter for each explanatory variable and derive a single parsimonious model of the response variable. In order to provide a single regression parameter for each explanatory variable we assume that the effect of each variable is the same for each binary comparison. This enables the effects to be averaged and a single parameter calculated representing the effect of the explanatory variable on the response variable. It is important, however, to test this assumption statistically (this is demonstrated later in this chapter, however, see Hoffmann, 2004, for a full description of testing the proportional odds assumption). When the binary comparisons are combined, the proportional odds model provides a single parameter to predict the probability of being in a higher compared to a lower category of the response variable as each explanatory variable changes. The model for multiple explanatory variables is shown in Equation 4.1 which basically models the effect that changes in the explanatory

The Proportional Odds Model

variables X_1 to X_k has on the log odds of Y being in a higher rather than a lower category.

$$\text{logit}[\Pr(Y > j)] = \alpha + \beta X_1 + \beta X_2 + \ldots + \beta X_k \tag{4.1}$$

where logit refers to the log odds,
Pr is the probability,
Y is the ordered response variable,
and j is the level of the response variable.

The data set used to illustrate the proportional odds model will be based on the ice cream consumption data set already used in the chapter that described OLS regression.[1] These data have been amended slightly to allow certain analyses to be conducted. Specifically, consumption is now represented as an ordered categorical variable as the original continuous consumption variable has been re-coded into 3 categories (low, medium and high). In addition to this, a hypothetical variable 'advertising' has been included in the data set to enable operations on an unordered categorical explanatory variable to be demonstrated and discussed later in this chapter. The variable 'advertising' shows the dominant advertising technique (radio, television or local posters) used during the period of data collection. The modified data are shown in Table 4.1 below.

4.2.1 Simple proportional odds

We will begin demonstrating the proportional odds model using the simple example of trying to predict level of ice cream consumption by using average outdoor temperature as an explanatory variable. The model for this is shown in Equation 4.2.

$$\text{logit}[\Pr(\text{consumption} > j)] = \alpha + \beta \text{ temperature} \tag{4.2}$$

You should note that this equation is almost exactly the same as that used to model consumption when it was recorded as a continuous variable (see Section 2.2.2). The only difference (in the equation, at least) is that we now model 'logit[Pr(consumption $> j$)]' rather than consumption directly. In this equation, the log odds that consumption is in a higher rather than a lower category may be predicted by the average outdoor temperature when the ice cream was sold. The relationship between consumption and temperature has been examined earlier in the OLS regression chapter and is depicted for the ordered data in Figure 4.1 below. It is obvious from the graph (and the previous analyses) that, as expected, the level of ice cream consumption appears to be higher at higher temperatures. The proportional odds model should demonstrate this and also provide the significance of the relationship between the two variables.

---

[1] The reason for using these data is that the relationships between the variables are easily understood and we already have a good idea from OLS regression as to the form and strength of the relationships between the variables. The relatively minor change in coding consumption (from continuous to ordered) will require a different analysis method, but the results should be similar.

Table 4.1 *Data: ice cream consumption represented as ordered categories*

Ice cream consumption	Price	Family income	Temperature	Advertising method
Low	0.277	79	24	Radio
Low	0.265	76	32	Television
Low	0.277	94	32	Posters
Low	0.282	82	28	Posters
Low	0.267	79	47	Television
Low	0.270	85	26	Posters
Low	0.287	87	40	Radio
Low	0.282	95	28	Radio
Medium	0.287	83	40	Posters
Medium	0.292	85	44	Television
Medium	0.285	92	27	Television
Medium	0.275	82	61	Posters
Medium	0.272	86	32	Radio
Medium	0.277	86	60	Radio
Medium	0.262	78	65	Television
Medium	0.265	96	33	Radio
Medium	0.282	79	56	Posters
Medium	0.265	94	41	Television
Medium	0.277	84	55	Radio
High	0.287	82	63	Posters
High	0.270	78	41	Radio
High	0.277	84	67	Posters
High	0.277	81	63	Television
High	0.272	76	69	Television
High	0.265	96	52	Posters
High	0.280	80	68	Radio
High	0.268	91	64	Television
High	0.277	78	72	Radio
High	0.280	80	72	Posters
High	0.260	90	71	Television

Source: Koteswara, 1970 (with amendments)

Checking the proportional odds assumption: Before we interpret any statistics from a proportional odds model, it is important to first test the proportional odds assumption that the effect of the explanatory variable is consistent across all levels of the response variable (i.e., is it appropriate to average the effect of the explanatory variable?). The test for this is to determine whether the odds ratios for the $j - 1$ individual binary comparisons are significantly different from each other. This test is commonly known as the parallel lines test and is available in most statistical analysis packages (either the parallel lines test, or a version of it).

The Proportional Odds Model

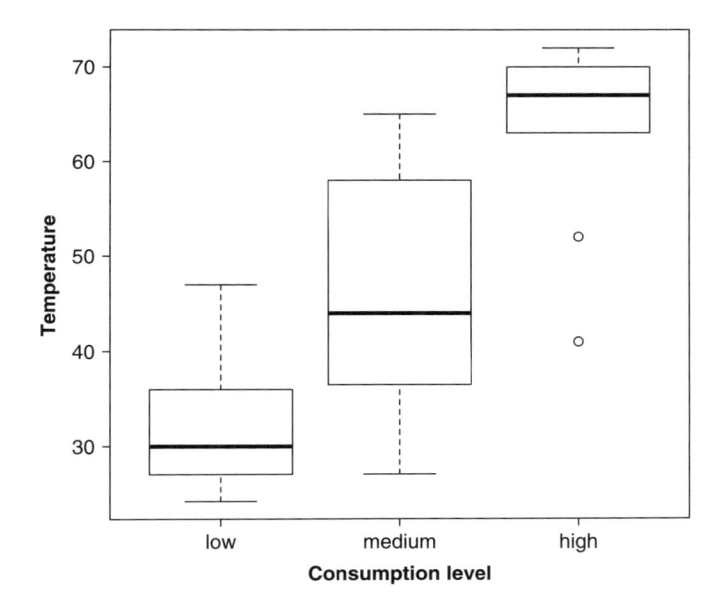

Figure 4.1 *Temperature and consumption level of ice cream*

The proportional odds assumption may also be tested using the likelihood-ratio test where the deviance of a multi-nomial logistic regression model of consumption (see Chapter 5) is compared to the deviance of a proportional odds model of consumption (as much of this book deals with deviances and the likelihood-ratio tests, this is the method we shall use to test the proportional odds assumption). As the proportional odds model (which treats the response variable as ordered categorical data) can be seen as a constrained model nested within the multi-nomial logistic regression model (which treats the response variable as unordered categorical data), the fit of the two models can be compared. The difference in deviance between the models is distributed as a χ^2 with df equivalent to the difference in the number of parameters between the models. Basically, if the multi-nomial logistic regression model fits better than the proportional odds model, the proportional odds assumption has not been met (i.e. accounting for the order has not improved the model which suggests that there may not be any order in the data to take account of). For this example, the deviance of the proportional-odds model

$$\text{logit}[\text{Pr}(\text{consumption} > j)] = \alpha + \beta \text{ temperature}$$

is compared to the deviance of the multi-nomial logistic regression model

$$\log \frac{\text{Pr}(\text{consumption} = j)}{\text{Pr}(\text{consumption} = j')} = \alpha + \beta \text{ temperature}$$

where one consumption category (j) is compared to the reference category (j'). This is the odds of being in one category compared to the other and is computed as a log, hence this is also a logit model (log odds). The results for this test are shown in Table 4.2 below. The non-significant difference between the models indicates that it may be appropriate to combine the parameters for the temperature variable.[2]

Table 4.2 *Test of the proportional odds assumption*

Model	Residual deviance	Difference in deviance	df	P-value
Multi-nomial logistic model	40.442	0.062	1	0.803
Proportional odds model	40.504			

It should be noted that there is some debate about the adequacy of the proportional odds assumption test, particularly in relation to its sensitivity to sample size (Scott et al. 1997). Even with this reservation, the test can provide useful information about the proportional odds model and will be used here as an indication of the test's appropriateness. For a full discussion of testing the proportional odds assumption using this technique see Fox, 2002 and Hoffmann, 2004.

Computing and interpreting model parameters: The model parameters for the simple proportional odds model discussed above (see Equation 4.2) were computed using software[3] and are shown in Table 4.3 below. You should note from the table that 2 intercepts are given whilst only one parameter is provided for temperature. This is because 2 comparisons are made between the levels of the response variable, one comparing low with medium and high (low | ≥medium) and the other comparing low and medium with high (≤medium | high). The effect of temperature for these 2 comparisons has been averaged (we can do this as the proportional odds assumption has been met) in order to create a single parameter for the explanatory variable.

Table 4.3 *Regression parameters*

	Estimate	Standard error	Odds ratio
Coefficients			
Temperature	0.146	0.039	1.157
Intercepts			
Low | ≥medium	5.078	1.573	
≤Medium | high	8.454	2.307	

Model: $\text{logit}[\Pr(\text{consumption} > j)] = \alpha + \beta \text{ temperature}$

---

[2] If the proportional odds assumption is rejected, it might not be appropriate to combine the parameters. In this case one may wish to consider the levels as unordered and use an unordered technique such as multi-nomial logistic regression to model the response variable.

[3] The software package used here is R (R Development Core Team, 2007).

The Proportional Odds Model

The parameters for the model shown in Table 4.3 can be interpreted as follows. For a unit increase in temperature, the log odds of being in a higher compared to a lower category increases by 0.146; this corresponds to an odds ratio of 1.157 ($e^{0.146}$). Put another way, the odds of being in a high category are 1.157 times higher than the odds of being in a medium or low category for each unit increase in temperature. Similarly, the odds of being in a high or a medium category are 1.157 times higher than being in a low category for each unit increase in temperature. The odds of moving up one category in consumption are 1.157 times higher for each unit increase in temperature. In general, as temperature increases, the more likely it is that the amount of ice cream consumed also increases. It should be noted that this interpretation of the parameters is very similar to that for the OLS regression model shown in Section 2.2.1. The only difference here is that we are modeling the probability of being in higher or lower categories of consumption rather than modeling an actual defined amount.

Using software, it is a simple matter to compute the confidence intervals for the parameter estimates.[4] Table 4.4 shows the 95% confidence intervals for temperature for both the log odds and odds ratios. We can see that for each unit increase in temperature, the odds of being in a higher compared to a lower category of consumption is expected to be between 1.072 and 1.250. As both of these estimates predict an increase (the odds are greater than 1.0 in each case), it appears that the effect of temperature is significant to the 95% level.

Table 4.4 *Confidence intervals*

	2.5%	50%	97.5%
Temperature			
Log odds	0.069	0.146	0.223
Odds ratio	1.072	1.157	1.250

Model: logit[Pr(consumption > j)] = $\alpha + \beta$ temperature

Predicted probabilities: Predictions can be made from the proportional odds model in much the same way as they were from the OLS and logistic regression models. However, as there is more than one model computed (leading to multiple intercepts) and an averaging procedure employed for the regression parameters, the calculations are not as simple but predictions can be made using statistical software.[5] For example, for the model

$$\text{logit}[\Pr(\text{consumption} > j)] = \alpha + \beta \text{ temperature}$$

predictions can be made of the probability of being in any one of the response categories for a given temperature. Table 4.5 shows the predicted probabilities of being in each response category for a selection of temperatures. We can see from the table

---

[4]These are also easy to compute manually, as the 95% confidence intervals for the parameters are simply the estimate ±1.96 times the standard error.

[5]The package R has been used to generate these statistics. Identical statistics can be obtained from a number of other packages.

Table 4.5 *Predicted consumption*

Temperature	Probability of being in category...		
	Low	Medium	High
24	0.828	0.165	0.007
32	0.600	0.378	0.022
32	0.600	0.378	0.022
40	0.318	0.614	0.068
44	0.206	0.677	0.116
27	0.757	0.232	0.011
72	0.004	0.108	0.887
72	0.004	0.108	0.887
71	0.005	0.123	0.872

Model: $\text{logit}[\Pr(\text{consumption} > j)] = \alpha + \beta \text{ temperature}$

that the probability of being in response category low when the temperature is 24 is 0.828. The probability of being in categories medium and high are 0.165 and 0.007 respectively. Similarly, when the temperature is 72 degrees, the probability of being in the high consumption category is 0.887 with the probabilities of being in the medium and low categories being 0.108 and 0.004 respectively. So, when the temperature is relatively high, consumption is likely to be in the high category, when it is relatively low, consumption is likely to be be in the low category, and when it is less extreme, consumption is likely to be in the medium category. The predicted probabilities of being in each category given temperature is shown in Figure 4.2 below.

Goodness-of-fit statistics: In addition to the model parameters, it is useful to have an indication of how well the model fits the data. For this we need to compute some model-fit statistics. There are, however, a number of aspects to assessing the model-fit. These can be utilized to assess the entire model (all the variables considered together), individual variables and individual categories within variables. There are a number of statistics that can be used to estimate significance and those used depend, to a large extent, on the software package being used. This chapter will utilize statistics based on the deviance measure ($-2LL$) to estimate the whole model and individual variables, but will use t-statistics to estimate the effect of individual categories within explanatory variables. Although it is possible to use statistics based on the deviance measure to estimate the significance of individual categories within variables, this is not particularly easy to achieve in software[6] and is therefore often estimated using t-statistics (or a comparable statistic). As this technique is commonly utilized in software, this technique will also be used in this discussion.

---

[6]The computation of $-2LL$ statistics for the individual categories of a variable often involves manually re-coding the data and then manually comparing nested models (see Hutcheson and Sofroniou, 1999, for a full description of this).

The Proportional Odds Model

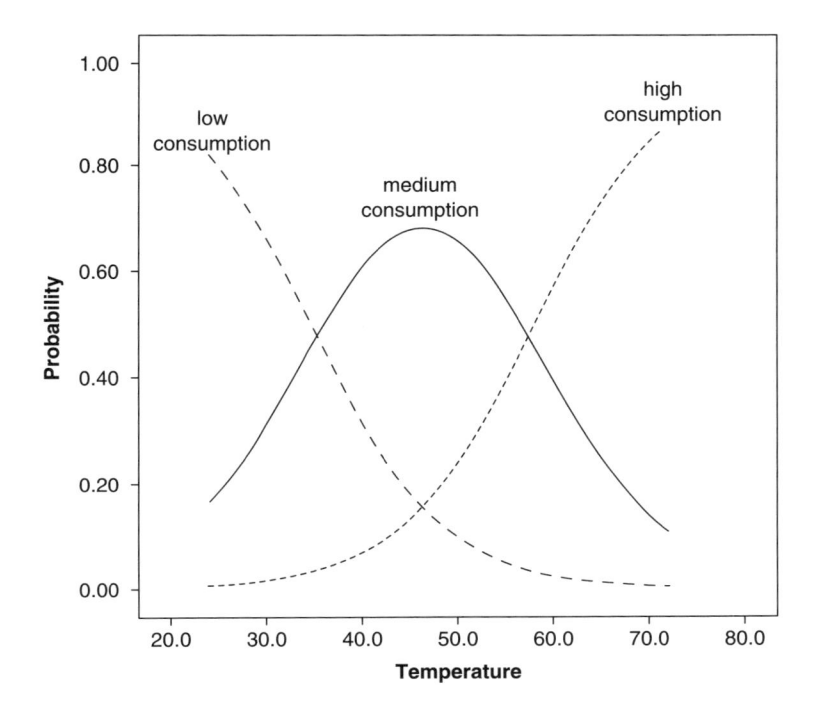

Figure 4.2 *Predicted probabilities for each group given temperature*

For a proportional odds model, model fit can be determined by comparing measures of deviance for nested models. The measure of deviance used is −2LL (see the chapter on logistic regression for a full discussion of this statistic) which is tested for significance using the chi-square distribution with the number of degrees of freedom equal to the difference in the number of terms between two nested models. For a simple proportional odds model, the effect of the single explanatory variable can be assessed by comparing the −2LL statistic for the full regression model with that for the null model (see Equation 4.3).

$$-2LL_{\text{diff}} = (-2LL_0) - (-2LL_1) \tag{4.3}$$

where $-2LL_0$ is the deviance in the null model $\text{logit}[\Pr(Y > j)] = \alpha$,
and $-2LL_1$ is the deviance in the model $\text{logit}[\Pr(Y > j)] = \alpha + \beta x$.

For the model 'logit[Pr(consumption > j)] = $\alpha + \beta$ temperature', the deviance statistics for the null and regression models and the significance of the change in deviance (-2LL$_{\text{diff}}$) are shown in Table 4.6. A model that just includes the response variable (the null model) has a deviance of 65.293. Adding the variable temperature to the model results in a model with a deviance equal to 40.504. This indicates that adding the variable temperature to the null model has reduced the variance by 24.789, which is a highly significant change, given that the models only differ by one parameter (hence the 1 df the change in deviance is tested on). Adding temperature to the model therefore significantly reduces the deviance and indicates that temperature is a significant predictor of consumption category.

Table 4.6 *Assessing significance by comparing model deviances*

Model	Residual deviance	Difference in deviance	df	P-value
Logit[Pr(Y > j)] = α	65.293	24.789	1	6.4e−07
Logit[Pr(Y > j)] = $\alpha + \beta$ temperature	40.504			

Y = ice cream consumption category

In many statistical packages, these model-fit statistics are provided in simple analysis of deviance tables as part of the analysis output. Table 4.7, shows this output for the simple proportional odds model of consumption. Although this table is redundant for this model (as the information has already been provided above), it is useful for multiple regression models and for models that include categorical explanatory variables and is included here for completeness.

Table 4.7 *Analysis of deviance table: the significance of variables*

	−2LL	df	P-value
Coefficient			
Temperature	24.789	1	6.4e − 07

Model: logit[Pr(consumption > j)] = $\alpha + \beta$ temperature

In addition to those statistics based on −2LL, the significance of the explanatory variables can be estimated using t-statistics. The t-statistics are simply the estimates divided by the standard error and tested for significance using $n - k - 1$ degrees of freedom (where n is the number of cases and k is the number of parameters excluding the constant). The t-statistic for temperature is therefore 0.146/0.039, which is 3.728 (this is the estimate from software, which uses many more decimal places than have been reported here). This value is then tested at 28 degrees of freedom and significance reported for a 2-tailed test (see Table 4.8). Using the t-statistic, we find that temperature is still significantly related to consumption level, albeit at a reduced level of significance.

In addition to the significance it is also useful to have an idea of the percentage of variation in the response variable that is 'explained' by the model. Similar to the logistic regression model (see Section 3.2.1), 'pseudo R^2' statistics can be computed. For the above model, Cox & Snell R Square = 0.562 and Nagelkerke R Square = 0.634. These statistics indicate that temperature 'explains' over 50% of the variation in consumption and corresponds quite well with the R^2 statistic from the OLS regression procedure for the similar model shown in Section 2.2.1 which showed an R^2 value of

The Proportional Odds Model

Table 4.8 *Estimating the significance of individual parameters using t-statistics*

	Estimate	Standard error	t-statistic	P-value
Coefficients				
Temperature	0.146	0.039	3.728	$8.7e-04$
Intercepts				
Low | $\geq$medium	5.078	1.573		
$\leq$Medium | high	8.454	2.307		

Model: $\text{logit}[\Pr(\text{consumption} > j)] = \alpha + \beta \text{ temperature}$

0.6. It should be noted that, similar to the logistic regression pseudo R^2 statistics, these should be used with caution and advisably only used as a supplementary statistic.

In conclusion, the simple proportional odds model of ice cream consumption suggests that, as expected, temperature is significantly related to consumption and explains over half of the variation. The test of parallel lines indicated that the proportional odds assumption was met, however, one may wish to investigate the model further using regression diagnostics (see, for example, Crawley, 2005; Draper and Smith, 1998; Everitt and Hothorn, 2006; Hoffman, 2004).

4.2.2 Multiple proportional odds

As is the case in OLS and logistic regression models, it is a simple matter to include more than one explanatory variable into a proportional odds model. These explanatory variables are entered into the model as additional terms. For example, the ordered categorical variable 'ice cream consumption' can be modeled using information about temperature, price and income. If the errors are independently distributed according to the standard logistic distribution, we get the ordered logit model shown in Equation 4.4.

$$\text{logit}[\Pr(\text{consumption} > j)] = \alpha + \beta_1 \text{ price } + \beta_2 \text{ family income } + \beta_3 \text{ temperature} \quad (4.4)$$

It is useful at this stage to investigate the relationships between each explanatory variable and the consumption category using boxplots. Figure 4.3 shows these relationships and suggests that whilst temperature appears to be related to consumption, income and price do not. We need to be careful, however, when evaluating these graphs as they do not take into account the relationships between the explanatory variables.

Relationships between the explanatory variables can have serious consequences for interpretation of the proportional odds model as they introduce a degree of multicollinearity (see Hutcheson and Sofroniou, 1999, for a detailed discussion). This is unlikely to be the case in this particular study as the explanatory variables are unlikely to be highly related to one another. Theoretically, it is unlikely that the explanatory variables would be related; for example, temperature is unlikely to be related to income or price (unless, for example, prices are made higher on hot days). Figure 4.4 shows a matrix scatterplot of the explanatory variables and suggests that they are not highly related to each other.

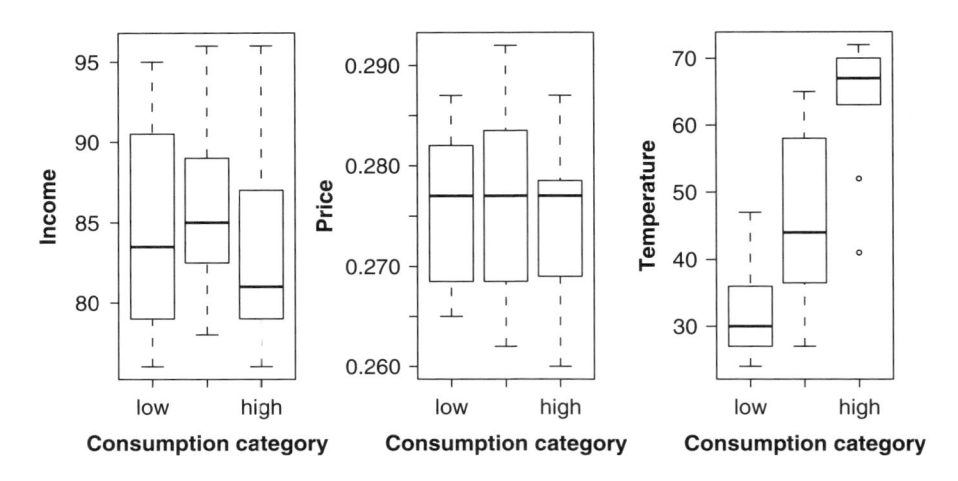

Figure 4.3 *Boxplots showing relationships between each explanatory variable and the level of consumption*

On the evidence from the graphs above it would appear that only temperature is likely to be related to consumption level. The proportional odds model should be able to illustrate this.

Checking the proportional odds assumption: Before we interpret the model statistics, it is important to test the proportional odds assumption. The test results are shown in Table 4.9 below and suggest that the proportional odds assumption cannot be rejected. The difference in deviance between the multi-nomial logistic regression model and the proportional odds model is tested at 3 degrees of freedom as there are now 3 parameters in the proportional odds model. For this example, it therefore looks appropriate to combine the parameters for the explanatory variables and use a proportional odds model.

Table 4.9 *Test of the proportional odds assumption*

Model	Residual deviance	Difference in deviance	df	P-value
Multi-nomial logistic model	38.257	0.450	3	0.930
Proportional odds model	37.807			

Model: $\text{logit}[\Pr(\text{consumption} > j)] = \alpha + \beta_1 \text{ price } + \beta_2 \text{ income } + \beta_3 \text{ temperature}$

Computing and interpreting model parameters: Table 4.10 shows the parameters for the multiple proportional odds model shown in Equation 4.4. Similar to the

The Proportional Odds Model

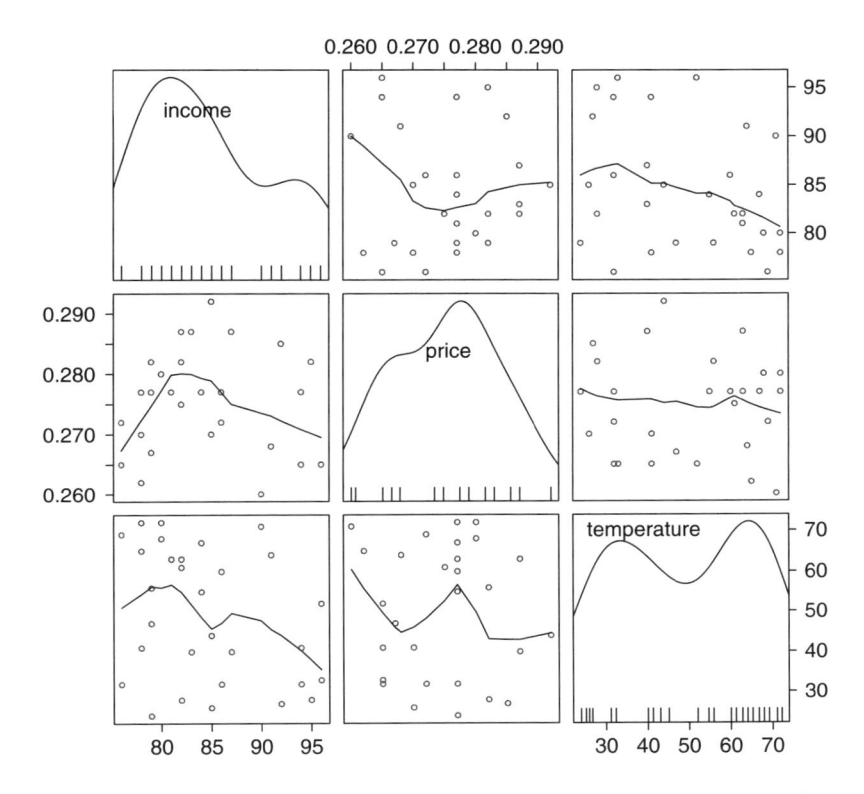

Figure 4.4 *Matrix scatterplot showing relationships between the explanatory variables*

simple proportional odds model, there are 2 intercepts representing the 2 comparisons modeled (low | ≥ medium, and ≤ medium | high) and a single parameter for each of the explanatory variables (these have been averaged across the models to provide single parameters). The parameters for this model are interpreted almost identically to the multiple OLS and multiple logistic regression models. For example, for a unit increase in price, when controlling for income and temperature, the log odds of being in a higher compared to a lower category increase by an average of 2.408. The odds ratio for price indicates that you are 11 times more likely to be in a higher category of consumption for each unit increase in price. Similarly, for a unit increase in temperature, when controlling for income and price, the log odds of being in a higher compared to a lower category increase by an average of 0.175. The odds ratio for temperature indicates that you are 1.191 times as likely to be in a higher category of consumption for each unit increase in temperature. It is a simple matter to also compute the confidence intervals for the parameter estimates. Table 4.11 shows the 95% confidence intervals for the log odds and odds ratios of all explanatory variables in the model.

Table 4.10 *Regression parameters*

	Estimate	Standard error	Odds ratio
Coefficients			
Price	2.408	2.388	11.112
Income	0.124	0.081	1.132
Temperature	0.175	0.048	1.191
Intercepts			
Low | $\geq$ medium	17.635	7.526	
$\leq$ Medium | high	21.233	7.945	

Model: $\text{logit}[\Pr(\text{consumption} > j)] = \alpha + \beta_1 \text{ price} + \beta_2 \text{ income} + \beta_3 \text{ temperature}$

Table 4.11 *Confidence intervals*

	2.5%	50%	97.5%
Price			
Log odds	−2.273	2.408	7.089
Odds ratio	0.103	11.112	119.708
Income			
Log odds	−0.035	0.124	0.283
Odds ratio	0.966	1.132	1.327
Temperature			
Log odds	0.081	0.175	0.269
Odds ratio	1.084	1.191	1.309

Model: $\text{logit}[\Pr(\text{consumption} > j)] = \alpha + \beta_1 \text{ price} + \beta_2 \text{ income} + \beta_3 \text{ temperature}$

You should note that the size of the parameter estimates do not give any indication of significance as they are related to the measurement scales used. The effect of price may look impressive when compared to temperature, but this may be due to the fact that a unit increase in price is a relatively large increase when compared to a unit increase in temperature (values of price range from 0.260 to 0.292, whilst values of temperature range from 24 to 72). In order to make statements about the significance of these parameters, one needs to look at the goodness-of-fit statistics presented below.

Predicted probabilities: Predictions can be made from a multiple proportional odds model in much the same way as they were for a simple model. Using statistical software, predictions can be made as to the probability of being in any one of the response categories for a given price, income and temperature. Table 4.12 shows the predicted probabilities of being in each response category for a selection of price, income and

The Proportional Odds Model

temperature values. We can see from the table that the probability of being in response category low when the price is 0.277, income is 79 and temperature is 24 is 0.950. The probability of being in categories medium and high are 0.048 and 0.001 respectively.

Table 4.12 *Predicted probabilities*

Price	Income	Temperature	Predicted probabilities of being in category...		
			Low	Medium	High
0.277	79	24	0.950	0.048	0.001
0.265	76	32	0.875	0.121	0.004
0.277	94	32	0.422	0.542	0.036
0.277	86	60	0.014	0.333	0.652
0.262	78	65	0.017	0.367	0.617
0.265	96	33	0.330	0.618	0.053
0.277	78	72	0.005	0.145	0.850
0.280	80	72	0.004	0.116	0.880
0.260	90	71	0.001	0.046	0.953

Model: logit[Pr(consumption > j)] = $\alpha + \beta_1$ price + β_2 income + β_3 temperature

Table 4.12 suggests that consumption is closely related to temperature, but this relationship is more difficult to see than in the previous simple model as there are now 3 interacting variables rather than a single variable acting on the response. However, in general, it still looks as if higher consumption is associated with higher temperatures.

Goodness-of-fit statistics: In addition to the model parameters, it is useful to have an indication of how well the model fits the data and how significantly each explanatory variable is related to the response. As with the simple proportional odds model discussed above significances may be estimated using statistics based on the deviance and on t-statistics. In this section, the significance of the variables is to be estimated using statistics based on $-2LL$, and the significance of individual categories within variables is to be estimated using t-statistics.

For a multiple proportional odds model, the effect of individual or groups of explanatory variables can be assessed by comparing the $-2LL$ statistics for 2 nested models (see Equation 4.5). The resulting statistic is tested for significance using the chi-square distribution with the number of degrees of freedom equal to the difference in the number of terms between the 2 models.

$$-2LL_{\text{diff}} = (-2LL_p) - (-2LL_{p+q}) \qquad (4.5)$$

where p is the smaller, nested model,
and $p + q$ is the larger model.

Table 4.13 shows the $-2LL$ statistics associated with a number of nested models and the significance of the differences in these scores.

Table 4.13 *Assessing significance by comparing model deviances*

	$-2LL$	df	$-2LL_{diff}$	df_{diff}	P-value
The overall effect of price, income and temperature					
Logit[Pr(Y > j)] = α	65.293	28	27.486	3	4.7e−06
Logit[Pr(Y > j)] = $\alpha + \beta_1$price + $\beta_2$income + $\beta_3$temp	37.807	25			
The effect of price					
Logit[Pr(Y > j)] = $\alpha + \beta_2$income + $\beta_3$temp	37.823	26	0.016	1	0.900
Logit[Pr(Y > j)] = $\alpha + \beta_1$price + $\beta_2$income + $\beta_3$temp	37.807	25			
The effect of temperature					
Logit[Pr(Y > j)] = $\alpha + \beta_1$price + $\beta_2$income	64.594	26	26.787	1	2.3e−07
Logit[Pr(Y > j)] = $\alpha + \beta_1$price + $\beta_2$income + $\beta_3$temp	37.807	25			

Y = ice cream consumption level

From Table 4.13, we can see that the effect of all explanatory variables on the prediction of Y is highly significant with a χ^2 value of 27.486 at 3 degrees of freedom ($p = 4.7e-06$). The effect of price on consumption in the model 'logit[Pr(consumption> j)] = $\alpha + \beta_1$ price + β_2 income + β_3 temperature' is non-significant ($\chi^2 = 0.016$ at 1 degree of freedom, $p = 0.9$), whilst temperature is highly significant, ($\chi^2 = 26.787$ at 1 degree of freedom, $p = 2.3e-07$). This information about the significance of each individual explanatory variable is also typically displayed in statistical packages in an analysis of deviance table similar to the one shown in Table 4.14.

In addition to those statistics based on $-2LL$, the significance of the explanatory variables can be estimated using t-statistics (the parameter estimates divided by the standard error and tested for significance using $n - k - 1$ degrees of freedom). The t-statistics for the multiple regression model of ice cream consumption are shown in Table 4.15. Using the t-statistics, we find similar relationships to those identified using the $-2LL$ statistics. Temperature is still the only variable significantly related to consumption level, albeit at a reduced level.

It is worth comparing these statistics with the ones computed using OLS regression for the original uncategorized consumption variable. Given that the data sets are very

The Proportional Odds Model

Table 4.14 *Analysis of deviance table: the significance of variables*

	−2LL	df	P-value
Coefficients			
Price	0.016	1	0.900
Income	2.680	1	0.102
Temperature	26.787	1	2.3e−07

Model: logit[Pr(consumption > j)] = $\alpha + \beta_1$ price + β_2 income + β_3 temperature

Table 4.15 *Estimating the significance of individual parameters using t-statistics*

	Estimate	Standard error	T-statistic	P-value
Coefficients				
Price	2.408	2.388	1.008	0.323
Income	0.124	0.081	1.531	0.138
Temperature	0.175	0.048	3.661	0.001
Intercepts				
Low | ≥ medium	17.635	7.526		
≤ Medium | high	21.233	7.945		

Model: logit[Pr(consumption > j)] = $\alpha + \beta_1$ price + β_2 income + β_3 temperature

similar, the results from the 2 models should also be similar. The 2 regression models are shown in Table 4.16 below. As expected, the statistics for the two models are similar, but do show some differences, particularly with respect to the variable 'income' which does not reach significance in the proportional odds model (this is perhaps due to the loss of some of the information that was encoded in the variable 'consumption' when it was transformed into three ordered categories). In general, though, the results and interpretation of the analyses are similar.

Similar to the simple proportional odds regression model, 'pseudo R^2' statistics can be computed for models containing multiple explanatory variables. For the above model containing price, income and temperature, Cox and Snell R Square = 0.600 and Nagelkerke R Square = 0.677, which compares to the R^2 value of 0.791 computed for the OLS multiple regression model in section 2.2.2. Using these indicators, it appears that the 3 variables together 'explain' about 60% of the variation in the categorized consumption variable, although, as before, one should treat these statistics as supplementary.

In conclusion, the multiple proportional odds model of ice cream consumption suggests that out of the 3 variables tested, only temperature is significantly related to consumption. From the pseudo R-Square statistics we find that all 3 variables explain about 60% of the variation in consumption. The test of the proportional odds assumption indicated that the proportional odds model can be used, however, one may

Table 4.16 *Comparing proportional odds and OLS regression models*

	OLS regression model	Proportional odds model
All variables	$F_{3,26} = 22.175, p = 2.45\text{e}-07$	$\chi^2 = 27.486, \text{df} = 3, p = 4.7\text{e}-06$
Price	$F_{1,26} = 1.567, p = 0.222$	$\chi^2 = 0.016, \text{df} = 1, p = 0.900$
Income	$F_{1,26} = 7.973, p = 0.009$	$\chi^2 = 2.680, \text{df} = 1, p = 0.102$
Temperature	$F_{1,26} = 60.252, p = 3.1\text{e}-10$	$\chi^2 = 26.787, \text{df} = 1, p = 2.3\text{e}-07$

OLS model: consumption = $\alpha + \beta_1$ price + β_2 income + β_3 temperature
Proportional odds model: logit[Pr(consumption > j)] = $\alpha + \beta_1$ price + β_2 income + β_3 temperature

wish to investigate the model further using regression diagnostics and maybe employ some variable selection techniques to choose a more parsimonious model that only includes those variables that reach a certain level of significance (see, for example, Draper and Smith, 1998; Hoffman, 2004; Maindonald and Braun, 2003).

4.2.3 Categorical explanatory variables

As with OLS and logistic regression, it is relatively simple to include categorical explanatory variables into a proportional odds model once the variable has been appropriately coded (this is usually carried out automatically by software). The technique for coding categorical variables in proportional odds regression models is identical to those for OLS and logistics regression described in Chapters 2 and 3 and will not be revisited here. It is, however, useful to show an example proportional odds analysis that includes an unordered categorical variable. The model we will demonstrate here is the ice cream consumption model shown in Section 4.2.2 with the addition of the unordered categorical variable 'advertising method' (see Table 4.1). The model is shown in Equation 4.6 below.

$$\text{logit}[\text{Pr}(\text{consumption} > j)] = \alpha + \beta_1 \text{ price} + \beta_2 \text{ family income} + \beta_3 \text{ temperature} + \beta_{4-5} \text{ advertising method} \quad (4.6)$$

Advertising method is a 3 group unordered categorical variable which designates the type of advertising predominantly used during the period of data collection (radio, posters or television). The 3 groups result in two parameters in the regression model (hence the 2 parameters associated with advertising, β_{4-5}, in Equation 4.6). It should be noted that adding the variable designating advertising method to the model will result in individual regression parameters being estimated on fewer data points. For example, predictions for each level of consumption are now divided between three methods of advertising. If there were, say, 9 observations in the low consumption category spread equally among the advertising methods, this will mean only 3 observations can be used for estimating each parameter, which can make the parameter

The Proportional Odds Model

estimates very unstable. As the number of cases in this data set are very limited, the inclusion of the categorical variable could well cause problems and needs to be recognized when interpreting the results. Even though there are likely to be difficulties caused by the limited sample size, we will continue with this analysis for the purpose of demonstration.

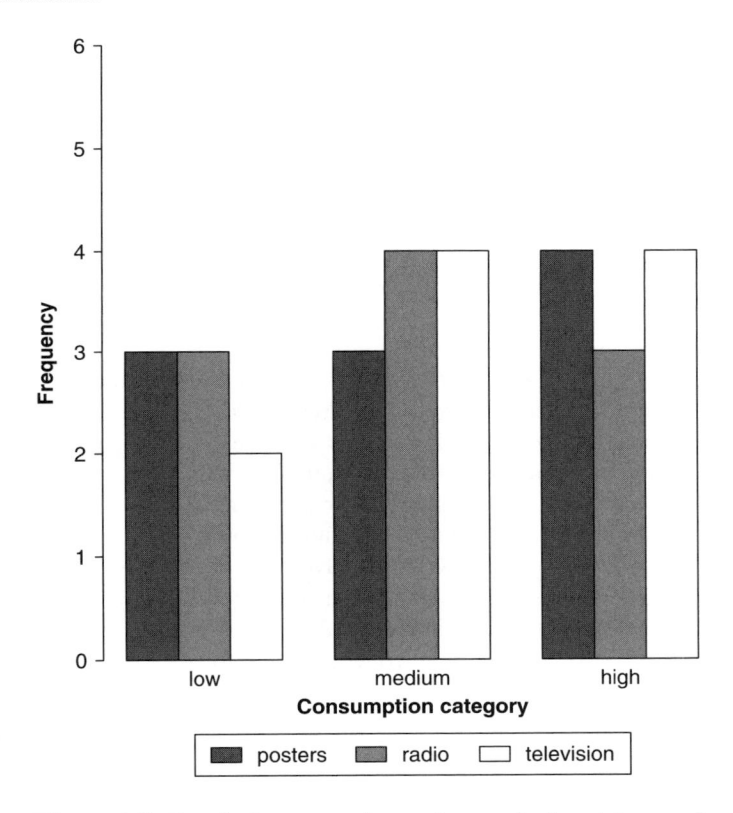

Figure 4.5 *Level of consumption and type of advertising used*

Figure 4.5 shows the relationship between consumption and advertising method in a graphical format. Posters and television advertising methods are associated with higher levels of consumption, but the relationship between radio and consumption level is inconsistent (as medium consumption is the highest category). In general, the graph shows little evidence of a strong relationship between the two variables (although this is confirmed in the forthcoming analysis, this variable is included in the model for the purpose of illustration).

Table 4.17 shows the test of the proportional odds assumption for the model and the non-significant result suggests that the assumption cannot be rejected. The difference in deviance between the multi-nomial logistic regression model and the proportional odds model is tested at 5 df as there are now 5 parameters in the proportional odds

Table 4.17 *Test of the proportional odds assumption*

Model	Residual deviance	Difference in deviance	df	P-value
Multi-nomial logistic model	37.774	0.056	5	0.99996
Proportional odds model	37.718			

Model: $\text{logit}[\Pr(\text{consumption} > j)] = \alpha + \beta_1 \text{ price } + \beta_2 \text{ income } + \beta_3 \text{ temperature } + \beta_{4-5} \text{ advertise}$

model. For this example, therefore, it looks appropriate to combine the parameters for the explanatory variables and use a proportional odds model.

The parameters for the proportional odds model of ice cream consumption are shown in Table 4.18. The interpretation of the parameters for the categorical variable 'advertise' is very similar to the interpretation of the categorical variable included in a logistic regression model (see Section 3.2.3). In this analysis, advertising method has been coded using treatment coding (hence the letter 'T' printed before the comparison group) so that each category is compared against a reference category, which in this case is the use of posters. Using radio to advertise compared to posters, when controlling for income, price and temperature, the log odds of being in a higher compared to a lower category of consumption increase by an average of 0.196. The odds ratio for radio (1.217) indicates that for this model, someone is more likely to be in a higher category of consumption when the advertising medium is radio compared to posters. For these data, the use of radio would appear to a more effective advertising tool than the use of posters. The estimate of 0.252 for television, suggests that the use of television to advertise is even more effective than posters (and, consequently, also more effective than radio).

It is also useful to look at the confidence intervals as these provide clues about the precision of the estimates. Table 4.19 shows the 95% confidence intervals for each of the parameters in Equation 4.6. It should be immediately obvious from this table (particularly when compared to the results in Table 4.11), that the variable 'price' may be problematic as it has huge estimates associated with it and these change dramatically when other variables are taken out of the model.[7] As we will find out later, price does not appear to be a significant variable in the model, but from this table it does look to have a significant effect (both confidence intervals for the odds ratio are above 1). This effect is most likely due to the fact that there are very few observations for this model. For example, at low consumption, there are only two observations for television and these observations are very close (0.265 and 0.267). On this information one would question the inclusion of this number of variables in the model and either increase the sample size, or reduce the number of variables (by, for example, removing those

---

[7] For instance, the parameter for price changes from 12.880 to −5.018 (with a standard error of 51.217), when income is removed from the model. This illustrates the imprecision of the estimate for price as income is only weakly associated with the response variable (and with price), and its removal should not, therefore, influence the model parameters to such a degree.

The Proportional Odds Model

Table 4.18 *Regression parameters*

	Estimate	Standard error	Odds ratio
Coefficients			
Price	12.880	2.503	3.9e+05
Income	0.129	0.082	1.138
Temperature	0.177	0.048	1.194
Advertise(T.radio)	0.196	1.041	1.217
Advertise(T.television)	0.252	1.022	1.287
Intercepts			
Low | ≥ medium	21.193	7.655	
≤ Medium | high	24.774	8.064	

Model: $\text{logit}[\Pr(\text{consumption} > j)] = \alpha + \beta_1 \text{ price} + \beta_2 \text{ income} + \beta_3 \text{ temperature} + \beta_{4-5} \text{ advertise}$

Advertise reference category = posters

Table 4.19 *Confidence intervals*

	2.5%	50%	97.5%
Price			
Log odds	7.975	12.880	17.786
Odds ratio	2.93+03	3.9e+05	5.3e+07
Income			
Log odds	−0.033	0.129	0.291
Odds ratio	0.968	1.138	1.338
Temperature			
Log odds	0.083	0.177	0.271
Odds ratio	1.087	1.194	1.311
Advertise (T.radio)			
Log odds	−1.843	0.196	2.235
Odds ratio	0.158	1.217	9.346
Advertise (T.television)			
Log odds	−1.753	0.252	2.256
Odds ratio	0.173	1.287	9.545

Model: $\text{logit}[\Pr(\text{consumption} > j)] = \alpha + \beta_1 \text{ price} + \beta_2 \text{ income} + \beta_3 \text{ temperature} + \beta_{4-5} \text{ advertise}$

Advertise reference category = posters

that are non-significant). Table 4.19 does show some interesting information about the categorical variable and suggests that the effect of radio and television, when compared to the use of posters is not significant when predicting consumption category (the confidence intervals for both variables contain 1).

The predicted probabilities of being in each response category for a selection of price, income, temperature and advertising values is shown in Table 4.20. The addition of the variable 'advertising' has made little difference to the predicted values when compared to the predictions made for a model that did not include advertising (these are shown in Table 4.12).

Table 4.20 *Predicted probabilities*

Price	Income	Temperature	Advertising	Predicted probabilities		
				Low	Medium	High
0.277	79	24	Radio	0.951	0.047	0.001
0.265	76	32	Television	0.885	0.111	0.004
0.277	94	32	Posters	0.454	0.513	0.032
0.277	86	60	Radio	0.013	0.314	0.672
0.262	78	65	Television	0.018	0.376	0.606
0.265	96	33	Radio	0.341	0.608	0.051
0.277	78	72	Radio	0.005	0.136	0.859
0.280	80	72	Posters	0.004	0.125	0.871
0.260	90	71	Television	0.001	0.045	0.953

Model: $\text{logit}[\Pr(\text{consumption} > j)] = \alpha + \beta_1 \text{ price } + \beta_2 \text{ income } + \beta_3 \text{ temperature } + \beta_{4-5} \text{ advertise}$

It is important, however, not to read too much into these statistics before the significances of the variables are determined. The significance associated with all explanatory variables is shown in Table 4.21 with the individual variables shown in Table 4.22 and the individual categories of the advertising variable shown in Table 4.23.

The significance of all explanatory variables can be computed by comparing the deviance in the full regression model (see Equation 4.6) with the deviance in the null model (ice cream consumption on it own). These statistics are shown in Table 4.21.[8] The significance of the change in deviances associated with individual variables are shown in Table 4.22. You will note that the significance of the variables price, income and temperature are tested at one degree of freedom as these variables are single parameters, whereas the variable advertising is tested at two degrees of freedom as this variable is represented using two parameters.

From Table 4.22, we can see that the variable 'advertising' is not significantly related to ice cream consumption when included in a model with the other explanatory

---
[8] These statistics may appear as the 'model chi-square' (or similar) in the output of your statistical package.

The Proportional Odds Model

variables. When the two parameters associated with advertising are removed from the full regression model, $-2LL$ reduces by 0.089, which is insignificant ($\chi^2 = 0.089, df = 2, p = 0.957$). Of all the explanatory variables in the model, only temperature is significant ($\chi^2 = 26.550, df = 1, p = 2.6e-07$). As one would expect, these results are very similar to those obtained for the multiple proportional odds model discussed earlier.

Table 4.21 Assessing significance by comparing model deviances

	$-2LL$	df	$-2LL_{diff}$	df_{diff}	P-value
Logit[Pr(Y > j)] = α	65.293	28	27.575	5	4.4e−05
Logit[Pr(Y > j)] = $\alpha + \beta_1$price + $\beta_2$income + $\beta_3$temp + β_{4-5}advert	37.718	23			

Y = ice cream consumption category

Table 4.22 Analysis of deviance table: the significance of variables

	$-2LL$	df	P-value
Coefficients			
Price	0.066	1	0.797
Income	2.686	1	0.101
Temperature	26.550	1	2.6e−07
Advertising	0.089	2	0.957

Model: logit[Pr(consumption > j)] = $\alpha + \beta_1$ price + β_2 income + β_3 temperature + β_{4-5} advertise

The significance of each individual parameter may be estimated using t-statistics. It is important to note that although the variable 'price' is significant using the t-statistic, this is not the case when it is tested using the change in deviance ($-2LL$).[9] As suggested before, this anomaly is likely due to the small sample size used. This example is useful, however, as a demonstration of the potential problems of small samples and the use of the significance tests to assess their contribution.

In conclusion, unordered categorical variables can be included simply in a multiple proportional odds model as the parameters and model-fit statistics for the categorical data are interpreted in much the same way as for other GLM models. In this case, it appeared that the categorical variable did not significantly contribute to the prediction of the response variable and may therefore be a candidate for removal (in addition to the other non-significant variables) in order to derive a simpler model of ice cream consumption.

---

[9] As these tests provide conflicting information, we would want to exercise caution when interpreting these results.

Table 4.23 *Estimating the significance of individual parameters using t-values*

	Estimate	Standard error	T-value	P-value
Coefficients				
Price	12.880	2.503	5.146	$2.9e-05$
Income	0.129	0.082	1.565	0.131
Temperature	0.177	0.048	3.682	0.001
Advertise(T.radio)	0.196	1.041	0.188	0.852
Advertise(T.television)	0.252	1.022	0.246	0.808
Intercepts				
Low | $\geq$ medium	21.193	7.655		
$\leq$ Medium | high	24.774	8.064		

Model: $\text{logit}[\Pr(\text{consumption} > j)] = \alpha + \beta_1 \text{ price } + \beta_2 \text{ income} + \beta_3 \text{ temperature} + \beta_{4-5} \text{ advertise}$

Advertise reference category = posters

P-values (2-tailed) are tested at $n - k - 1$ degrees of freedom

4.3 Analyzing Simple Experimental Designs for Ordered Data

The analysis of ordered data from simple experimental or quasi-experimental studies has traditionally been conducted through the use of non-parametric tests such as the Mann-Whitney, Kruskal-Wallis, Wilcoxon and Friedman tests (see, for example, Agresti and Finlay, 1997; Crawley, 2005; Everitt and Hothorn, 2006; Kanji, 1999; Moutinho et al., 1998; Siegel and Castellan, 1988). These grouped data can also be analyzed using regression methods; in particular, the proportional odds model for ordered data. The analysis of such data can be viewed in a similar way to the modeling techniques already discussed earlier in this chapter. Namely, an outcome variable can be predicted to some extent using information about other variables. In this case an ordered variable (management grade, ability, rank, position in class, etc.) can be predicted to some extent using information about group membership (teaching method used, gender, ethnic origin, university attended). To use the regression model terminology,

examination grade *can be predicted by* teaching method

managerial level *can be predicted by* gender

level of satisfaction *can be predicted by* reputation of store.

The aim is to represent the hypothesis in the form of an equation that can be subjected to a regression modeling technique. In an independent groups design the response variable is predicted using information about group membership, whereas in a dependent groups design the additional information about subject also needs to be included.

A GLM model allows a number of advantages over the more traditional tests, not least the ability to include a number of additional variables in the model (those that are not controlled experimentally) and the use of a general technique to replace multiple tests.[10] It is also possible to apply a full range of model selection techniques and model diagnostics, although these are beyond the scope of the present book.

The following discussion will describe the analysis of simple experimental and quasi-experimental data from unrelated and related groups designs using proportional odds regression models and compare these results with the more traditional non-parametric hypothesis tests.[11]

4.3.1 Unrelated groups design

In an unrelated groups design, the cases in the groups are independent of one another. That is, different cases have been chosen for each group (e.g. a random sample of 40 people are exposed to condition A and a different random sample of 40 people are exposed to condition B). There is no direct relationship between the members of the 2 groups.

In order illustrate the analysis of an unrelated groups design we will use the data set showing the price of whiskey and its relationship to the type of ownership.[12] This data set is identical to that used in Chapter 2, except that the response variable (price of whiskey) has been recoded into an ordered categorical variable. The four ordered categories relate to the original continuous variable as follows; category 1 = ≤ 4.19, category 2 = ≥ 4.20 and ≤ 4.60, category 3 = ≥ 4.61 and ≤ 4.89, category 4 = ≥ 4.90 and are shown in Table 4.24. For a full description of the original data set, see Section 2.4.1.

A pictorial representation of this design is shown in Figure 4.6 below and shows the 30 companies are unrelated to one another across the 3 groups (state-funded, privately-funded or state–private funded). The regression model that will test the relationship between the groups and the price of whiskey is shown in Equation 4.7. As the data to be modeled (the response variable) is ordered a proportional odds regression model can be used.

$$\text{logit}[\Pr(\text{price} > j)] = \alpha + \beta \text{ funded} \tag{4.7}$$

Before interpreting the model parameters, it is useful to test the proportional odds assumption to see if it is appropriate to use this model on these data. Table 4.25 shows the test of the proportional odds assumption and the non-significant result indicates that the assumption cannot be rejected. The proportional odds model may therefore be appropriately applied to these data.

---

[10]This is particularly useful for teaching purposes as a single technique can replace a number of individual tests.

[11]As the GLM is a general technique, this section is very similar to the discussion in Chapter 2 that described the use of OLS regression to analyze experimental designs for continuous data. Readers are advised to familiarize themselves with this material.

[12]This data set has the advantage of being quite simple and also enables the results to be compared with those from the OLS regression analysis.

Table 4.24 *Data: ranked price of whiskey*

State-funded	Privately-funded	State–private partnership
3	3	3
2	4	4
1	3	1
1	4	4
2	2	2
2	4	4
1	4	4
1	4	3
1	2	2
3	3	3

Chance, 1991 (with amendments).
Reported in Hand et al., 1994

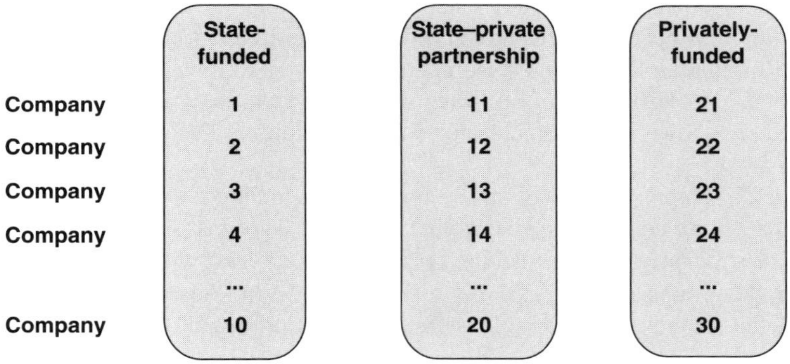

	State-funded	State–private partnership	Privately-funded
Company	1	11	21
Company	2	12	22
Company	3	13	23
Company	4	14	24
	...	...	...
Company	10	20	30

Figure 4.6 *A pictorial representation of an unrelated groups design*

Table 4.25 *Test of the proportional odds assumption*

Model	Residual deviance	Difference in deviance	df	P-value
Multi-nomial logistic model	66.784	2.594	4	0.628
Proportional odds model	69.378			

Model: $\text{logit}[\Pr(\text{price} > j)] = \alpha + \beta$ funded

Table 4.26 shows the parameter estimates for the model shown in Equation 4.7. There are 3 intercepts shown, which correspond to the 3 comparison logit models computed for the 4 levels of the response variable. The parameters have been averaged across these multiple logit models to provide single estimates for each explanatory variable (this is appropriate as the test of the proportional odds assumption was insignificant). From the table we can see that the type of funding has been dummy coded using the indicator method to provide treatment contrasts (signified by the 'T.' before the category identifier), which mean that each identified category is compared to the reference category (which in this example is state–private partnership). The log odds of being in a higher price category for a privately-owned company is 0.531 higher than for a state–private partnership. This equates to an odds ratio of 1.701. The price of whiskey in a privately-funded company is more likely to be higher than for a state–private partnership. The log odds of being in a higher price category for a state-owned company is 2.542 units lower than for the reference category. This equates to an odds ratio of 0.079. The price of whiskey in a state-owned company is more likely to be lower than for a state–private partnership. Looking at this in a slightly different way, one can say that a state-owned company is 12.658 (1/0.079) times as likely to be in a lower price category than a state-private partnership.

It is useful to also compute the confidence intervals for the regression coefficients. Table 4.27 shows these intervals for the variable 'funded'. These intervals are quite wide and show the imprecision of the estimates. Of particular interest is the fact that the odds ratio for 'funded (T.private)' include 1.0, which suggests that this parameter is not significant (the 95% confidence intervals predict an increase in price as well as a decrease). The odds ratio for 'funded (T.state)' does not include 1.0, which suggests that this parameter is significant at the 95% level (both of the 95% confidence intervals predict a decrease in price).

Once we have the model, it is a simple matter to obtain the estimated probabilities of each of our funding groups falling into any of the categories of the response variable. These statistics are shown in Table 4.28 and clearly show the greater probability that

Table 4.26 *Regression parameters*

	Estimate	Standard error	Odds ratio
Coefficients			
Funded (T.private)	0.531	0.843	1.701
Funded (T.state)	−2.542	0.952	0.079
Intercepts			
Level 1 | ≥level 2	−2.570	0.835	
≤Level 2 | ≥level 3	−0.964	0.658	
≤Level 3 | level 4	0.530	0.629	

Model: $\text{logit}[\Pr(\text{price} > j)] = \alpha + \beta_{1-2}$ funded
Funded reference category = state-private partnership

Table 4.27 *Confidence intervals*

	2.5%	50%	97.5%
Funded (T.private)			
Log odds	−1.122	0.531	2.184
Odds ratio	0.326	1.701	8.882
Funded (T.state)			
Log odds	−4.408	−2.542	−0.676
Odds ratio	0.012	0.079	0.509

Model: logit[Pr(price > j)] = $\alpha + \beta_{1-2}$ funded
Funded reference category = state-private partnership

state funded companies have of being in a low price category compared to other types of funding. Similarly, privately-funded companies have a greater probability of being in the highest price category compared to the other types of ownership.

Table 4.28 *Predicted probabilities*

How funded	Predicted probability of being in ...			
	Category 1 lowest price	Category 2	Category 3	Category 4 highest price
State	0.493	0.336	0.127	0.044
Private	0.043	0.140	0.317	0.500
State–private Partnership	0.071	0.205	0.353	0.371

Model: logit[Pr(price > j)] = $\alpha + \beta_{1-2}$ funded

It is important to determine the significance of the estimated effects of the grouping variable. The significance of this variable can be determined by comparing the deviance measures (−2LL) for two nested models; one that includes the variable 'funding' and one that does not. The significance of the differences between the individual categories of the variable can be estimated by looking at the t-statistics in the output table provided the software package (the actual statistic used to estimate significance depends on the package used and can be represented using t-, z-, or Wald statistics). It should be noted that −2LL statistics can also be used to assess the significance of individual categories by comparing nested models, but this often requires the variable to be manually dummy-coded; see Hutcheson and Sofroniou, 1999, for a full discussion of this). For simplicity, here we will use −2LL to assess the overall significance of the variable 'ownership' and the t-statistics to assess the significance of individual categories of the variable 'ownership'. The −2LL statistics are shown in Table 4.29 and the t-statistics are shown in Table 4.30.

Analysing Simple Experimental Designs for Ordered Data

Table 4.29 *Assessing significance by comparing model deviances*

Model	Residual deviance	Difference in deviance	df	P-value
Logit[Pr(Y > j)] = α	82.507	13.129	2	1.4e − 03
Logit[Pr(Y > j)] = $\alpha + \beta_{1-2}$ funded	69.378			

Y = price category

Adding the variable 'funded' to the model results in a reduction in deviance of 13.129, which, at 2 degrees of freedom is highly significant (p< 0.005). There would appear to be a significant relationship between the type of funding and the price of whiskey.

Table 4.30 *Estimating the significance of individual parameters using t-values (reference category for variable 'funded' = state–private partnership)*

	Estimate	Standard error	t-value	P-value
Coefficients				
Funded (T.private)	0.531	0.843	0.630	0.534
Funded (T.state)	−2.542	0.952	−2.671	0.013
Intercepts				
Level 1 | ≥level 2	−2.570	0.835		
≤Level 2 | ≥level 3	−0.964	0.658		
≤Level 3 | level 4	0.530	0.629		

Model: logit[Pr(price > j)] = $\alpha + \beta_{1-2}$ funded
Funded reference category = state–private partnership
P-values (2-tailed) are tested at $n - k - 1$ degrees of freedom

We can see from the t-statistics in Table 4.30 that the two categories 'funded (T.private)' and 'funded (T.partnership)' (the identified category compared to the reference category) are not significantly different at the 0.1 level (t = 0.630, df = 27, p = 0.534), whereas 'funded (T.state)' is significantly different from 'funded (T.partnership)' (t = −2.671, df = 27, p = 0.013).[13] It is a simple matter to obtain statistics comparing state-funded and privately-funded companies. This can be achieved by changing the reference category to either state or private. Table 4.31 shows the analysis when the reference category has been defined as private-funded. If you run this analysis, you should note that all model-fit statistics are the same as for the model with a different reference category. All that have changed are the comparisons.

---

[13] df = n − k − 1, where n is the number of cases and k is the number of parameters (excluding the constant). Significance is quoted using a 2-tailed test.

It appears that the parameter 'funded (T.state)' is significantly different from 'funded (T.private)' and this appears to be the most significant difference between all the categories (t = −3.142, df = 28, p = 0.004). Privately-funded would appear to be the most expensive followed by the partnership and then state-funded. The only significant differences are between state-funded and the other categories, with the most significant difference being between state and privately funded. These results are illustrated in the boxplot shown in Figure 4.7.

Table 4.31 *Estimating the significance of individual parameters using t-values (reference category for variable 'funded' = private)*

	Estimate	Standard error	t-value	P-value
Coefficients				
Funded (T.partner)	−0.531	0.843	−0.630	0.534
Funded (T.state)	−3.073	0.978	−3.142	0.004
Intercepts				
Level 1 | ≥level 2	−3.101	0.870		
≤Level 2 | ≥level 3	−1.495	0.685		
≤Level 3 | level 4	−0.001	0.611		

Model: $\text{logit}[\Pr(\text{price} > j)] = \alpha + \beta_{1-2}$ funded
Funded reference category = private
P-values (2-tailed) are tested at $n - k - 1$ degrees of freedom

The results for the proportional odds analysis of the whiskey ownership data are broadly similar to the more traditional non-parametric hypothesis tests that can also be used. For a multiple group analysis such as this, the Kruskal-Wallis rank sum test may be used. Using this technique, the groups are also shown to be significantly different with respect to the price of whiskey (Kruskal-Wallis chi-square = 11.238, df = 2, p-value = 0.004). The proportional odds technique does, in this case, provide a more significant estimate of the difference between the groups.

In conclusion, the proportional odds model suggests that privately-owned companies are associated with more expensive whiskey and this association is highly significant. It would be unwise to interpret this relationship as causal however, as the data are only quasi-experimental and the groups self-selected to some extent.[14] Although the results from the proportional odds model are in broad agreement with those from the non-parametric Kruskal-Wallis test, we would argue that the consistent theoretical underpinnings of the proportional odds model and the additional information available to the analyst (model diagnostics, ability to add additional explanatory variables, etc.) make it a superior technique for analyzing these data.

---

[14]The privately-owned companies might operate more in the well-established and affluent parts of the country. The price of whiskey may be affected by geographical considerations that also affect type of ownership. It would be incorrect in this case to state that type of ownership 'causes' price differentials.

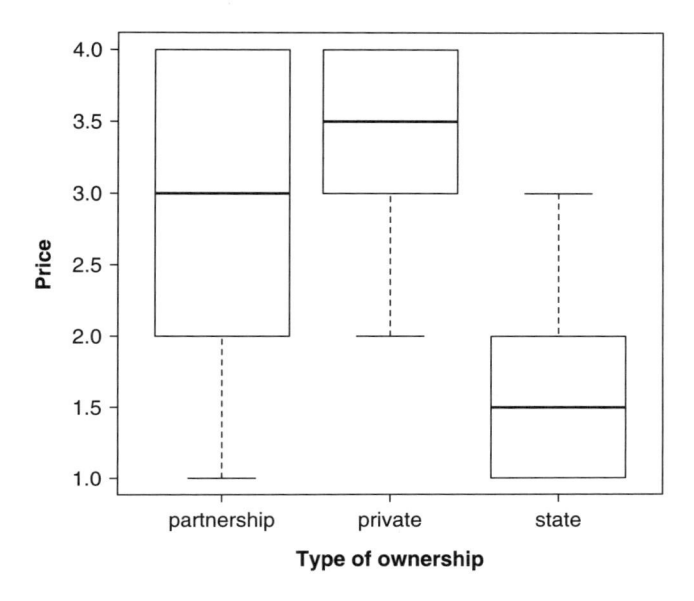

Figure 4.7 *Average ranked price of whiskey for each type of ownership*

4.3.2 Related groups design

It is relatively simple for the proportional odds model to also deal with related groups designs (also knows as dependent groups). In a related groups design, the individual cases in the groups are the same (repeated measures) or they are matched (matched groups). That is, the same case (or matched cases) takes part in each phase of the experiment (e.g. 40 people are exposed to both condition 1 and condition 2). The analysis of these studies is different to the independent groups, as an additional source of variation needs to be accounted for; the variation between cases as well as between groups. This design is illustrated pictorially in Figure 4.8.

This extra source of information (the subject) can be simply added to the model as an unordered categorical variable. For example, if there are two conditions that are applied to individual subjects, we are interested in comparing the results from the two conditions (to see if the two conditions are different), but we also have to take account of the fact that the subject scores may be related. So, the information we have to include in the model (the sources of variation) are condition and subject, which are both unordered categorical variables. If the response variable is ordered, a proportional odds model may be appropriate and this is shown in Equation 4.8). You will note that this is the same equation as for an independent groups analysis (see Equation 4.7), except that subject is now added to the model.

$$\text{logit}[\Pr(\text{outcome} > j)] = \alpha + \beta_1 \text{ condition} + \beta_2 \text{ subject} \quad (4.8)$$

The data we are to use here to demonstrate the analysis are shown in Table 4.32. These data show repeated measurements taken from individual subjects and show the

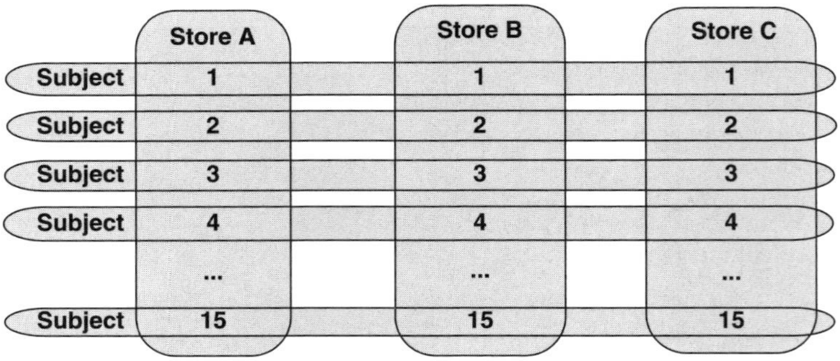

Figure 4.8 *A pictorial representation of a dependent groups design*

perceived quality of 3 stores that they have been asked to rate. The rating of quality is from a 5-point ordered scale indicating low to high quality.

Table 4.32 *Data: ranked quality ratings of stores*

Subject	Store A	Store B	Store C
1	1	5	4
2	3	3	1
3	3	4	2
4	1	5	5
5	1	4	4
6	3	2	1
7	2	3	2
8	2	4	1
9	3	1	3
10	5	2	5
11	4	4	2
12	2	3	3
13	1	4	4
14	2	5	3
15	1	2	3

The three stores are represented by two regression parameters and the 15 subjects are represented by 14 parameters in the model of quality. The proportional odds model for quality is shown below in Equation 4.9.

$$\text{logit}[\Pr(\text{quality} > j)] = \alpha + \beta_{1-2}\,\text{store} + \beta_{3-16}\,\text{subject} \qquad (4.9)$$

Before interpreting any model parameters, it is useful to test the proportional odds assumption to see if it is appropriate to use this model on these data. Table 4.33 shows the test and the non-significant result indicates that the proportional odds

Analysing Simple Experimental Designs for Ordered Data 115

Table 4.33 *Test of the proportional odds assumption*

Model	Residual deviance	Difference in deviance	df	P-value
Multi-nomial logistic model	62.276	62.646	48	0.076
Proportional odds model	124.922			

Model: $\text{logit}[\Pr(\text{quality} > j)] = \alpha + \beta_{1-2} \text{ store} + \beta_{3-16} \text{ subject}$

assumption cannot be rejected. The proportional odds model may therefore be appropriately applied to these data.

Table 4.34 shows the parameter estimates for the model shown in Equation 4.9. There are 4 intercepts shown, which correspond to the 4 comparison logit models computed for the 5 levels of the response variable. The parameters have been averaged across these multiple logit models providing single estimates for each explanatory variable (this is appropriate as the test of the proportional odds assumption was insignificant). From the table we can see that 'store' and 'subject' have been dummy coded using the indicator method to provide treatment contrasts (signified by the 'T.' before the category identifier), which means that each identified category is compared to the reference category (which in this example is 'store A' and 'subject 01'). The log odds of store B being rated in a higher quality category than store A is 1.872, which corresponds to an odds ratio of 6.501. The odds of a subject being 1 category of perceived quality higher for store B are 6.501 times what they are for store A. Store A therefore appears to be associated with lower quality. Similarly, store C would appear to also be associated with higher quality ratings when compared to store A, but with only 2.243 times the odds. The parameters for the subjects are not particularly informative as we are primarily interested in comparing the quality of the stores, rather than comparing subjects. The subjects are included in the model as we need to control for the effect of the repeated observations. These statistics are presented here for completeness, but may often be left out of the output in presentations. In general, the model parameters suggest that store B is associated with the highest quality ratings, followed by store C and with store A being associated with the lowest ratings. This is exactly what we find when we chart the average rated quality of each store; see Figure 4.9 (although this is not taking into account subject, the boxplot is useful in illustrating the difference between the stores).

As with the other models described in this chapter, it is useful to also compute the confidence intervals for the regression coefficients. Table 4.35 shows these intervals for the variables 'store' and 'subject' (as the parameters for the different subjects are not particularly informative, only the log odds for two subjects are shown in the table). These intervals are quite wide and show the imprecision of the estimates. Of particular interest is the fact that the odds ratio for 'store(T.B)' does not include 1.0, which suggests that this parameter is significant (the 95% confidence intervals both predict that store B is higher quality than store A). The odds ratio for store C does contain 1.0, which suggests that a non-significant result. Although store B appears to be

Table 4.34 *Regression parameters*

	Estimate	Standard error	Odds ratio
Coefficients			
Store[T.B]	1.872	0.737	6.501
Store[T.C]	0.808	0.695	2.243
Subject[T.02]	−1.973	1.621	0.139
Subject[T.03]	−0.891	1.524	0.410
Subject[T.04]	1.097	1.839	2.995
Subject[T.05]	−0.866	1.588	0.421
Subject[T.06]	−2.624	1.671	0.073
Subject[T.07]	−1.849	1.505	0.157
Subject[T.08]	−1.814	1.595	0.163
Subject[T.09]	−1.614	1.653	0.199
Subject[T.10]	1.966	1.882	7.142
Subject[T.11]	−0.424	1.577	0.654
Subject[T.12]	−1.420	1.502	0.242
Subject[T.13]	−0.866	1.588	0.421
Subject[T.14]	−0.343	1.552	0.710
Subject[T.15]	−2.595	1.624	0.075
Intercepts			
Level 1 | ≥level 2	−1.993	1.334	
≤Level 2 | ≥level 3	−0.774	1.325	
≤Level 3 | ≥level 4	0.573	1.316	
≤Level 4 | level 5	2.343	1.330	

Model: $\text{logit}[\Pr(\text{quality} > j)] = \alpha + \beta_{1-2} \text{ store} + \beta_{3-16} \text{ subject}$

significantly different from store A, the confidence intervals are very large and range between 1.543 and 27.55 for the odds.

Also of use when interpreting this model are the estimated probabilities of each of the stores falling into any of the categories of the response variable. These statistics are shown in Table 4.36 and clearly show the greater probability that store B has of being in higher levels of the response variable and the higher probability that store A has of being in a lower level of rated quality.

The significance of these variables can be determined by comparing the deviance measures (−2LL) for nested models. The significance of both variables together can be assessed by comparing the deviance of the model that includes both of the variables with a model that includes neither. The significance of the variable 'store' in Equation 4.9 can be assessed by comparing the full model with one that does not includes the variable 'store'. Similarly, the significance of the variable 'subject' can be assessed by comparing the deviance of the full model with one that does not include 'subject'. These statistics are shown below in Tables 4.37 and 4.38.

The significance of the differences between the individual categories of the variables can be estimated by looking at the t-statistics in the output table provided in

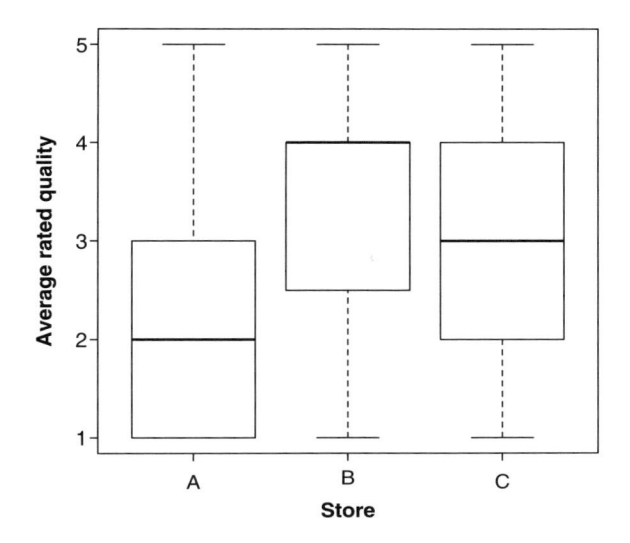

Analysing Simple Experimental Designs for Ordered Data

Figure 4.9 *Average rated quality for each store*

Table 4.35 *Confidence intervals*

	2.5%	50%	97.5%
STORE			
Store(T.storeB)			
Log odds	0.428	1.872	3.316
Odds ratio	1.534	6.501	27.550
Store(T.storeC)			
Log odds	−0.555	0.808	2.171
Odds ratio	0.574	2.243	8.767
SUBJECT			
Subject (T.sub2)			
Log odds	−5.150	−1.973	1.205
↓	↓	↓	↓
Subject (T.sub15)			
Log odds	−5.778	−2.595	0.589

Model: logit[Pr(quality > j)] = $\alpha + \beta_{1-2}$ store + β_{3-16} subject

Table 4.39.[15] In general, this table provides similar information to that provided in the previous tables, but also enables us to investigate the individual categories in more detail. Of particular interest here is the finding that stores B and A are significantly

---

[15]The significance of individual categories can also be assessed by comparing the deviances of nested models. However, the t-values will be used here as they are commonly available in statistical software.

Table 4.36 *Predicted probabilities*

How funded	Predicted average probability of being in ...				
	Category 1 Lowest	Category 2	Category 3	Category 4	Category 5 Highest
Store A	0.316	0.233	0.221	0.160	0.070
Store B	0.081	0.129	0.237	0.309	0.244
Store C	0.188	0.204	0.255	0.227	0.126

The predicted probabilities shown are the average probabilities for all subjects.

Table 4.37 *Assessing significance by comparing model deviances*

	$-2LL$	df	$-2LL_{diff}$	df_{diff}	P-value
Logit[Pr(Y > j)] = α	143.193	41	18.271	16	0.308
Logit[Pr(Y > j)] = $\alpha + \beta_{1-2}$ store + β_{3-16} subject	124.922	25			

Table 4.38 *Analysis of deviance table: significance of variables*

	$-2LL$	df	P-value
Store	6.9589	2	0.031
Subject	12.4076	14	0.574

Model: logit[Pr(consumption > j)] = $\alpha + \beta_1$ price + β_2 income + β_3 temperature + β_{4-5} advertise

different at the 0.05 level ($t_{28} = 2.541$; $p = 0.017$). Stores C and A are, however, not significantly different ($t_{28} = 1.162$; $p = 0.255$). By changing the reference category and re-estimating the model one can show that the difference between stores B and C is also not significant ($t_{28} = 1.556$; $p = 0.129$). The comparisons of subjects are not particularly informative and shows no significant difference between the subjects (when compared to subject 1).

The data above could also have been analyzed using the non-parametric Friedman test[16] that is frequently used on related group designs with ordered data (see Greene and D'Oliveira, 2005, for a discussion of this). The results of the Friedman test show $\chi^2 = 4.588$, df $= 2$, asymptotic significance $= 0.101$, and suggest that the three stores are not significantly different at the 0.05 level after controlling for the effect of subject. This is different from the results obtained using the proportional odds model, which suggests that stores are significantly different at the 5% level after controlling for subject ($\chi^2 = 6.959$, df $= 2$, p $= 0.031$). The proportional odds model has provided, in this case, a more significant result and has also enabled a number of additional conclusions to be drawn about the analysis.

---

[16]This has been computed using SPSS.

Conclusion

Table 4.39 *Estimating the significance of individual parameters using t-values*

	Estimate	Standard error	t-statistic	P-value
Coefficients				
Store(T.B)	1.872	0.737	2.541	0.017
Store(T.C)	0.808	0.695	1.162	0.255
Subject[T.02]	−1.973	1.621	−1.217	
Subject[T.03]	−0.891	1.524	−0.585	
Subject[T.04]	1.097	1.839	0.596	
Subject[T.05]	−0.866	1.588	−0.545	
Subject[T.06]	−2.624	1.671	−1.570	
Subject[T.07]	−1.849	1.505	−1.228	
Subject[T.08]	−1.814	1.595	−1.138	
Subject[T.09]	−1.614	1.653	−0.977	
Subject[T.10]	1.966	1.882	1.045	
Subject[T.11]	−0.424	1.577	−0.269	
Subject[T.12]	−1.420	1.502	−0.946	
Subject[T.13]	−0.866	1.588	−0.545	
Subject[T.14]	−0.343	1.552	−0.221	
Subject[T.15]	−2.595	1.624	−1.597	
Intercepts				
Level 1 | ≥level 2	−1.9928	1.3338	−1.4941	
≤Level 2 | ≥level 3	−0.7736	1.3254	−0.5837	
≤Level 3 | ≥level 4	0.5734	1.3160	0.4357	
≤Level 3 | level 4	2.3433	1.3297	1.7622	

Model: $\text{logit}[\Pr(\text{price} > j)] = \alpha + \beta_{1-2}\,\text{store} + \beta_{3-16}\text{subject}$

In conclusion, the analysis of the related groups data suggests that subjects do rate stores differently in terms of quality. The only difference between this analysis and the previous one conducted on independent groups, was the addition of the variable subject into the model to take account of the experimental design. Although the more traditional non-parametric tests are often used to analyze these data (e.g. the Friedman), we would argue that the proportional odds model is a superior technique as it has a consistent theoretical basis as part of the generalized linear model and allows the analyst to use the full range of techniques available for these class of models (for example, model diagnostics and the addition of additional explanatory variables).

4.4 Conclusion

This chapter looked at the proportional odds technique for modeling ordered categorical data. This model is particularly useful as it allows continuous and categorical explanatory variables to be included in the model which allows the analysis of simple experimental designs as well as correlational studies. The analyses presented concentrated on the interpretation of the regression parameters and on the use of the deviance statistic to determine the significance of the variables in the model. A major goal of this chapter was to illustrate the similarities between this model and the other generalized linear modeling techniques so far covered.

The proportional odds model is a powerful technique for analysing ordered categorical data and also provides an alternative to the older hypothesis tests for ordered data. The proportional odds model greatly simplifies the choice of test as it can be applied to 2 or more groups which are part of an independent or related design. When there are 2 groups being compared, the Wilcoxon test may be used for related designs whilst the Mann-Whitney test may be applied to unrelated designs. However, if there are more than 2 groups, the Friedman test and Page's L-trend test may be used for related designs, whilst the Kruskal-Wallis and Jonckheere trend test may be used for unrelated designs. These are just a few of the tests available, however, if one uses the generalized linear model, the choice of test is simple as they are all proportional odds models. In addition to this simplicity, the proportional odds model offers greater power and flexibility to the analyst than the hypothesis tests.

There are a number of areas that we have not touched upon including the use of diagnostic tests, data transformation, techniques of model selection and the extension of the proportional odds model to hierarchical (multi-level) data. These topics are beyond the scope of the present book, however, information about these topics may be found in Agresti, 1996; Agresti and Finlay, 1997; Clogg and Shihadeh, 1994; Crawley, 2005; Everitt and Hothorn, 2006; Fox, 2002, Franses and Paap, 2001; Hoffmann, 2004; Powers and Xie, 1999; Raudenbusch and Bryk, 2002.

CHAPTER 5
Modeling Unordered Data

This chapter introduces the multi-nomial logistic regression model which can be used to model unordered categorical response variables. The chapter covers the theory behind the technique and the interpretation of the parameters and the model-fit statistics. It also shows how it can be used to analyse data from simple experimental studies when the response variable is unordered categorical.

Before we commence with describing the multi-nomial logistic regression model, it is important to distinguish it from the log-linear model, a technique that can also be used to model unordered categorical data. The basic difference is that multi-nomial logistic regression models a single response variable using information from explanatory variables, whereas a log-linear model essentially treats every variable as explanatory (it models the cell count rather than an actual variable). The 2 techniques are, however, similar as evidenced by the fact that when all explanatory variables are categorical the multi-nomial logistic regression model can be made to correspond to a log-linear model. As we are concerned with predicting single response variables (in order to maintain consistency with the other techniques presented in this book), we will concentrate on the multi-nomial logistic regression technique which has the advantage of being a simple generalization of the logistic regression model. A full description of log-linear models is beyond the scope of this chapter, however, detailed information may be found in Agresti (1990), Anderson (1997), Christensen (1997), Simonoff (2003) and Zelterman (2006).

5.1 The Generalized Linear Model

In previous chapters we have seen how generalized linear models can be used to model continuous data using the technique of OLS regression, binary data using logistic regression and ordered categorical data using the proportional odds model. In this chapter we will demonstrate how the GLM framework (more particularly, the logit model) can be extended to predict unordered categorical data. When we have an unordered categorical response variable, an extension of the binary logit model called a multi-nomial logit model can be used. This model implies that an ordinary logit model holds for each pair of response categories. As a multi-nomial logistic regression is an extension of logistic regression it can be interpreted in much the same way. As it is a generalized linear model, methods of assessing model fit and interpreting parameters are similar to those for OLS, logistic and the proportional odds regression models.

5.2 The Multi-nomial Logistic Regression Model

The multi-nomial logistic regression model can most simply be understood as an extension of logistic regression. This technique allows each category of an unordered response variable to be compared to an arbitrary reference category providing a number of logistic regression models. A binary logistic regression model compares one dichotomy (for example, passed–failed, died–survived, etc.) whereas the multi-nomial logistic regression model compares a number of dichotomies by using a series of binary comparisons. The multinomial logistic regression procedure outputs a number of logistic regression models that make specific comparisons. When there are j categories, the model consists of $j - 1$ logit equations which are fit simultaneously. Multi-nomial logistic regression is basically multiple logistic regressions conducted on a multi-category unordered response variable that has been dummy coded.

Multinomial logistic regression allows each category of an unordered response variable to be compared to a reference category providing a number of logistic regression models. For example, if one were to model which of 3 supermarkets was chosen by a customer, 2 models could be computed; one comparing supermarket A with the reference category (supermarket C) and one comparing supermarket B with the reference category (supermarket C). The choice between 3 supermarkets can therefore be represented using 2 (i.e. $j - 1$) logit models.

$$\log \frac{\Pr(Y = \text{supermarket A})}{\Pr(Y = \text{supermarket C})} = \alpha + \beta_1 X_1 + \beta_2 X_2 + \ldots + \beta_k X_k$$

$$\log \frac{\Pr(Y = \text{supermarket B})}{\Pr(Y = \text{supermarket C})} = \alpha + \beta_1 X_1 + \beta_2 X_2 + \ldots + \beta_k X_k$$

The models above provide 2 estimates for the effect that each explanatory variable has on the response. This is useful information as the effect of the explanatory variables (X_k) can be assessed for each logit model (i.e. the effect of X_1 on the choice between supermarkets A and C) and also for the model as a whole (i.e. the effect of X_1 across all supermarkets). It is also useful to interpret a single parameter for each explanatory variable in order to derive a single parsimonious model of the response variable. The multi-nomial logistic regression model allows the effects of the explanatory variables to be assessed across all the logit models and provides estimates of the overall significance (i.e. for all comparisons rather than each individual comparison). The general multi-nomial logistic regression model is shown in Equation 5.1 below:

$$\log \frac{\Pr(Y = j)}{\Pr(Y = j')} = \alpha + \beta_1 X_1 + \beta_2 X_2 + \ldots + \beta_k X_k \qquad (5.1)$$

where j is the identified supermarket

and j' is the reference supermarket.

As we will see, software provides estimates of model-fit statistics for the individual comparisons as well as estimates for the overall model (in the regression parameter and analysis of deviance tables). To demonstrate this technique we will use an example of supermarket choice behavior (see Moutinho and Hutcheson, 2007, for a more complete description of these data). The data used here are a subset of those used in the original study with variables chosen in order to provide a description of the technique rather than a complete analysis of supermarket choice behavior. The aim of this analysis is to model which supermarket someone is likely to choose given their salary and whether they use a car or not.[1] The data set is taken directly from the original study and includes a number of missing data points which have been coded as NA (unsurprisingly, a number of respondents were unwilling to provide information about their salary, even though the questionnaire used divided salary into just a few categories).

5.2.1 Simple multi-nomial logistic regression

We will begin demonstrating the multi-nomial logistic regression model using the simple example of trying to predict supermarket choice by using average salary as an explanatory variable. This model is shown in Equation 5.2.

$$\log \frac{\Pr(Y = j)}{\Pr(Y = j')} = \alpha + \beta \text{ salary} \tag{5.2}$$

where j is the identified supermarket
and j' is the reference supermarket.

Equation 5.2 simply represents a comparison between one supermarket ($Y = j$) and the reference supermarket ($Y = j'$). In this equation, the log odds of choosing one supermarket compared to the reference category may be predicted, at least to some extent, by salary. It is useful at this point to illustrate the relationship between supermarket choice and salary using a graph such as the box plot shown in Figure 5.1. The graph shows that the average salary appears to be related to the supermarket consumers selected and suggests that Sainsburys and Asda tend to be chosen by consumers with relatively high salaries compared to those consumers who chose Solo and Kwik Save. A multi-nomial logistic regression model should demonstrate this relationship and also provide the significance of the relationship between the variables and the supermarket categories.

Computing and interpreting model parameters: The model parameters for the simple multi-nomial logistic regression model discussed above (see Equation 5.2) were computed using software[2] and are shown in Table 5.2 below. You should note from the table that parameters for 3 comparisons are provided as 3 comparisons are made

---

[1] The original data contains many more variables, these have just been chosen for the purpose of illustration.
[2] The software package used here is R (R Development Core Team, 2007).

Table 5.1 Data: supermarket choice

Supermarket	Salary	Car	Supermarket	Salary	Car	Supermarket	Salary	Car	Supermarket	Salary	Car
Solo	NA	yes	Kwik Save	125	no	Kwik Save	200	yes	Asda	80	yes	Asda	200	yes
Solo	NA	no	Kwik Save	80	no	Kwik Save	80	yes	Asda	125	no	Sainsburys	625	yes
Solo	NA	no	Solo	125	no	Kwik Save	NA	yes	Asda	375	no	Sainsburys	625	yes
Solo	80	no	Solo	80	no	Kwik Save	NA	yes	Sainsburys	750	no	Sainsburys	750	yes
Solo	80	no	Solo	80	no	Sainsburys	375	no	Sainsburys	NA	yes	Asda	NA	yes
Solo	80	no	Kwik Save	200	no	Solo	375	yes	Sainsburys	80	yes	Sainsburys	NA	yes
Solo	125	no	Asda	200	yes	Asda	200	yes	Solo	NA	yes	Sainsburys	375	yes
Solo	60	no	Asda	625	yes	Solo	NA	yes	Solo	375	yes	Sainsburys	375	yes
Solo	200	yes	Sainsburys	375	no	Solo	NA	yes	Sainsburys	375	yes	Sainsburys	375	yes
Solo	200	no	Sainsburys	375	no	Solo	NA	yes	Sainsburys	NA	yes	Kwik Save	80	yes
Kwik Save	NA	yes	Sainsburys	200	yes	Kwik Save	200	yes	Kwik Save	375	yes	Kwik Save	80	yes
Kwik Save	NA	yes	Asda	200	no	Solo	80	yes	Sainsburys	NA	yes	Sainsburys	375	yes
Kwik Save	NA	yes	Asda	200	no	Solo	200	no	Kwik Save	125	yes	Sainsburys	625	yes
Kwik Save	NA	yes	Sainsburys	200	yes	Solo	200	yes	Kwik Save	200	yes	Asda	NA	yes
Kwik Save	NA	yes	Sainsburys	125	yes	Kwik Save	60	no	Kwik Save	125	yes	Asda	200	yes
Kwik Save	NA	yes	Sainsburys	375	yes	Kwik Save	125	yes	Kwik Save	125	yes	Kwik Save	NA	yes
Kwik Save	NA	yes	Kwik Save	375	yes	Kwik Save	125	yes	Kwik Save	200	yes	Sainsburys	375	yes
Kwik Save	80	yes	Solo	125	yes	Solo	125	yes	Kwik Save	NA	yes	Sainsburys	375	yes
Kwik Save	80	no	Kwik Save	80	no	Solo	125	yes	Kwik Save	200	yes	Sainsburys	375	yes
Kwik Save	80	no	Asda	125	yes	Sainsburys	80	no	Kwik Save	375	yes	Asda	375	yes
Kwik Save	80	no	Sainsburys	625	yes	Asda	80	no	Sainsburys	125	yes	Solo	200	yes
Kwik Save	125	yes	Sainsburys	NA	no	Kwik Save	125	no	Solo	125	yes	Solo	125	yes
Kwik Save	125	yes	Sainsburys	200	yes	Sainsburys	60	no	Solo	125	yes	Solo	125	yes
Kwik Save	200	yes	Kwik Save	125	yes	Asda	200	yes	Sainsburys	80	yes	Sainsburys	375	yes
Kwik Save	200	no	Kwik Save	80	yes	Solo	80	no	Asda	80	yes	Asda	375	yes
Kwik Save	125	yes	Solo	375	yes	Solo	80	no	Kwik Save	NA	yes	Asda	375	yes
Kwik Save	200	yes	Asda	200	no	Kwik Save	200	yes	Kwik Save	200	yes	Asda	375	yes
Kwik Save	200	yes	Sainsburys	200	yes	Solo	60	no	Kwik Save	200	yes	Sainsburys	200	yes
Kwik Save	375	yes	Asda	625	yes	Solo	80	no	Sainsburys	60	yes	Sainsburys	375	yes
Kwik Save	NA	yes	Kwik Save	80	yes	Solo	80	no	Kwik Save	60	yes	Sainsburys	375	yes
Sainsburys	NA	yes	Kwik Save	125	yes	Sainsburys	60	yes	Sainsburys	60	yes	Sainsburys	200	yes
Sainsburys	80	yes	Sainsburys	125	no	Kwik Save	125	no	Solo	125	yes	Sainsburys	375	yes
Sainsburys	125	yes	Kwik Save	375	yes	Kwik Save	125	yes	Kwik Save	125	yes	Kwik Save	375	yes
Sainsburys	125	yes	Kwik Save	200	yes	Kwik Save	NA	yes	Sainsburys	200	yes	Sainsburys	375	yes
Sainsburys	NA	yes	Asda	375	no	Solo	200	yes	Solo	375	yes	Kwik Save	125	yes
Sainsburys	200	yes	Sainsburys	375	yes	Solo	200	no	Sainsburys	375	yes	Kwik Save	NA	no
Sainsburys	200	yes	Kwik Save	125	yes	Asda	80	no	Sainsburys	375	no	Asda	375	yes
Sainsburys	200	yes	Sainsburys	NA	yes	Sainsburys	375	yes	Sainsburys	80	no	Kwik Save	125	yes

Source: Moutinho and Hutcheson, 2007.

The Multi-nomial Logistic Regression Model

between the 4 categories of the response variable, one comparing each supermarket with the reference category.

Table 5.2 *Regression parameters*

Supermarket	Parameter	Estimate	Standard error	Odds ratio
Asda	(intercept)	−0.722	0.498	
	salary	0.000	0.001	1.000
Solo	(intercept)	2.034	0.496	
	salary	−0.012	0.003	0.988
Kwik Save	(intercept)	1.987	0.395	
	salary	−0.007	0.001	0.993

Model: $\log \frac{\Pr(Y=j)}{\Pr(Y=j')} = \alpha + \beta \text{ salary}$

j' = reference category = Sainsburys

The parameters for the model shown in Table 5.2 can be interpreted as follows. For a unit increase in salary, the log odds of a consumer selecting Solo as opposed to Sainsburys decreases by 0.012. This equates to an odds ratio of 0.988 ($e^{-0.012}$). For each unit increase in salary, the odds of someone selecting Solo decreases by 0.012. Put simply, consumers with higher salaries tend to select Sainsburys compared to Solo (this is consistent with the information provided in Figure 5.1). Whilst this might appear to be quite a small difference, one needs to recognizse that a unit increase in

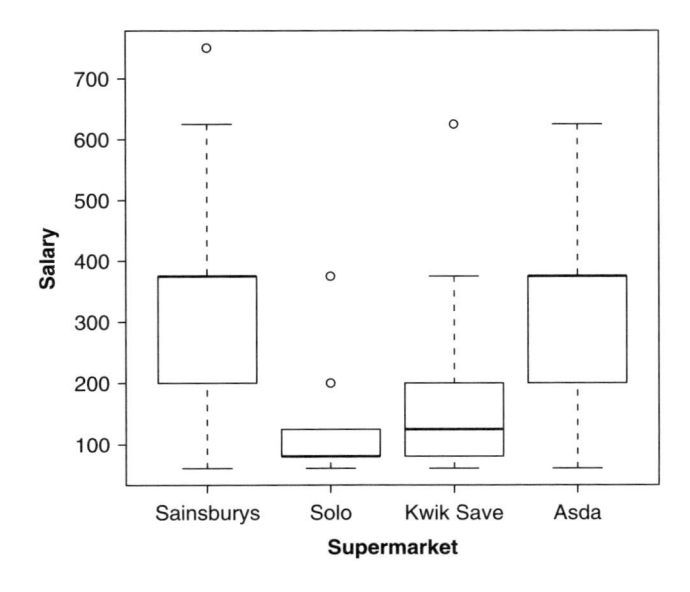

Figure 5.1 *Selected supermarket and average salary*

salary is a small measure and that consumers' salaries can differ by large amounts. For a unit increase in salary, there is no difference to 3 decimal places in the log odds of a consumer selecting Asda as opposed to Sainsburys. Consumers of these two supermarkets therefore appear to be similar, at least with respect to their salaries (this finding is also consistent with the information provided in Figure 5.1).

Using software, it is a simple matter to compute the confidence intervals for the parameter estimates in Table 5.2.[3] The 95% confidence intervals for salary for both the log odds and odds ratios are shown in Table 5.3 below:

Table 5.3 *Confidence intervals*

Supermarket	Parameter	Confidence intervals		
		2.5%	50%	97.5%
Asda	salary (log odds)	−0.002	0.000	0.003
	salary (odds ratio)	0.998	1.000	1.003
Solo	salary (log odds)	−0.018	−0.012	−0.007
	salary (odds ratio)	0.982	0.988	0.993
Kwik Save	salary (log odds)	−0.010	−0.007	−0.004
	salary (odds ratio)	0.990	0.993	0.996

Model: $\log \frac{\Pr(Y=j)}{\Pr(Y=j')} = \alpha + \beta$ salary

j' = reference category = Sainsburys

We can see that for each unit increase in salary, the odds of a consumer selecting Solo as opposed to Sainsburys is expected to be between 0.982 and 0.993; as both of these predict a reduction in the odds that someone will choose Solo, this relationship looks to be significant at the 95% level (this is confirmed in Table 5.7, which shows that consumers selecting Solo and Sainsburys have significantly different salaries). Similarly, for a unit increase in salary, the odds of a consumer selecting Asda as opposed to Sainsburys is expected to be between 0.998 and 1.003. As these limits include 1.0, this relationship looks to be non-significant at the 95% level (this is also confirmed in Table 5.7, which shows that the salaries of consumers selecting Asda and Sainsburys are not significantly different).

Predicted probabilities: Predictions can be made from the multi-nomial logistic regression model in much the same way as they were from the OLS, logistic and proportional odds regression models. For example, for the model

$$\log \frac{\Pr(Y=j)}{\Pr(Y=j')} = \alpha + \beta \text{ salary}$$

---

[3] These are also easy to compute manually, as the 95% confidence intervals for the parameters are simply the estimate ±1.96 times the standard error (see Faraway, 2006).

The Multi-nomial Logistic Regression Model

predictions can be made of the probability of consumers who earn certain salaries selecting particular supermarkets. Table 5.4 shows the predicted probabilities of a consumer selecting each supermarket for a number of different salaries.[4] From the table we can clearly see that consumers with higher salaries are more likely to select Sainsburys and Asda (this is precisely what we would expect given the results shown in Figure 5.1 and Table 5.2).

Table 5.4 *Predicted probabilities*

Salary	Probability of selecting supermarket ...			
	Asda	Kwik Save	Sainsburys	Solo
80	0.058	0.492	0.117	0.333
200	0.128	0.461	0.249	0.161
375	0.248	0.257	0.460	0.034
625	0.344	0.060	0.594	0.002

Model: $\log \frac{\Pr(Y=j)}{\Pr(Y=j')} = \alpha + \beta \text{ salary}$

Goodness-of-fit statistics: In addition to the model parameters, it is useful to have an indication of how well the model fits the data. For this we need to compute some model-fit statistics. There are, however, a number of aspects to assessing the model-fit. These can be utilized to assess the entire model (all the variables considered together), individual variables and individual categories within variables. There are a number of statistics that can be used to estimate significance and those used depend, to a large extent, on the software package being used. This chapter will utilize statistics based on the deviance measure ($-2LL$) to estimate the whole model and individual variables, but will use Wald statistics to estimate the effect of individual categories within explanatory variables (and also provide additional estimates of the significance of individual variables).

For a multi-nomial logistic regression model, model fit can be determined by comparing measures of deviance for nested models. The measure of deviance used is $-2LL$ (see the chapter on logistic regression for a full discussion of this statistic) which is tested for significance using the chi-square distribution with the number of degrees of freedom equal to the difference in the number of terms between 2 nested models. For a simple multi-nomial logistic regression model, the effect of the single explanatory variable can be assessed by comparing the $-2LL$ statistic for the full regression model with that for the null model (see Equation 5.3).

$$-2LL_{\text{diff}} = (-2LL_0) - (-2LL_1) \qquad (5.3)$$

where $-2LL_0$ is the deviance in the null model '$\log \frac{\Pr(Y=j)}{\Pr(Y=j')} = \alpha$'

and $-2LL_1$ is the deviance in the model '$\log \frac{\Pr(Y=j)}{\Pr(Y=j')} = \alpha + \beta$ salary'

---

[4]The package R has been used to generate these statistics. Identical statistics can however be obtained from a number of other packages.

The deviance statistics for the null and regression models and the significance of the change in deviance ($-2LL_{diff}$) are shown in Table 5.5. A model that just includes the response variable (the null model) has a deviance of 482.401. Adding the variable 'salary' to the model results in a model with a deviance equal to 427.644. This indicates that adding the variable 'salary' to the null model has reduced the deviance by 54.757, which is a highly significant change, given that the models only differ by three parameters (hence the 3 df the change in deviance is tested on – it is 3 degrees of freedom as the effect of the explanatory variable is assessed across the three comparisons that have been made between the supermarkets). Adding salary to the model therefore significantly reduces the deviance and indicates that salary is a significant predictor of store choice.

Table 5.5 *Assessing significance by comparing model deviances*

Model	Residual deviance	df	Difference in deviance	df	P-value
$\text{Log} \frac{\Pr(Y=j)}{\Pr(Y=j')} = \alpha$	482.401	549	54.757	3	7.7e−12
$\text{Log} \frac{\Pr(Y=j)}{\Pr(Y=j')} = \alpha + \beta \text{ salary}$	427.644	546			

In many statistical packages, these model-fit statistics are provided in simple analysis of deviance tables as part of the analysis output. Table 5.6, shows this output for the simple multi-nomial logistic regression model of store choice. Although this table is redundant for this model (as the information has already been provided above), it is useful for multiple regression models and for models that include categorical explanatory variables and is included here for completeness.

Table 5.6 *Analysis of deviance table: significance of variables*

	−2LL	df	P-value
Coefficient salary	54.757	3	7.7e-12

Model: $\log \frac{\Pr(Y=j)}{\Pr(Y=j')} = \alpha + \beta \text{ salary}$

It is also useful to look at the model-fit statistics for the explanatory variables comparing individual categories of the response variable. Although it is possible to use statistics based on the deviance measure to do this, this is not particularly easy to achieve in software[5] and is therefore often estimated using Wald statistics (or a comparable statistic). It should be noted, however, that several authors have identified

---

[5] The computation of −2LL statistics for the individual categories of a variable often involves manually

The Multi-nomial Logistic Regression Model

problems with their use. For example, Menard (1995) warns that for large coefficients, standard error is inflated, lowering the Wald statistic value and Agresti (1996) states that the likelihood-ratio test is more reliable for small sample sizes than the Wald test. Even with these reservations, the Wald and z-statistics are discussed here as they are commonly utilized in software. These statistics are shown in Table 5.7.

Table 5.7 *Estimating the significance of individual parameters using Wald and z-statistics (reference supermarket = Sainsburys)*

Supermarket	Parameter	Estimate	Standard error	z	Wald	P-value
Asda	(Intercept)	−0.722	0.498			
	salary	0.000	0.001	0.202	0.041	0.840
Solo	(Intercept)	2.034	0.496			
	salary	−0.012	0.003	−4.550	20.703	5.4e − 06
Kwik Save	(Intercept)	1.987	0.395			
	salary	−0.007	0.001	−4.582	20.995	4.6e − 06

Model: $\log \frac{\Pr(Y=j)}{\Pr(Y=j')} = \alpha + \beta$ salary

j' = reference category = Sainsburys

The significance of salary when comparing consumers who selected Asda compared to Sainsburys can be estimated from the z-statistic, which is simply the estimate divided by the standard error (allowing for rounding error, this equals 0.202). Testing this for significance using a 2-tailed test (i.e. $\Pr(>|z|)$) indicates that this change in deviance is not significant. Salary does not distinguish between consumers who choose Asda and those who choose Sainsburys.

$$z = 0.202, df = 1, p = 0.840$$

The Wald statistic is z^2, and is distributed as a chi-square with one degree of freedom. This statistic provides the same information as the z-statistic and shows exactly the same level of significance (it is used here as it is often included in statistical software output):

$$\chi^2 = 041, df = 1, p = 0.840$$

Looking at these results, it would appear that the biggest differences between the supermarkets with respect to the salaries of consumers is between Sainsburys and Solo and between Sainsburys and Kwik Save, which is what is expected from Figure 5.1. At the moment we do not have comparisons between Asda, Kwik Save and Sainsburys,

---

re-coding the data and then manually comparing nested models (see Hutcheson and Sofroniou, 1999, for a full description of this).

however, it is a relatively simple matter to obtain these comparisons by changing the reference category.[6] For example, in order to compare Solo and Kwik Save, we can change the reference category to Solo and re-run the model. From Figure 5.1 we would expect the difference between these 2 to be small, which is what we find in Table 5.8, which re-run the model using Solo as the reference category supermarket.

Table 5.8 *Estimating the significance of individual parameters using Wald and z-statistics (reference supermarket = Solo)*

Supermarket	Parameter	Estimate	Standard error	z	Wald	P-value
Asda	(Intercept)	−2.756	0.573			
	salary	0.013	0.003	4.471	19.990	7.8e − 06
Kwik Save	(Intercept)	−0.048	0.410			
	salary	0.005	0.003	2.090	4.368	0.037
Sainsburys	(Intercept)	−2.034	0.496			
	salary	0.012	0.003	4.550	20.703	5.4e − 06

Model: $\log \frac{\Pr(Y=j)}{\Pr(Y=j')} = \alpha + \beta$ salary

j' = reference category = Solo

In conclusion, the simple multi-nomial logistic regression model of supermarket choice suggests that salary is significantly related to choice and that the main differences are between two supermarkets that attract relatively high earners (Sainsburys and Asda) and two supermarkets that attract relatively low earners (Kwik Save and Solo). We will now develop this model into a multiple multi-nomial logistic regression by considering the effect of an additional variable on supermarket choice.

5.2.2 Multiple multi-nomial logistic regression including categorical variables

As is the case in OLS, logistic and proportional odds regression models, it is a simple matter to include more than one explanatory variable into a multi-nomial logistic regression model. These explanatory variables may be numeric or categorical and are simply entered into the model as additional terms. For example, the unordered categorical variable 'supermarket' can be modeled using information about salary and car use. If the errors are independently distributed according to the standard logistic distribution, we get the unordered logit model shown in Equation 5.4.

$$\log \frac{\Pr(Y=j)}{\Pr(Y=j')} = \alpha + \beta_1 \text{ salary} + \beta_2 \text{ car} \tag{5.4}$$

---

[6]refer to the software manuals for information about how this can be achieved in specific packages.

The Multi-nomial Logistic Regression Model

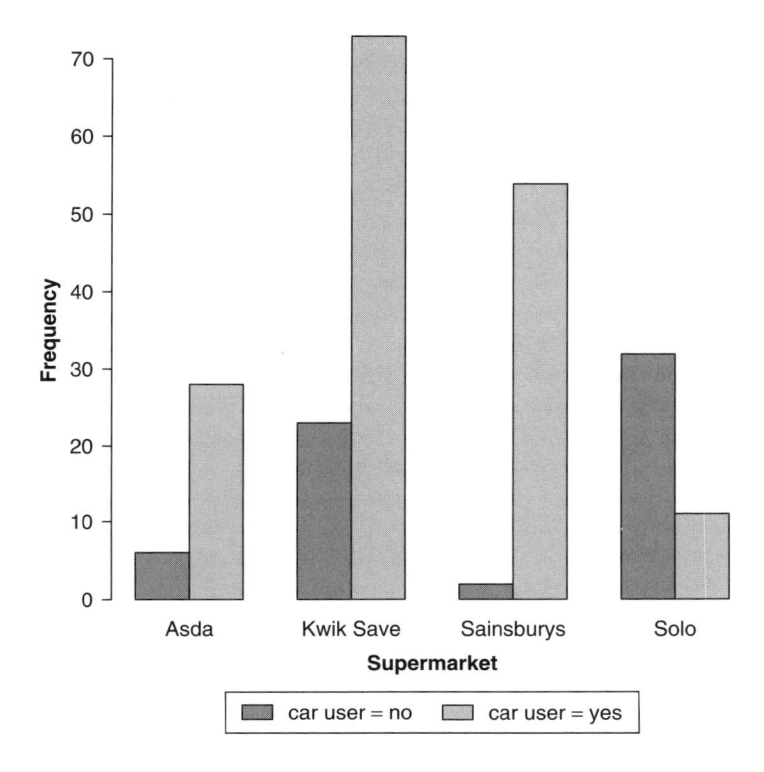

Figure 5.2 *Selected supermarket, average salary and car use*

The additional variable added to the model is 'car', which identifies whether the consumer uses a car. This variable is a simple binary classification of car use. It is useful at this stage to investigate the relationship between this variable and supermarket choice using a graph. Figure 5.2 shows a clustered bar chart that illustrates that consumers who choose different supermarkets are quite different with respect to whether they use a car or not. Whilst consumers who select Sainsburys, Asda and Kwik Save tend to be predominantly car users, those consumers who select Solo tend to not use a car. The biggest difference between the supermarkets in car use also appears to be between Solo and Sainsburys. This finding should be reinforced in the following analysis.

It is also useful to investigate the relationship between the explanatory variables 'salary' and 'car use'. The boxplot in Figure 5.3 shows that these two variables are related with higher salaries associated with car use. This information is important as it is necessary to control for salary when assessing the influence of car use on supermarket selection.

Computing and interpreting model parameters: Table 5.9 shows the parameters for the multiple multi-nomial logistic regression model shown in Equation 5.4. Similar to the simple multi-nomial logistic regression model, there are 3 sets of parameters

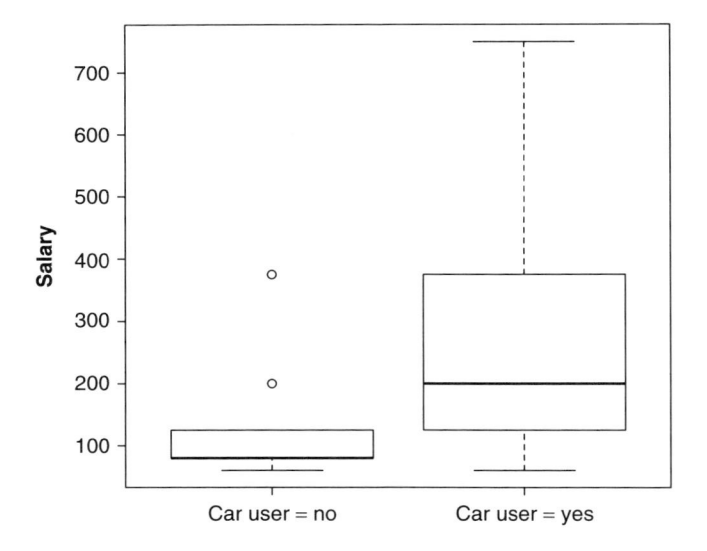

[Figure 5.3 box plot: Salary (y-axis) vs Car user = no / Car user = yes]

Figure 5.3 *Relationship between average salary and car use*

representing the 3 comparisons made between the 4 supermarkets. The following discussion will concentrate on the interpretation of the unordered categorical variable 'car', as this is the variable that has been added to the model.

Table 5.9 *Regression parameters*

Supermarket	Parameter	Estimate	Standard error	Odds ratio
Asda	(Intercept)	0.288	0.941	
	salary	0.001	0.001	1.001
	Car(T.yes)	−1.249	0.981	0.287
Solo	(Intercept)	3.526	0.829	
	salary	−0.007	0.003	0.993
	Car(T.yes)	−3.789	0.867	0.023
Kwik Save	(Intercept)	3.098	0.778	
	salary	−0.006	0.002	0.994
	Car(T.yes)	−1.468	0.793	0.230

Model: $\log \frac{\Pr(Y=j)}{\Pr(Y=j')} = \alpha + \beta_1 \text{ salary} + \beta_2 \text{ car}$

$j' = $ reference category $= $ Sainsburys

The parameters for the model shown in Table 5.9 can be interpreted as follows. For a unit increase in salary whilst controlling for car use, the log odds of a consumer

The Multi-nomial Logistic Regression Model 133

selecting Solo as opposed to Sainsburys decreases by 0.007. This equates to an odds ratio of 0.993 ($e^{-0.007}$). Even after controlling for car use, consumers with higher salaries tend to select Sainsburys.

Car use has been dummy coded using treatment coding method which means that the identified category is compared to the reference. In this case, the identified category is car user (hence the (T.yes) designation in the tables). The log odds of a car user selecting Solo compared to Sainsburys is -3.789, which equates to an odds ratio of 0.023 ($e^{-3.789}$). Car users are therefore much more likely to select Sainsburys than Solo even after controlling for salary (this result confirms the impression of the data provided in Figure 5.2).

Using software, it is a simple matter to compute the confidence intervals for the parameter estimates.[7] Table 5.10 shows the 95% confidence intervals for salary and car use for both the log odds and odds ratios. From this table we can see that for each unit increase in salary, the odds of a consumer selecting Solo as opposed to Sainsburys is expected to be between 0.988 and 0.999; as both of these predict a reduction in the odds that someone will choose Solo, this relationship looks to be just significant at the 95% level. Similarly, we find that Solo's customers are much less likely to use cars than Sainsbury's customers as the 95% confidence intervals both show a reuction in the odds (0.004 to 0.124). When investigating car use for consumers who choose Asda compared to Sainsburys we find that the confidence intervals for the odds ratio predict both an increase and a decrease (the confidence intervals for the odds ratio include 1.0) and indicate that the relationship is not significant to the 0.05 level. The significance values for these relationships are discussed later in this chapter and confirm these findings.

Predicted probabilities: Predictions can be made from a multiple multi-nomial logistic regression model in much the same way as they were for a simple model. Using statistical software, predictions can be made as to the probability of being in any one of the response categories for a given salary and category of car use. Table 5.11 shows the predicted probabilities of being in each response category for a selection of salaries and car use.[8]

The effect of car use is particularly noticeable when comparing Solo and Sainsburys (as was expected from the graph). We can also clearly see the effect of salary. From these predictions we would expect car use to be significant (particularly for the comparison between Solo and Sainsburys) and salary to also be important in distinguishing between stores as it appears clear that even once car use is taken into account, there is still a large effect of salary (for example, those consumers on higher salaries are more likely to choose Asda and Sainsburys, whereas those on lower incomes are more likely to select Kwik Save).

---

[7]These are also easy to compute manually, as the 95% confidence intervals for the parameters are simply the estimate ±1.96 times the standard error.

[8]Note that the high probabilities associated with Kwik Save is affected by the larger number of people that have selected this store.

Table 5.10 *Confidence intervals*

Supermarket	Parameter	2.5%	50%	97.5%
		Confidence intervals		
Asda	Salary (log odds)	−0.002	0.001	0.004
	Salary (odds ratio)	0.998	1.001	1.004
	Car(T.yes) (log odds)	−3.171	−1.249	0.673
	Car(T.yes) (odds ratio)	0.042	0.287	1.960
Solo	Salary (log odds)	−0.012	−0.007	−0.001
	Salary (odds ratio)	0.988	0.890	0.999
	Car(T.yes) (log odds)	−5.488	−3.789	−2.091
	Car(T.yes) (odds ratio)	0.004	0.023	0.124
Kwik Save	Salary (log odds)	−0.009	−0.006	−0.003
	Salary (odds ratio)	0.991	0.994	0.997
	Car(T.yes) (log odds)	−3.021	−1.468	0.086
	Car(T.yes) (odds ratio)	0.049	0.230	1.090

Model: $\log \frac{Pr(Y=j)}{Pr(Y=j')} = \alpha + \beta_1 \text{ salary} + \beta_2 \text{ car}$

j' = reference category = Sainsburys

Table 5.11 *Predicted probabilities*

Salary	Car use	Asda	Kwik Save	Sainsburys	Solo
		Probability of selecting supermarket ...			
80	yes	0.081	0.630	0.200	0.089
80	no	0.040	0.382	0.028	0.550
125	yes	0.101	0.578	0.242	0.079
125	no	0.054	0.381	0.037	0.529
375	yes	0.242	0.252	0.478	0.028
375	no	0.231	0.299	0.131	0.339

Model: $\log \frac{Pr(Y=j)}{Pr(Y=j')} = \alpha + \beta_1 \text{ salary} + \beta_2 \text{ car}$

Goodness-of-fit statistics: In addition to the model parameters and predictions, it is useful to have an indication of how well the model fits the data and how significantly each explanatory variable is related to the response. As with the simple multi-nomial logistic regression model discussed above, significances may be estimated using statistics based on the deviance and on z- and Wald statistics. In this section, the significance of the variables is to be estimated using statistics based on the measure of deviance (−2LL), and the significance of the variables when comparing individual categories of the response variable is to be estimated using z- and Wald statistics.

The Multi-nomial Logistic Regression Model

For a multiple multi-nomial logistic regression model, the effect of individual or groups of explanatory variables can be assessed by comparing the $-2LL$ statistics for two nested models (see Equation 5.5). The resulting statistic is tested for significance using the chi-square distribution with the number of degrees of freedom equal to the difference in the number of terms between the 2 models.

$$-2LL_{\text{diff}} = (-2LL_p) - (-2LL_{p+q}) \tag{5.5}$$

where $-2LL_p$ is the smaller, nested model

and $-2LL_{p+q}$ is the larger model.

Table 5.12 shows the significance of each of the explanatory variables and both explanatory variables together computed using the change in deviance. From the table we can see that both explanatory variables together reduce the deviance in the response variable by 91.123. This is tested at 6 degrees of freedom (the models differ by 2 parameters for each of the 3 supermarket comparisons). This result is highly significant. When car use is removed from the model, the deviance increases by 36.366, which when tested at 3 degrees of freedom (1 parameter difference for each of the 3 supermarket comparisons) also proves to be highly significant.

Table 5.12 *Assessing significance by comparing model deviances*

Model	Deviance	$-2LL_{\text{diff}}$	df	P-value
Determining the effect of all explanatory variables				
$\text{Log } \frac{\Pr(Y=j)}{\Pr(Y=j')} = \alpha$	482.401	91.123	6	1.8e−17
$\text{Log } \frac{\Pr(Y=j)}{\Pr(Y=j')} = \alpha + \beta_1 \text{ salary} + \beta_2 \text{ car}$	391.278			
Determining the effect of salary				
$\text{Log } \frac{\Pr(Y=j)}{\Pr(Y=j')} = \alpha + \beta \text{ car}$	418.156	26.878	3	6.2e−06
$\text{Log } \frac{\Pr(Y=j)}{\Pr(Y=j')} = \alpha + \beta_1 \text{ salary} + \beta_2 \text{ car}$	391.278			
Determining the effect of car use				
$\text{Log } \frac{\Pr(Y=j)}{\Pr(Y=j')} = \alpha + \beta \text{ salary}$	427.644	36.366	3	6.3e−08
$\text{Log } \frac{\Pr(Y=j)}{\Pr(Y=j')} = \alpha + \beta_1 \text{ salary} + \beta_2 \text{ car}$	391.278			

Information about the significance of each individual explanatory variable is also typically displayed in statistical packages in an analysis of deviance table similar to the one shown in Table 5.13.

Table 5.13 *Analysis of deviance table: significance of variables*

	−2LL	df	P-value
Coefficient			
salary	26.878	3	$6.2e-06$
Car use	36.366	3	$6.3e-08$

Model: $\log \frac{Pr(Y=j)}{Pr(Y=j')} = \alpha + \beta_1 \text{ salary} + \beta_2 \text{ car use}$

In addition to those statistics based on −2LL, the significance of the explanatory variables for individual supermarket comparisons can be estimated using z and Wald statistics. The z-statistic is simply the estimate divided by the standard error and tested for significance using a 2-tailed test (i.e. $Pr(>|z|)$). The Wald statistic can also be used to test for significance, which is z^2, and is distributed as a chi-square with one degree of freedom. Table 5.14 shows the z and Wald statistics and the associated level of significance for each parameter in the model for each supermarket comparison.

Table 5.14 *Estimating the significance of individual parameters using Wald and z-statistics*

Market	Parameter	Estimate	Standard error	z	Wald	P-value
Asda	(Intercept)	0.288	0.941			
	salary	0.001	0.001	0.521	0.271	0.603
	Car(T.yes)	−1.249	0.981	−1.274	1.623	0.203
Solo	(Intercept)	3.526	0.829			
	salary	−0.007	0.003	−2.389	5.707	0.017
	Car(T.yes)	−3.789	0.867	−4.373	19.123	$1.2e-05$
Kwik Save	(Intercept)	3.098	0.778			
	salary	−0.006	0.002	−3.923	15.390	$8.7e-05$
	Car(T.yes)	−1.468	0.793	−1.852	3.430	0.064

Model: $\log \frac{Pr(Y=j)}{Pr(Y=j')} = \alpha + \beta_1 \text{ salary} + \beta_2 \text{ car use}$

j' = reference category = Sainsburys

It is interesting to compare the results from Table 5.14 with the results from the simple multi-nomial logistic regression model that did not include the variable 'car use' (see Tables 5.7 and Table 5.8). Although salary and car use are both highly significant the effect of these variables is very different depending on which supermarkets are being compared. Asda and Sainsburys appear to be quite similar as both explanatory variables are insignificant. Sainsburys and Solo are differentiated on the basis of car use, whereas Sainsburys and Kwik Save appear to be differentiated on the basis of salary. It would appear that Kwik Save attracts consumers who have relatively low salaries and Solo attracts consumers who do not use cars.

In conclusion, the multiple multi-nomial logistic regression model has identified that salary and car use are significantly related to supermarket choice. The relationship between these variables and choice behavior is, however, dependent upon which supermarkets are compared. For this analysis, the multi-nomial logistic regression model has allowed the significance of the explanatory variables to be determined for the model as a whole and for each category of the response variable compared with the reference category. These statistics have allowed detailed analysis of an unordered categorical variable.

5.3 Analyzing Simple Experimental Designs for Unordered Data

The analysis of unordered data from simple experimental or quasi-experimental studies has traditionally been conducted through the use of chi-square analysis (see, for example, Anderson, 1997). These grouped data can also be analyzed using regression methods; in particular, the multi-nomial logistic regression model. The analysis of such data can be viewed in a similar way to the modeling techniques already discussed earlier in this chapter. Namely, an outcome variable can be predicted to some extent using information about other variables. In this case an unordered categorical variable (management style, store chosen etc.) can be predicted to some extent using other information (teaching method used, gender, ethnic origin, university attended). The aim is to represent the hypothesis in the form of an equation that can be subjected to a regression modeling technique.

A GLM model has a number of advantages over the more traditional hypothesis tests, not least the ability to include a number of additional variables in the model (those that are not controlled experimentally) and the use of a general technique to replace multiple tests. It is also possible to apply a full range of model selection techniques and model diagnostics, although these are beyond the scope of the present book. The following discussion will describe the analysis of data from simple experimental and quasi-experimental unrelated and related groups designs using multi-nomial logistic regression models.[9]

5.3.1 Unrelated groups design

In an unrelated groups design, the cases in the groups are independent of one another. That is, different cases have been chosen for each group (e.g. a random sample of 40 people are exposed to condition A and a different random sample of 40 people are exposed to condition B). There is no direct relationship between the members of the two groups.

---

[9] As the GLM is a general technique, this section is very similar to the discussions in Chapters 2 and 4 that described the use of OLS regression and the proportional odds model to analyze experimental designs for continuous and ordered data. Readers are advised to familiarize themselves with this material.

We will use hypothetical data here showing an unordered categorical outcome variable (the response variable) which can be one of 3 values; accept, decline or undecided. These data are considered to be unordered as the 3 categories are very different outcomes. There are 3 groups that take part in the study (identified by the grouped explanatory variable), each group having received a different type of training. Each group comprises 15 randomly selected subjects (there are 45 subjects in total). The aim of the study is to see if the type of training (represented by the variable 'group') has an effect on the customer's decision (represented by the variable 'outcome'). The regression model to test this hypothesis is shown in Equation 5.6 with a pictorial representation of the experiment shown in Figure 5.4.

$$\log \frac{\Pr(Y = j)}{\Pr(Y = j')} = \alpha + \beta \text{ group} \tag{5.6}$$

where j is the identified category
and j' is the reference category.

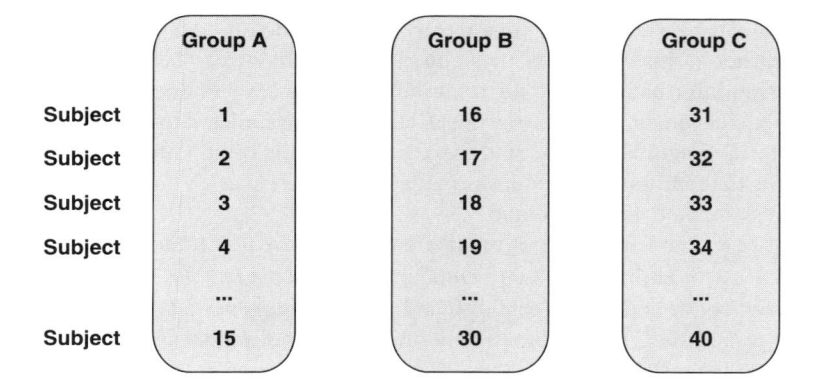

	Group A	Group B	Group C
Subject	1	16	31
Subject	2	17	32
Subject	3	18	33
Subject	4	19	34
	...	...	...
Subject	15	30	40

Figure 5.4 *A pictorial representation of an unrelated groups design*

Table 5.15 shows the data from the experiment shown in tabular form.[10] These types of data are often recorded in a table of cell frequencies as shown in Table 5.16 below.

Before we run the model, it is useful to illustrate the data using an association plot (Cohen, 1980; Friendly, 1992; R Development Core Team, 2007). Figure 5.5 shows a Cohen-Friendly association plot which indicates the deviations from independence

---

[10] As these data are hypothetical it is easy to experiment with them (change values and add and delete cases etc.) to see the effects certain changes can have on the model. Readers who are interested in the application of these methods to real-life data sets are directed to one of the many sources that deal with these models and provide real-world example data sets (see, for example, Agresti, 1996; Anderson, 1997; Everitt and Hothorn, 2006; Hand et al., 1994).

Analyzing Simple Experimental Designs for Unordered Data

Table 5.15 *Data: unordered categorical data from an unrelated groups design*

Group A	Group B	Group C
Accept	Accept	Decline
Undecided	Undecided	Decline
Decline	Decline	Decline
Decline	Undecided	Accept
Accept	Accept	Decline
Undecided	Decline	Undecided
Decline	Undecided	Undecided
Accept	Decline	Decline
Accept	Decline	Undecided
Decline	Undecided	Undecided
Accept	Decline	Decline
Decline	Decline	Undecided
Accept	Accept	Accept
Accept	Decline	Undecided
Decline	Decline	Decline

(see also, extended association plots; Meyer et al., 2003 and 2006). The area of the rectangles is proportional to the difference in observed and expected frequencies (if the variables are independent). For observed frequencies that are below expected, the rectangles are depicted below the baseline, with observed frequencies that are greater than expected being depicted above the baseline. The association plot suggests that Group A is associated with more acceptances and fewer undecided responses than the other groups and Group C is associated with more undecided and fewer acceptances than the other groups. The most noticeable difference appears to be between groups A and C in the response categories accept and undecided. Keeping this information in mind, we now analyze the data using the multi-nomial logistic regression model.

Table 5.16 *Contingency table*

	Group A	Group B	Group C
Accept	7	3	2
Decline	6	8	7
Undecided	2	4	6

Table 5.17 shows the parameter estimates for the model shown in Equation 5.6. You will note that there are 2 sets of parameters, one corresponding to each of the comparisons made between the identified category and the reference category of the response variable. There are, therefore, 2 models in this output, one that compares 'decline' with 'accept' and another that compares 'undecided' with 'accept'. In these

models the variable 'group' have been dummy-coded and are represented as 2 parameters (β_{1-2}).

$$\log \frac{\Pr(Y = \text{decline})}{\Pr(Y = \text{accept})} = \alpha + \beta_{1-2} \text{ group}$$

$$\log \frac{\Pr(Y = \text{undecided})}{\Pr(Y = \text{accept})} = \alpha + \beta_{1-2} \text{ group}$$

Although there is no direct comparison between the categories "decline" and "undecided", it is a simple matter to change the reference category to enable this comparisons to be made (for instruction on how to do this, refer to the manual for the software you are using). From Table 5.17 we can see that the type of training (represented by the

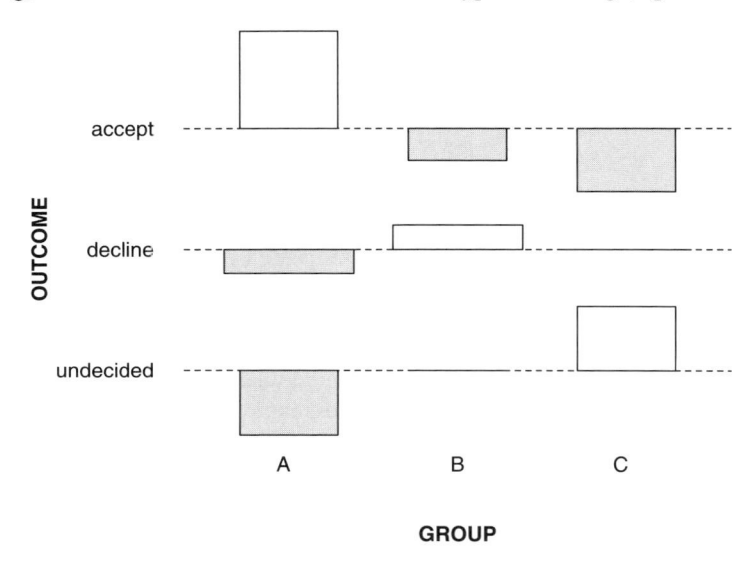

Figure 5.5 *An association plot*

explanatory variable "group") has been dummy coded using the indicator method to provide treatment contrasts (signified by the "T." before the category identifier), which means that each identified category is compared to the reference category (which in this example is group A). Each parameter therefore provides information about the log odds of being in one particular response category compared to the reference outcome category "accept" for each identified training group compared to group A. For example, the parameter estimate of 1.135 for the outcome category "decline" and group(T.B) shows the log odds of someone in group B compared to group A being in the category 'decline' as opposed to "accept". The odds ratio of 3.111 shows that someone in group B has over 3 times the odds of being in the category "decline"

Table 5.17 *Regression parameters*

	Estimate	Standard error	Odds ratio
Coefficients			
Outcome = decline			
Intercept	−0.154	0.556	
Group (T.B)	1.135	0.876	3.111
Group (T.C)	1.407	0.976	4.084
Outcome = undecided			
Intercept	−1.253	0.802	
Group (T.B)	1.540	1.107	4.665
Group (T.C)	2.352	1.144	10.507

Model: $\log \frac{\Pr(Y=j)}{\Pr(Y=j')} = \alpha + \beta_{1-2}$ group

Outcome reference category = accept

as opposed to "accept" than someone in group A. Similarly, the parameter estimate of 2.352 for the outcome category "undecided" and group (T.C) shows the log odds of someone in group C compared to group A being in the category "undecided" as opposed to "accept". The odds ratio of 10.507 shows that someone in group C has over 10 times the odds of being in the category 'undecided' as opposed to "accept" than someone in group A. These results confirm the picture of the data provided in the association plot shown in Figure 5.5. From the association plot and the parameter estimates, the major difference appears to be between groups A and C between the categories "accept" and "undecided".

In addition to the parameter estimates, it is also useful to compute the confidence intervals for the regression coefficients. Table 5.18 shows these intervals for the parameters shown in Table 5.17. These intervals are quite wide and show the imprecision of the estimates. Of particular interest is the observation that only one parameter appears to be significant (i.e. both confidence intervals for the odds ratio predict either an increase or decrease; that is, the confidence intervals for the odds ratio include 1.0). According to the table, group C compared to group A has more undecided responses compared to accept responses (the confidence intervals do not include 1.0 as they predict a value from 1.115 to 98.890). This result is confirmed in the association plot as these are the 4 biggest deviations as shown in the deviation plot (i.e. the accept and undecided responses of group A and group C).

Once we have the model, it is a simple matter to obtain the estimated probabilities of each of our training groups being in any of the categories of the response variable. These statistics are shown in Table 5.19 and clearly show the greater probability that members of group A have of being in the category "accept" and the greater probability that members of group C have of being in the category "undecided".

It is important to determine the significance of the estimated effects of the grouping variable. The significance of this variable can be determined by comparing the deviance measures ($-2LL$) for 2 nested models; one that includes the grouping variable and one

Table 5.18 *Confidence intervals*

	2.5%	50%	97.5%
Outcome = decline			
Group (T.B)			
Log odds	−0.583	1.135	2.852
Odds ratio	0.558	3.111	17.322
Group (T.C)			
Log odds	−0.506	1.407	3.320
Odds ratio	0.603	4.084	27.660
Outcome = undecided			
Group (T.B)			
Log odds	−0.630	1.540	3.711
Odds ratio	0.533	4.665	40.895
Group (T.C)			
Log odds	0.109	2.352	4.594
Odds ratio	1.115	10.507	98.890

Model: $\log \frac{\Pr(Y=j)}{\Pr(Y=j')} = \alpha + \beta_{1-2} \text{ group}$

Table 5.19 *Predicted probabilities*

Outcome	Predicted probability of being in category ...		
	Accept	Decline	Undecided
Group (T.A)	0.467	0.400	0.133
Group (T.B)	0.200	0.533	0.267
Group (T.C)	0.133	0.467	0.400

that does not. The significance of the differences between the individual categories of the variable can be estimated by comparing nested models using the −2LL statistics (see Hutcheson and Sofroniou, 1999, for a full discussion of this), but can also be estimated using the Wald statistics in the output table provided by software (the actual statistic used to estimate significance depends on the package used and can be represented using z- or Wald statistics). For simplicity, here we will use −2LL to assess the overall significance of the variable "group" and the Wald statistic to assess the significance of individual categories of the variable "group".[11] The −2LL statistics for the variable "group" are shown in Table 5.20 and the Wald statistics showing the significance of each category in the variable "group" are shown in Table 5.22.

From Table 5.20, we can see that adding the variable 'group' to the model results in a reduction in deviance of 5.716, which, at 4 degrees of freedom (two parameters for group in the two $(j-1)$ logit models comparing outcomes) is not significant

---

[11] This approach has been used as these are typical statistics provided by software.

Table 5.20 *Assessing significance by comparing model deviances*

Model	Residual deviance	Difference in deviance	df	P-value
$\text{Log}\ \frac{\Pr(Y=j)}{\Pr(Y=j')} = \alpha$	95.454			
		5.716	4	0.221
$\text{Log}\ \frac{\Pr(Y=j)}{\Pr(Y=j')} = \alpha + \beta_{1-2}\ \text{group}$	89.739			

(p = 0.221). There does not appear to be a relationship between the types of training used (the variable 'group') and the outcome. These statistics are commonly provided in an analysis of deviance table such as that shown in Table 5.21 below:

Table 5.21 *Analysis of deviance table: significance of variables*

	−2LL	df	P-value
Coefficient			
Group	5.716	4	0.221

Model: $\log \frac{\Pr(Y=j)}{\Pr(Y=j')} = \alpha + \beta_{1-2}\ \text{group}$

Although one should be careful when interpreting the significance of the differences between individual categories when the overall group is not significant, for demonstration purposes we will show these statistics here. Table 5.22 shows the z- and Wald statistics for the model. The z-statistic is simply the estimate divided by the standard error, whilst the Wald statistic is the square of the estimate divided by the square of the error (see Agresti and Finlay, 1997, for an explanation of this).

The significance of the variable group (T.B) compared to group (T.A) for the category decline compared to accept, can be estimated from the Wald statistic, which is simply $1.135^2/0.876^2 = 1.677$ (allowing for rounding error). The Wald statistic is distributed as a chi-square with one degree of freedom (there is one parameter associated with the statistic). The significance of the statistic can therefore be calculated as:

$$\chi^2 = 1.677, \text{df} = 1, p = 0.195$$

The corresponding z-statistic is 1.295, which provides the same estimate for significance on a 2-tailed test (i.e. $\Pr(>|z|)$):

$$z = 1.295, p = 0.195$$

From this analysis, it appears that groups A and C are significantly different (Wald = 4.223, p = 0.040) when comparing the outcomes 'accept' and 'undecided', although we need to be careful not to attach too much importance to this as the variable 'group' was not significant overall (see Table 5.20). The table does not provide an explicit comparison between the outcome categories of 'decline' and 'undecided'. Table 5.23 shows the results of the model when the category 'undecided' is defined

Table 5.22 *Estimating the significance of individual parameters using Wald and z-statistics (outcome reference category = accept)*

	Estimate	Standard error	z-statistic	Wald statistic	P value
Coefficients					
Outcome = decline					
Intercept	−0.154	0.556	−0.277	0.077	
Group (T.B)	1.135	0.876	1.295	1.677	0.195
Group (T.C)	1.407	0.976	1.442	2.079	0.149
Outcome = undecided					
Intercept	−1.253	0.802	−1.563	2.443	
Group (T.B)	1.540	1.107	1.391	1.935	0.164
Group (T.C)	2.352	1.144	2.055	4.223	0.040

Model: $\log \frac{Pr(Y=j)}{Pr(Y=j')} = \alpha + \beta_{1-2}\, \text{group}$

Outcome reference category (j') = accept

as the reference category for the response variable (Group A is still defined as the reference category for the explanatory variable).

Table 5.23 *Estimating the significance of individual parameters using Wald and z-statistics (outcome reference category = undecided)*

	Estimate	Standard error	z-statistic	Wald statistic	P value
Outcome = decline					
Intercept	1.099	0.816	1.346	1.812	
Group (T.B)	−0.405	1.021	−0.397	0.158	0.691
Group (T.C)	−0.944	0.988	−0.956	0.914	0.339
Outcome = accept					
Intercept	1.253	0.802	1.562	2.440	
Group (T.B)	−1.540	1.107	−1.391	1.935	0.164
Group (T.C)	−2.351	1.144	−2.055	4.223	0.040

Model: $\log \frac{Pr(Y=j)}{Pr(Y=j')} = \alpha + \beta\, \text{group}$

Outcome reference category = undecided

From Table 5.23 we can see that group A does not differ significantly from groups B and C when comparing the outcome categories of 'decline' and 'undecided'. The results for 'accept' compared to 'undecided' are the same as in Table 5.22, as exactly the same comparison is being made.

In conclusion, the multi-nomial logistic regression model suggests that the type of training someone receives does not have a significant effect on the outcome. There is some evidence, however, that groups A and C differ when comparing the outcomes 'accept' and 'undecided', but we would not wish to over-interpret this result as the grouping variable was not significant overall.

5.3.2 Related groups design

It is relatively simple for the multi-nomial logistic regression model to also deal with related groups designs (also known as dependent groups). In a related groups design, the individual cases in the groups are the same (repeated measures) or they are matched (matched groups). That is, the same case (or matched cases) takes part in each phase of the experiment (e.g. the same or matched 40 people are exposed to both condition 1 and condition 2). The analysis of these studies is different from the independent groups' design, as an additional source of variation needs to be accounted for; the variation between cases as well as between groups. This design is illustrated pictorially in Figure 5.6.

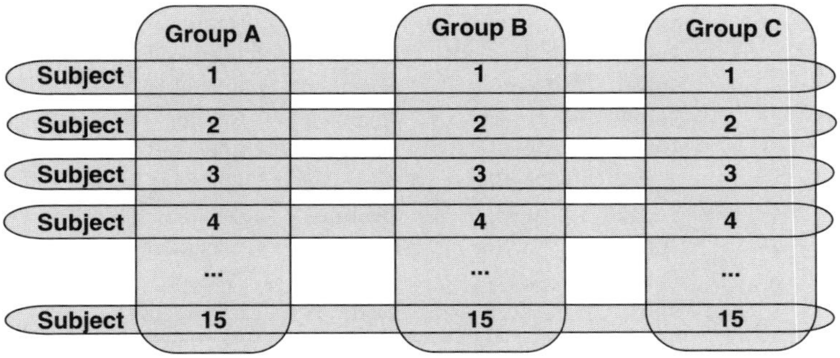

	Group A	Group B	Group C
Subject	1	1	1
Subject	2	2	2
Subject	3	3	3
Subject	4	4	4
	...	...	...
Subject	15	15	15

Figure 5.6 *A pictorial representation of a dependent groups design*

This extra source of information (the subject) can be simply added to the model as an unordered categorical variable. For example, if there are 2 conditions that are applied to individual subjects, we are interested in comparing the results from the 2 conditions (to see if the 2 conditions are different), but we also have to take account of the fact that the subject scores may be related. So, the information we have to include in the model (the sources of variation) are condition and subject, which are both unordered categorical variables. If the response variable is unordered, a multi-nomial logistic regression model may be appropriate and this is shown in Equation 5.7). You will note that this is the same equation as for an independent groups analysis (see Equation 5.6), except that the variable 'subject' is now added to the model.

$$\log \frac{\Pr(Y = j)}{\Pr(Y = j')} = \alpha + \beta \text{ group} + \beta \text{ subject} \quad (5.7)$$

where j is the identified category

and j' is the reference category.

The data we are to use here to demonstrate the analysis is shown in Table 5.24. These hypothetical data show repeated measurements taken from matched subjects who were exposed to one of three conditions (Groups A, B and C) and show an outcome decision (accept, decline, undecided). The data are essentially identical to that used for the unrelated groups' design except that this time the group members have been matched.

Table 5.24 *Data: Unordered categorical data from a related groups design*

Subject	Group A	B	C
Sub01	Accept	Accept	Decline
Sub02	Undecided	Undecided	Decline
Sub03	Decline	Decline	Decline
Sub04	Decline	Undecided	Accept
Sub05	Accept	Accept	Decline
Sub06	Undecided	Decline	Undecided
Sub07	Decline	Undecided	Undecided
Sub08	Accept	Decline	Decline
Sub09	Accept	Decline	Undecided
Sub10	Decline	Undecided	Undecided
Sub11	Accept	Decline	Decline
Sub12	Aecline	Decline	Undecided
Sub13	Accept	Accept	Accept
Sub14	Accept	Decline	Undecided
Sub15	Decline	Decline	Decline

The 3 conditions are represented by two regression parameters and the 15 matched subjects are represented by 14 parameters in the model of decision outcome. The multi-nomial logistic regression model for outcome is shown below in Equation 5.8.

$$\log \frac{\Pr(Y=j)}{\Pr(Y=j')} = \alpha + \beta_{1-2} \text{ group} + \beta_{3-16} \text{ subject} \tag{5.8}$$

Table 5.25 shows the parameter estimates for the model shown in Equation 5.8. From the table we can see that "group" and "subject" have been dummy coded using the indicator method to provide treatment contrasts (signified by the "T." before the category identifier), which means that each identified category is compared to the reference category (which in this example is "group A" and "subject 01").

The log odds of someone in group B being "decline" as opposed to "accept" is 3.060, which corresponds to an odds ratio of 21.328. A subject in Group B has over 21 times the likelihood of declining as opposed to accepting compared to a subject in group A. Group B subjects therefore tend to decline more than accept compared to group A subjects, even after controlling for the repeated observations. This result is

Table 5.25 *Regression parameters*

	Estimate	Standard error	Odds ratio
Outcome = decline			
Intercept	−3.616	2.044	0.027
Group[T.groupB]	3.060	1.569	21.328
Group[T.groupC]	4.060	1.898	57.974
Subject[T.sub02]	22.540	0.856	6.15e+09
Subject[T.sub03]	25.667	0.000	1.40e+11
Subject[T.sub04]	1.866	2.492	6.462
Subject[T.sub05]	0.000	2.010	1
Subject[T.sub06]	22.540	0.856	6.15e+09
Subject[T.sub07]	22.540	0.856	6.15e+09
Subject[T.sub08]	2.293	2.319	9.905
Subject[T.sub09]	1.866	2.492	6.462
Subject[T.sub10]	22.540	0.856	6.15e+09
Subject[T.sub11]	2.293	2.319	9.905
Subject[T.sub12]	21.546	0.860	2.3e+09
Subject[T.sub13]	−41.100	0.000	1
Subject[T.sub14]	1.866	2.492	6.462
Subject[T.sub15]	25.667	0.000	1.40e+11
Outcome = undecided			
Intercept	−20.950	1.411	$8.0e-10$
Group[T.groupB]	4.058	1.920	57.858
Group[T.groupC]	6.232	2.272	5.1e+02
Subject[T.sub02]	39.643	0.856	1.6e+17
Subject[T.sub03]	−8.308	0.000	$2.5e-04$
Subject[T.sub04]	17.710	1.955	4.9e+07
Subject[T.sub05]	−24.850	0.000	$1.6e-11$
Subject[T.sub06]	39.643	0.856	1.6e+17
Subject[T.sub07]	39.643	0.856	1.6e+17
Subject[T.sub08]	−17.821	0.000	$1.8e-08$
Subject[T.sub09]	17.710	1.955	4.9e+07
Subject[T.sub10]	39.643	0.856	1.6e+17
Subject[T.sub11]	−17.821	0.000	$1.8e-08$
Subject[T.sub12]	37.004	0.860	1.2e+16
Subject[T.sub13]	−28.859	0.000	$2.9e-13$
Subject[T.sub14]	17.710	1.955	4.9e+07
Subject[T.sub15]	−8.308	0.000	$2.5e-04$

Model: $\log \frac{\Pr(Y=j)}{\Pr(Y=j')} = \alpha + \beta_{1-2} \text{ group} + \beta_{3-16} \text{ subject}$

Outcome reference category = accept

consistent with the association plot in Figure 5.5 that shows the relationship between the outcome and group membership. Similarly, from the regression coefficients, a person in group C would appear to be more likely to be "undecided" and "decline" compared to someone in group A. The parameters for the subjects are not particularly informative as we are primarily interested in comparing the different groups rather than comparing subjects. The subjects are included in the model as we need to control for the effect of the repeated observations. These statistics are presented here for completeness, but may often be left out of the output in presentations.

As with the other models described in this chapter, it is useful to also compute the confidence intervals for the regression coefficients. Table 5.26 shows these intervals for the variable "group" (as the parameters for the different subjects are not particularly informative, they are not shown in the table). These intervals are quite wide and show the imprecision of the estimates.

Table 5.26 *Confidence intervals*

	2.5%	50%	97.5%
Outcome = decline			
Group (T.B)			
Log odds	−0.015	3.060	6.136
Odds ratio	0.985	21.328	4.6e+02
Group (T.C)			
Log odds	0.340	4.060	7.779
Odds ratio	1.405	57.974	2.4e+03
Outcome = undecided			
Group (T.B)			
Log odds	0.296	4.058	7.821
Odds ratio	1.344	57.858	2.5e+03
Group (T.C)			
Log odds	1.780	6.232	10.684
Odds ratio	5.930	5.1e+02	4.4e+04

Model: $\log \frac{\Pr(Y=j)}{\Pr(Y=j')} = \alpha + \beta_{1-2} \text{ group} + \beta_{3-16} \text{ subject}$

Of particular interest here is that the odds ratios associated with the groups all include 1.0, apart from group B when comparing "decline" with "accept" (although these parameters only just include 1.0 which suggests that the difference is close to significance). We would, therefore, expect these relationships to be significant at the 95% level, apart from when comparing group B with group A for 'decline' as opposed to "accept". This is what we find in the results in Table 5.30.

Once we have the model, it is a simple matter to obtain the estimated probabilities of each of our groups being in any of the categories of the response variable. These statistics are shown in Table 5.27 and clearly show the greater probability that members of group A have of being in the category "accept" and the greater probability that members of group C have of being in the category "undecided". You will note that this table is exactly the same as Table 5.19 as the effect of subject has been averaged across each group. The results are presented here for completeness.

Table 5.27 *Predicted probabilities*

Outcome	Predicted probability of being in category...		
	Accept	Decline	Undecided
Group (T.A)	0.467	0.400	0.133
Group (T.B)	0.200	0.533	0.267
Group (T.C)	0.133	0.467	0.400

It is important to determine the significance of the estimated effects of the grouping variable and subject. The significance of these variables can be determined by comparing the deviance measures ($-2LL$) for nested models. The significance of the differences between the individual categories of the variables can be estimated by comparing nested models using the $-2LL$ statistics (see Hutcheson and Sofroniou, 1999, for a full discussion of this), but can also be estimated using the Wald statistics in the output table provided by software (the actual statistic used to estimate significance depends on the package used and can be represented using z- or Wald statistics). For simplicity, here we will use $-2LL$ to assess the overall significance of the variables "group" and "subject" and the Wald statistic to assess the significance of individual categories of the variables for different comparisons of the response variable categories.[12] The $-2LL$ statistics for the variables "group" and "subject" are shown in Table 5.28 with the associated ANOVA table output shown in Table 5.29 and the Wald statistics showing the significance of each individual category shown in Table 5.30.

From Table 5.28, we can see that adding the variables "group" and "subject" to the model results in a reduction in deviance of 54.407, which, at 32 degrees of freedom

Table 5.28 *Assessing significance by comparing model deviances*

Model	Residual deviance	Difference in deviance	df	P-value
Effect of group and subject				
$\log \frac{Pr(Y=j)}{Pr(Y=j')} = \alpha$	95.454			
		54.407	32	0.008
$\log \frac{Pr(Y=j)}{Pr(Y=j')} = \alpha + \beta_{1-2}$ group $+ \beta_{3-16}$ subject	41.047			

continued on next page ...

---

[12] This approach has been used as these are typical statistics provided by software.

Model	Residual deviance	Difference in deviance	df	P-value
Effect of group				
$\log \frac{\Pr(Y=j)}{\Pr(Y=j')} = \alpha + \beta_{3-16}$ subject	54.147			
		13.100	4	0.011
$\log \frac{\Pr(Y=j)}{\Pr(Y=j')} = \alpha + \beta_{1-2}$ group $+\beta_{3-16}$ subject	41.047			
Effect of subject				
$\log \frac{\Pr(Y=j)}{\Pr(Y=j')} = \alpha + \beta_{1-2}$ group	89.739			
		48.691	28	0.009
$\log \frac{\Pr(Y=j)}{\Pr(Y=j')} = \alpha + \beta_{1-2}$ group $+\beta_{3-16}$ subject	41.047			

...continued from previous page

(2 parameters for group and 14 parameters for subject in the 2 $(j-1)$ logit models comparing outcomes) is significant (p = 0.008). There appears to be a relationship between the types of training used (the variable "group") and the outcome once the repeated measurements are taken account of (the variable "subject"). These statistics are commonly provided in an analysis of deviance table such as that shown in Table 5.29 below:

Table 5.29 *Analysis of deviance table: significance of variables*

	$-2LL$	df	P-value
Coefficient			
Group	13.100	4	0.011
Subject	48.691	28	0.009

Model: $\log \frac{\Pr(Y=j)}{\Pr(Y=j')} = \alpha + \beta_{1-2}$ group $+ \beta_{3-16}$ subject

The significance of each category in the model can be estimated from the Wald statistic, which is simply the squared estimate divided by the squared standard error. The Wald statistic is distributed as a chi-square with one degree of freedom. Table 5.30 shows the Wald (and z-) values for each category. As it is the variable "group" which is of interest here, the Wald and associated significance statistics are only provided for these parameters.

When comparing the response variable categories "decline" and "accept" (the top half of the table), subjects in group C and A are statistically different from the 95% level. As expected from Table 5.26, the difference between groups B and C just fails to reach significance. When comparing the response variable categories "undecided" and "accept" (the bottom half of the table) groups A and B, and groups A and C are significantly different. As suggested in Figure 5.5, it is the difference between groups

Analyzing Simple Experimental Designs for Unordered Data

Table 5.30 *Estimating the significance of individual parameters using Wald and z-statistics*

	Estimate	Standard error	z statistic	Wald statistic	P value
Outcome = decline					
intercept	−3.616	2.044			
group[T.groupB]	3.060	1.569	1.950	3.802	0.051
group[T.groupC]	4.060	1.898	2.139	4.575	0.032
subject[T.sub02]	22.540	0.856	26.335		
subject[T.sub03]	25.667	0.000	1.7e+09		
subject[T.sub04]	1.866	2.492	0.749		
subject[T.sub05]	0.000	2.010	4.7e−05		
subject[T.sub06]	22.540	0.856	26.335		
subject[T.sub07]	22.540	0.856	26.335		
subject[T.sub08]	2.293	2.319	0.989		
subject[T.sub09]	1.866	2.492	0.749		
subject[T.sub10]	22.540	0.856	26.335		
subject[T.sub11]	2.293	2.319	0.989		
subject[T.sub12]	21.546	0.860	25.064		
subject[T.sub13]	−41.100	0.000	−6.6e+16		
subject[T.sub14]	1.866	2.492	0.749		
subject[T.sub15]	25.667	0.000	1.7e+09		
Outcome = undecided					
intercept	−20.950	1.411			
group[T.groupB]	4.058	1.920	2.114	4.469	0.035
group[T.groupC]	6.232	2.272	2.744	7.530	0.006
subject[T.sub02]	39.643	0.856	46.318		
subject[T.sub03]	−8.308	0.000	−4.0e+20		
subject[T.sub04]	17.710	1.955	9.060		
subject[T.sub05]	−24.850	0.000	−8.7e+17		
subject[T.sub06]	39.643	0.856	46.318		
subject[T.sub07]	39.643	0.856	46.318		
subject[T.sub08]	−17.821	0.000	−1.9e+15		
subject[T.sub09]	17.710	1.955	9.060		
subject[T.sub10]	39.643	0.856	46.318		
subject[T.sub11]	−17.821	0.000	−2.4e+15		
subject[T.sub12]	37.004	0.860	43.046		
subject[T.sub13]	−28.859	0.000	−1.8e+19		
subject[T.sub14]	17.710	1.955	9.060		
subject[T.sub15]	−8.308	0.000	−4.0e+20		

Model: $\log \frac{Pr(Y=j)}{Pr(Y=j')} = \alpha + \beta_{1-2}\ \text{group} + \beta_{3-16}\ \text{subject}$

Outcome reference category = accept

A and C between the response variable categories "undecided" and "accept" that is the most significant. The significant results for the related groups design analysis are particularly interesting as the same data gave insignificant results when the variable subject was not controlled for.

5.4 Conclusion

This chapter looked at the multi-nomial logistic regression technique for modeling unordered categorical data. This model is particularly useful as it allows continuous and categorical explanatory variables to be included in the model which allows the analysis of experimental designs as well as correlational studies. The analyses presented concentrated on the interpretation of the regression parameters and on the use of the deviance statistic to determine the significance of the variables in the model. A major goal of this chapter was to illustrate the similarities between this model and the other generalized linear modeling techniques so far covered.

The multi-nomial logistic regression model is a powerful technique for analysing unordered categorical data and also provides an alternative to the older hypothesis tests for unordered data. The multi-nomial logistic regression model greatly simplifies the choice of test as it can be applied to 2 or more groups which are part of an independent or related design.

There are a number of areas that we have not touched upon, including the use of diagnostic tests, data transformation, techniques of model selection and the extension of the model to hierarchical (multi-level) data. These topics are beyond the scope of the present book, but information about these topics may be found in Agresti, 1990, 1996; Agresti and Finlay, 1997; Crawley, 2005; Faraway, 2006; Fox, 2002, Hoffmann, 2004; Raudenbusch and Bryk, 2002.

CHAPTER 6
Neural Networks

Recent business research has identified the potential for the use of neural networks in areas where statistical and structural equation modeling approaches have been traditionally used. Where little is yet known about the research area, a neural network analysis may be more useful in establishing a pattern of relationships. In a situation where there is strong previous research evidence for believing that the latent variables influence both sets of outer variables, structural equation models are likely to be the chosen technique.

The human brain processes information by interconnecting the five senses, sight, touch, smell, hearing and taste. The actual processing of this information occurs via nerves and the 10,000 million neurons which make up the average human brain. Currently, it is probably feasible using current silicon digital technology, notwithstanding cost, to achieve neural-based computers with 1 million processing elements ('neurons') and 100 million interconnects, i.e. with 1/10,000th the latent processing power of the average human brain!

6.1 Cognitive Theory – Nodes and Links – Mental Manipulation of Data

6.1.1 Roots: A parallel Model of the Brain

The starting point of the approach is based on the workings of the brain, which is taken to comprise an interconnected set of 'neurons'. The interconnections are referred to as 'synapses'. The neural networks approach (hereafter designated as NN) is also described as connectionism. NN models attempt to replicate the brain's own problem solving processes, whereby 'input neurons' receive direct stimuli which are then fed into through a pattern matching process to produce a conclusion or response. The signals input into a NN can identify certain patterns. Pattern matching operations translate well into the Marketing Environment, to the extent that we are concerned with perceptions, cognition and stimuli (impact of advertising on consumer motivation, opportunity and ability [MOA]). The simplest form of NN consists only of two sets or 'layers' of neurons – input and output layers. Each input is potentially linked to each output. The input neurons record or are activated by sensors. The output neurons would relate to either specific recognized stimuli or to decisions regarding specific outcomes. This simple model is the 'Perceptron' model.

The original inspiration for the Neural Networks approach came from physiology and psychology. The aim is to work with a direct analogy of the human brain as a set of interconnected processing nodes operating in parallel, copying the lower level computational actions (as opposed to cognitive operations) carried out by the brain. Knowledge is acquired by the NN through a process of learning from examples presented to it, and thus NNs can be viewed not just in terms of the replication of human intelligence but also as a mechanism for machine learning. Neural Networks originated as models of the operation of the brain and its processes. The motivation was to escape from problems of knowledge representation and knowledge acquisition which seriously constrain developers of expert systems. With NNs there is no need for an explicit or 'symbolic' representation of expert knowledge and no requirement for processes of inference.

6.1.2 Neural networks embody a process of learning

NN models originated as models of the operation of the brain. The main aim was to delve into physical details (rather than concentrate on concepts, cognition). The motivation was to escape from problems of knowledge representation and knowledge acquisition which seriously constrain developers of Expert Systems (ES). With NN there is no need for an explicit or 'symbolic' representation of expert knowledge and no regiment for processes of inference. Instead, early NN models date back to 'Perceptron' model (Rosenblatt 1958). Interest in the potential of NN has gone far beyond their potential use as representations of the brain and its processes. The best way to think of this is in terms of NN as alternatives to more traditional statistical procedures (regression and discriminant analysis). This arises because NN embody a process of learning (learning can be looked at from logical angle) and NN belong also to the study of machine learning.

Neural networks learn directly from data using pattern recognition to simulate human learning and make predictions. Neural computing attempts to model directly the biological structure of the human brain and the way it processes information (albeit at a somewhat simple level). NNs incorporate knowledge and memory in terms of the interaction of separate neurons. They amount to a 'sub-symbolic' or direct physical representation, equivalent to working not with a conceptual view of the human (or indeed animal) thought process but with the brain's equivalent of electrical circuitry.

NNs embody intelligence in the interconnections between physical neurons. This 'connectionist' approach is in contrast to the main alternative philosophy of artificial intelligence (AI) which deals with symbolic computation and seeks direct representation of human knowledge rather than embedding knowledge in interactions between neurons. If an expert system is like a trained professional, neural nets are like idiot savants (idiot savants are mentally impaired individuals who exhibit extraordinary genius in particular areas such as music or higher mathematics).

One implication of neural networks to computing technology is that they may offer new approaches to processes that have not been easily susceptible to conventional computing, e.g. those that involve a large element of 'gut feel'. Typically such processes require integration of disparate types of data, including current, past (experience) and future data (expectations) as well as the use of data that is incomplete. Neural computing may therefore provide a useful tool for marketing management seeking to escape from the simple extension of past trends which traditional computing processes imply.

Neural networks are good at inexact problems. The more fuzzy the problem, the more likely a neural net can give a more optimized solution than a conventional approach. If you don't know how to solve a problem, you can throw a neural net at it. It can take as little as an hour to configure a system where a conventional analysis and programming technique could take six months.

In contrast to traditional modeling techniques that start with hypotheses about relevant causes and effects, the user of neural networks can start with a chaotic mass of historic data or mixed forms; some may be certain and quantified, others uncertain and prone to error ('noisy'), some missing and some categorical.

Neural computers are also particularly effective at predicting the behavior of nonlinear or 'chaotic' systems. This is a task that conventional statistical techniques find very difficult to perform. Applying neural network technology to analyze and predict customer purchase patterns has resulted in fairly good predictions of a customer's next product choice.

In the UK, neural computers such as customer predictor and data builder are being used experimentally to derive predictions of customer behavior that can be used for direct marketing and advertising media planning. For database marketers, neural computers offer the benefit that they can easily handle missing and categorical data – a frequent occurrence in marketing databases.

However, one drawback to using neural network technology to make sense of historic data on markets and customers, etc. is that the reasoning that underpins a neural network's predictions can be very difficult to understand and to interpolate into rules.

This means that although you might use a neural network system to provide cost-effective customer purchasing predictions, you will not be able to benefit from investigating, understanding and even developing the system's reasoning. Therefore, alternative systems are being developed which, like neural networks, develop rules from data but also, and unlike neural networks, explain the reasoning process. One such product is data mariner, a system which combines traditional statistical cluster analysis with an inductive machine-learning algorithm.

The internal workings of a neural network behave largely as a 'black box', in that it is not possible to tell how the network achieved its results, only that it does. Unlike knowledge-based systems, which make their reasoning processes fully explicit, and data processing systems, whose behavior can be traced step by step, a neural network cannot explain its reasoning very easily, since its knowledge or 'program' is implicitly encoded as numerical weights distributed across the network.

A neural computer consists of a number of elementary units called neurons. A neuron is a simple mathematical processing unit, which takes one or more inputs and produces an output. Each input into the neuron is called a connection and each connection has an association weight that determines the 'intensity' of an input.

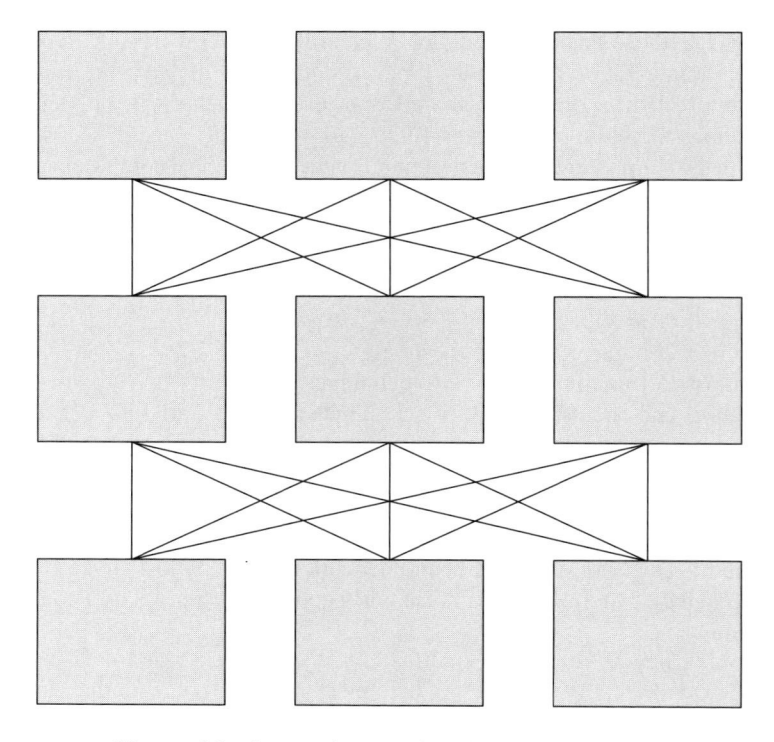

Figure 6.1 *A neural network with one hidden layer*

For many problems one hidden layer is sufficient to give the model much greater representational power. The outputs of the neural network are functions of hidden layer nodes which in turn are functionally dependent on inputs. Hidden layer nodes receive signals which are represented as weighted linear functions of inputs. The NN model amounts to a complex non-linear representation of the output variables in terms of the inputs. The hidden layers in such a model are of interest to the marketer in that the hidden layer nodes can be regarded as latent or unobservable variables, which can be named or described through considering their links with measurable input and output variables. The underlying philosophy is related to that of a structural equation model, or of factor analysis.

These layers are the 'hidden layers' in that they do not contain directly measurable variables. In terms of the brain analogy they can be related to the internal workings of the brain rather than its physical exterior. It provides a richer modeling platform, permitting the inclusion of more real-world structures. Also, the multi-layer model has the advantage that the intermediate layers may frequently be linked to important concepts. This is particularly valuable where these concepts are not susceptible to direct measurement. The hidden layers may add valuable features, e.g. the (Kohonen) self-organizing [network] contains a first layer which is seen to direct stimuli towards those neurons which are particularly able to process certain patterns.

6.1.3 Implementation of NNs

In formal terms, a NN model may be expressed in terms of the interconnections between its neurons. These interconnections can be regarded as weights – a kind of sophisticated regression analysis. The network learns from a set of examples. There are many techniques (called training algorithms) for training a neural network. One of the most powerful training methods is supervised training. For a particular layer above the first input layer we have each neuron that is functionally dependent on neurons in the layer immediately below it. A vital feature of the approach is that the values of the weights are established by 'training', whereby they are induced from example connections. In 'supervised training', the network is fed training pairs or related inputs and outputs.

In 'unsupervised training' it is forced to rely only on input vectors and learns by means of clustering methods. The fact that a network can learn from experience, reduces the need for an extensive process of knowledge acquisition, and so is an advantage over rule-based systems.

Learning depends very heavily on correct selection of training examples. Learning takes place through a statistically based procedure of iteratively adjusting the weights.

For supervised training, this is done in order to arrive at values for the weights which minimize the distances between actual output levels of neurons in the 'training set' and the values of the output neurons predicted from the inputs.

A 'backpropagation' algorithm is used whereby inputed values are calculated for hidden layer neurons. These are calculated by using values of neurons in the previous layer.

Rules may be derived a posteriori by interpretation of layers and their weights.

NN techniques, in that they deal with the inner workings of a process in numeric terms, employ what may be called 'sub-symbolic' computation. The model provides a framework for parameter estimation which permits the inclusion of intermediate layers of essentially non-measurable psychological variables.

There are several possibilities of combining NN with a rule-based formulation. The two could combine alternative sources of knowledge: NN could generate statistically based knowledge from examples.

The network is trained from a set of 'examples'. Where examples consist of both input layer and output layer values learning is said to be 'supervised', a condition equivalent to statistical estimation. 'Unsupervised' learning corresponds to the statistical problem of classification or discrimination.

Examples may consist of both inputs and outputs ('supervised learning', which corresponds to statistical estimation of the outputs), or inputs only ('unsupervised learning', which corresponds to statistical classification or discrimination).

A vital feature of the approach is that the values of the weights are established by 'training', whereby they are induced from example connections.

- Supervised training: the network is fed training pairs of related inputs and outputs.

- Unsupervised training: the network is forced to rely only on input vectors and learns by means of clustering methods.

The key task performed by a neural computer, which lies at the heart of most of the current applications of the technology is pattern recognition, which involved matching an input pattern with a stored bank of known patterns with the aim of finding the closest fit. Pattern recognition is an extremely difficult task for conventional computers to perform since it is very difficult to describe the solution to this task and all the possible input situations which can arise. Neural networks, however, have proved to be very effective at performing this task.

A number of analytical tasks can be identified which use pattern matching in one form or another.

1 Classification

2 Prediction

3 Assessment

4 Diagnosis.

For the 'Perceptron' model the most common scheme for supervised learning is through an iterative procedure known as the 'Delta' rule, whereby the weights for each node are adjusted in proportion to the difference between the given values of the output nodes in the training set and the values generated or predicted by the network.

The most common learning scheme for NN implementations with supervised learning, and the one used in the model discussed in this chapter, is known as the 'backpropagation algorithm'. This is an extension of the 'Delta rule', whereby the weights for each node are adjusted in proportion to the 'errors', which represent the differences between the given values of the output nodes in the training set of examples and the values predicted by the network. It is of course impossible to compute prediction errors for the hidden layer nodes. The algorithm circumvents this problem by calculating inputed values for these errors at each stage, by dividing the output layer error pro rata between the hidden nodes. Backpropagation refers to this process of calculating errors by working backwards from the output nodes.

Although it is technically not possible to calculate the errors for hidden nodes, the algorithm is made feasible by 'propagating' errors backwards from output nodes to hidden nodes. These inputed errors are then used to compute the adjustments to the weights at each stage.

6.1.4 The backpropagation algorithm (BP)

Here the weights (parameter values) are to be adjusted in proportion to the 'errors', which represent the differences between the given values of the nodes in the output layer and the values 'predicted' by the network.

The 'backpropagation algorithm': this is an extension of an iterative procedure known as the 'Delta rule', whereby the weights for each node are adjusted in proportion to the difference between the given values of the output nodes in the training set of examples and the values predicted by the network. For the hidden layer, the algorithm calculates inputed values for these errors at each stage, by dividing the output layer

Cognitive Theory – Nodes and Links – Mental Manipulation of Data

error between the hidden nodes. An element of non-linearity is brought in through the use of threshold levels for each hidden layer node. The threshold effect is modeled by a suitable continuous function, in this case the Sigmoid function which maps values to a range of plus one to minus one. For small input signals the function slopes steeply, but as the signal becomes stronger the differential impact becomes progressively lower.

An overview of the backpropagation training method is as follows:

1 A set of example cases for training the network is assembled. Each case consists of a problem statement (which represents the input into the network) and the corresponding solution (which represents the desired output from the network).

2 Some case data are entered into the network via the input layer.

3 Each neuron in the network processes the input data with the resultant values steadily 'percolating' through the network, layer by layer, until a result is generated by the output layer.

4 The output of the network is compared to what it should have been for that particular input. This results in an error value, representing the discrepancy between given input and expected output. On the basis of this error value all of the connection weights in the network are gradually adjusted, working backwards from the output layer, through the hidden layer, and back to the input layer, until the correct output is produced. Fine tuning the weights in this way has the effect of teaching the network how to produce the correct output for a particular input, i.e. the network learns.

The process that a neuron performs is quite straightforward :

1 Multiply each of the connection values by its respective weight.

2 Add up the resulting numbers for all the connections.

3 Filter this result through a 'squashing' or threshold function such as the Sigmoid equation commonly used in backpropagation.

If the result of the addition and multiplication process carried out by the network is less than the threshold value then no signal in output (or, in some cases, some form of 'negative' or inhibitory signal may be generated).

As the addition of hidden layers in a completely linear model would provide no additional representational power, it is also usual for an element of non-linearity to be brought in through the use of threshold levels for each hidden layer node. Networks are most commonly presumed to be linear in structure. The problem is, however, that adding hidden layers in a completely linear model provides no added representational value. It is usual therefore for an element of non-linearity to be brought in through the use of threshold levels for each hidden layer node. Thresholds could be modeled by a simple step function, whereby a node is activated only if the weighted sum of its inputs exceeds a given level. A more interesting scheme is to model the threshold effect by means of a suitable continuous function. The most interesting scheme is to model the threshold effect by means of a suitable continuous function. The most common scheme uses the Sigmoid function.

$$Y = \phi(x) = \frac{1}{(1+e^{-x})} \tag{6.1}$$

This is shown in the figure below. The threshold effect is modeled by a suitable continuous function, in this case the Sigmoid function which maps values to a range of one to zero. For small input signals the function slopes steeply, but as the signal becomes stronger the differential impact becomes progressively lower.

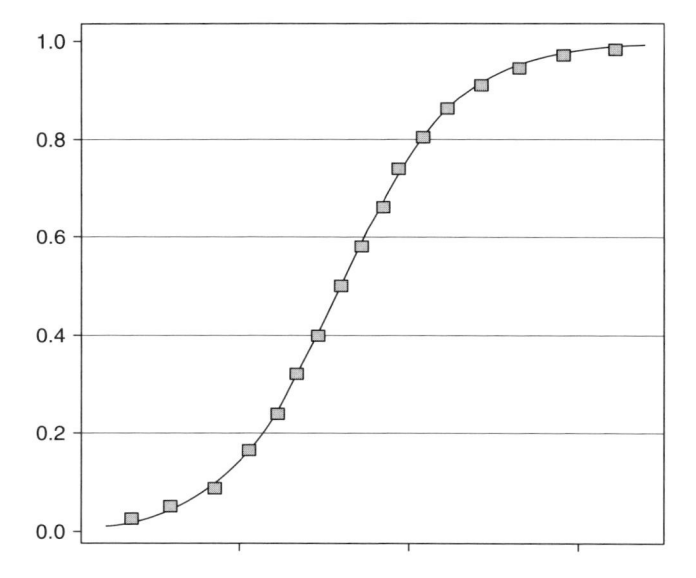

Figure 6.2 *The Sigmoid function*

The Sigmoid function and other trigonometric squashing functions offer almost infinite flexibility, to the extent that it is often stated that NNs are 'universal approximators' capable of fitting themselves to almost any arbitrary functional relationship.

The process by which NN learn (or are trained) is close to the statistician's idea of estimation, especially in the case of complex non-linear models in which it is necessary to estimate using a search procedure.

This can be seen looking more closely at the learning processes embodied in the multi-layer Perceptron (MLP) model, the term commonly used to denote the model of Rumerlhart et al., (1986). In the simplest case of a single layer network, the outputs of the network are functions of hidden layer nodes which in turn are functionally dependent on the inputs. Hidden layer nodes receive signals which are represented as weighted linear functions of inputs. In addition, an 'activation' function is used whereby a hidden node only operates if it receives a suitably strong incoming signal. Simple step functions could be used for this purpose but it is usual to adopt a more fuzzy approach in which the input signal is 'squashed' into a narrow interval such as 0,1. The classical Rumerlhart version of this used the Sigmoid function (see Equation 6.1).

Other similar trigonometric functions may also be adopted. Output nodes receive signals from the hidden nodes which are also represented linearly. It is also possible to transform these signals through a squashing function. The process of learning in such a model amounts to a search for the parameter weights. Conventionally, the weights are chosen to minimize RMS or MSE error. Hence, the process is entirely equivalent to non-linear regression models in which numerical search procedure is employed to carry out the actual least squares estimation. This begs the question of the appropriate error metric to use, which must be dependent on a formal error structure being inserted into the model, for example, one may derive the quadratic or lease squares error metric from a maximum likelihood approach to estimation, but only given a suitable 'well behaved' error term. Aside from considerations of error terms the NN model amounts to a complex non-linear representation of the output variables in terms of the inputs. This complex relationship amounts to sums of Sigmoid expressions. As well as regression, the approach is equivalent to discriminant analysis and other procedures whereby data points are classified by means of a function of a set of independent input variables. Much of the differences are simply a matter of terminology. A formal demonstration of these ideas was developed by White (1989) whose highly generalized and sophisticated methods yield formal proofs that NNs are susceptible to a classical statistical treatment. The particular method used by Rumerlhart et al. is backpropagation which has become by far the most popular approach. Here the weights (i.e parameter values) are progressively adjusted in response to differences between the actual outputs and the values predicted by the network. To counter the fact that errors for hidden nodes are by definition impossible to compute, errors at the output level are propagated backwards through the network: in other words imputed errors are calculated for hidden nodes by pro rata allocation of output errors. This procedure is equivalent to optimizing the error metric (minimizing the root mean square (RMS) error) by gradient descent methods. These methods change parameter weights in accordance with the first derivative of the error function with respect to the parameters. They are however known to generate local optima.

Details of the algorithm: Both the delta rule and the BP algorithm may be viewed as applications of gradient descent methods, whereby the parameter space is searched in such a way as to move always in the direction which gives the largest improvement in the objective functional. Rumerlhart et al. (1986) offer a proof that the method will find an optimum. This proof is worth examining since it shows the importance of the threshold function, particularly useful for this purpose being the properties of the Sigmoid function. It is assumed for the purposes of exposition that network has a single hidden layer. Output, hidden layer and input nodes are denoted by Y, Z and X variables respectively. Weights are expressed as vectors α and β.

The value of each node in the hidden layer depends on the input 'squashed' by the sigmoid function (ϕ).

$$Z_i = \phi(\sum_{j=1}^{n} \beta_j X_j) \qquad (6.2)$$

The output layer in turn receives a linear combination of these activated signals from the hidden layer.

$$Y_k = \sum_{j=1}^{m} \alpha_i Z_i \qquad (6.3)$$

The advantage of the sigmoid model is that it possesses a very convenient first derivative:

$$\frac{dy}{dx} = y(1-y) \qquad (6.4)$$

This expression is both simple and tractable and also has the added advantage of being parameter free. Gradient descent involves adjusting the weights in response to the first derivative of the function to be optimized (the error function).

Thus, despite the enormous popularity of BP methods and variations on the same theme that other numeric routines should be adopted.

Key parameters in the running of neural networks are the following:

Learning rate: the change in weight as a proportion of the prediction error at each iteration.

Learning momentum: is an extra refinement whereby the adjustment to a weight depends not only on the prediction error but also, proportionately, on the adjustment carried out at the previous iteration.

Learning threshold (of convergence): learning stops when the errors for all sample cases fall below this level.

Net weight change: (learning rate) * (error) + (momentum) * (last weight change).

A neural network (NN) can be defined as a collection of interrelated nodes. Definitions of this nature remove the need to rely on analogies of the brain and take us into more general domains, in which the nodes amount to what are known more familiarly as variables. Neural network techniques have become an accepted part of the 'toolkit' available to researchers in numerous fields. There are other less well-known NN techniques which also hold much potential, and perhaps the most notable of these is the Kohonen SOM. Self-organization can be described as the progressive formation within the system of sequential, ordered relationships between the interacting dynamic variables. One might also describe the phenomenon as 'adaptation'. The SOM provides, quite literally, a picture or map of a set of a data, but it does so in an adaptive or 'intelligent' way. On the other hand, NNs in general, including those which apply supervised learning, are also self-organizing in a similar sense: e.g. the hidden nodes in Perceptron models provide approximations to an underlying function and can act to filter the data.

The Kohonen self-organizing map (SOM) belongs to the general discipline of neural networks (NNs). This holds to the extent we may regard a neural net as a set of interrelated processing nodes. The SOM does not, however, form part of what may be termed the NN 'orthodoxy'. It involves unsupervised learning (i.e. without targets or outputs) and is more closely related to statistical clustering techniques than it is to methods such as regression analysis. It offers a rather novel approach to clustering.

NN techniques have become an accepted part of the 'toolkit' available to marketing researchers. There is a tendency, however, as in other disciplines where NNs have been popularized, towards the establishment of an orthodoxy in these matters. The orthodoxy is characterized by use of the multi-layer perceptron (MLP) with Sigmoid activation, which may be labelled more informatively as a 'feedforward logistic network'. The learning algorithm used in the orthodox approach is some variant of backpropagation (although other methods are available which offer potentially superior performance).

It is quite common for authors simply to note the usual distinction between supervised and unsupervised learning and thence to proceed to use the MLP, which effectively means that the network model is being used in a way equivalent to non-linear regression or discriminant analysis. The advantage of NNs in this context is that no prior specification is required for functional forms, relying on the so-called 'universal approximation' property. The capacity of networks to adapt to arbitrary target functions is a crucial part of their attractiveness.

Unsupervised learning implies the absence of what in more conventional terminology means of a dependent variable. It applies separately or independently to a set of network inputs. In statistical terms (let us not forget the NN applications in very many disciplines are statistical in nature), we are dealing with techniques of data transformation or data reduction.

The Kohonen self-organizing map (SOM) may be regarded as a form of clustering analysis, where in contrast to more conventional methods of clustering, the transformation does not involve the same space as the data, but rather a two dimensional grid of nodes. The idea is that a set of input data or input vectors is subject to a topology preserving transformation such that they are effectively described by the 'prototypes' (the SOM equivalent of clusters). Each node in the grid is a prototype in the sense that it possesses a set of weights which are values for the set of inputs. The position of each node in the grid vis-à-vis its neighboring nodes is of major importance, particularly during the training process.

In what follows we examine the details of the SOM approach and examine its potential through the 'market maps' that are obtained. At this point we may also note one important aspect. We referred above to the universal approximation property of feedforward networks, noting that non-linear approximation is perhaps their single most important advantage. SOMs can also be considered in a similar way, although little emphasis has been placed on this aspect in the literature on their applications. More specifically, the SOM has been shown (Mulier and Cherkassy, 1995) as being implied kernel smoothing process. Kernel methods are another interesting statistical technique for non-linear modeling without assumed functional forms, and Mulier and Cherkassy have pointed out that there are important formal similarities between kernel estimates and the implied non-linear transformation carried out in the SOM.

The SOM amounts to a relationship between a set of input nodes and a set of nodes connected to these inputs which perform the operations of transformation and grouping. There is no output node serving the role of predicted or target value and hence in NN terminology we have 'unsupervised learning'. Specifically these 'Kohonen' nodes are arranged in a 2-dimension grid, with each node being connected to each of the inputs.

Interestingly, the actual spacing of the Kohonen nodes has no meaning: what is important is their grouping together. This is because each node is regarded as a 'prototype', a set of cognate values of the attributes of the input data. An equivalent term is 'reference vector'. These values are the weights of the node. As discussed below, each vector of observed values, which may be continuous, discrete or categorical, will be closest in terms of Euclidean distance to one particular prototype node. The latter nodes serve to classify or cluster inputs, but the proximity of each node to its neighbors in the grid is a key element, which distinguishes the SOM from conventional statistical clustering techniques. Whereas Cluster Analysis (CA) operated in the space of actual values, the SOM operates within its own 2-dimensional grid. Standard methods of CA are almost invariably designed to produce non-overlapping clusters (Everitt, 1993), but the prototypes of the SOM are not mutually exclusive. This means that the final feature map, instead of showing several distinct clusters with differing characteristics, shows neighboring nodes which have many similar characteristics but differ perhaps on one or two, or in degree of intensity of characteristics.

In the terminology of the SOM, the grid preserves the 'topological structure' of the data or alternatively may help us uncover such structure. The *Concise Oxford Dictionary* defines topology as 'study of geometrical properties and spatial relations left unchanged by the continuous change of shape or size of figure'. The topological structure emerges as a 'feature map' in which the prototypes are related and subject to potential overlaps. Topology preservation implies that input vectors close together in input space map to close nodes in the grid. Thus, not only are the prototypes intended to reflect 'typical' values of the inputs in their respective neighborhoods, but their grid positions reflect the relative positioning and density of the original data. No such ordering exists for the clusters which merge from CA.

6.1.5 Basic properties of the SOM

The Kohonen network model can be considered has having two main groupings of nodes. In the first place we have input nodes, which are essentially the same as inputs in more standard networks. Each node represents a measurable attribute relating to data points. An input vector is a collection of attribute measures for each data unit, e.g. a firm or consumer.

What gives the SOM its primary distinctive feature is the 2-dimensional grid of Kohonen nodes. The grid serves to relate the nodes together, rather than them being

Cognitive Theory – Nodes and Links – Mental Manipulation of Data

taken as separate clusters. Each node in the grid is a 'prototype' rather than a cluster in the conventional sense. It represents a particular set of attribute values, these being comprised of its weights. For each Kohonen node, therefore, the number of weights is the same as the number of inputs to the network. The structure of the network is illustrated in Figure 6.3 below.

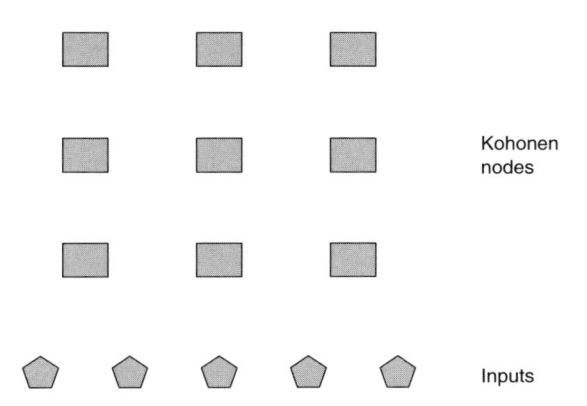

Figure 6.3 *Connections operate between all inputs and all Kohonen nodes*

Once the weights have been established, the network operates simply finding the Kohonen node which is the nearest match to a given input vector, measured in terms of the Euclidean distance between the input vector and the weights of the node. This classifies the input data by linking each data point to a single prototype.

Actually establishing the weights ('training' in NN parlance) involves a similar theme, giving rise to 'competitive' or 'winner takes all' learning. Input vectors are presented repeatedly to the network, as with more conventional models, and at each presentation the 'winning' Kohonen node is identified. This being the prototype for which the weights are the best representation of a particular input vector, the weights are then adjusted to move nearer toward it. The actual adjustment is such that the change in each weight of the prototype is proportional to the Euclidean distance between the current weights and the current input vector. The adjustment proportion, denoted by λ, is referred to as the learning constant.

Where the SOM becomes more interesting, however, is through the fact that it is not only the winning node which is adjusted. Other nodes within a defined 'neighborhood' of the winner are also subject to adjustment, thus exploiting the fact that the nodes are positioned with a grid. These neighboring nodes are themselves subjected to proportionate adjustment, with the proportion in this case being known as the 'interaction term', denoted by ϵ.

We have noted how, once 'trained', the network classifies a data point by identifying the nearest Kohonen node. As regards the training process, a similar principle is adopted. As is common in NN operation, data points are presented randomly to the network, and at each stage the nearest Kohonen node is identified. This is referred to as the 'winning' node and the learning mechanism itself as 'competitive learning' or 'winner takes all learning'. The weights of the winning node are adjusted so as to move towards the current data point, in which case the training process involves allowing the weights of each node to reflect or describe the data. The topological structure of the data is preserved because not only is the winning node updated, but also its neighboring nodes are. The shape of the neighborhood may take various forms, such as square or diamond. It is also possible to model the proximity of nodes by a Gaussian decay function.

More formally, we denote the input data by an $m \times n$ matrix X, each row of which contains a data point comprising observed values of the n inputs. Each node k in the SOM grid is characterized by a $1 \times n$ vector $w^{(k)}$ of weights. The Euclidean distance between the kth node and the jth input vector is then given by

$$D = \sum_i (W_i^{(k)} - X_{ji})^2 \tag{6.5}$$

where the observed values of the attributes of each data vector are indexed by i.

During training, the winning node is that with the smallest distance from the current data vector. The distance is in fact modified to allow for the frequency with which nodes have previously been 'winners', a so-called 'conscience mechanism' through which an additional egality is inserted. The adjusted distance is given by

$$D^* = D - \gamma (NF_k - 1) \tag{6.6}$$

where N is the number of Kohonen nodes, F is the relative frequency with which the kth of these nodes has been the winning node, and is a constant between zero and unity. For nodes whose frequency is the average for all nodes, i.e. $1/N$, the adjustment is zero. Nodes winning with higher or lower frequencies have the distances adjusted downward or upward respectively. The frequency values are estimates adjusted at each iteration.

The weight adjustment process involves finding the node nearest to the data vector in terms of adjusted distance D^*, and this node, p say, has its weights updated. The actual adjustment used is such that the change in each weight of the prototype is proportional to the Euclidean distance between the current weights and the current input vector. The adjustment proportion λ is referred to as the learning constant. Hence we have

$$W_i^{(p)*} = W_i^{(p)} + \lambda (X_{ji} - W_i^{(p)}) \tag{6.7}$$

Where $W_i p^{(p)*}$ and $W_i^{(p)}$ respectively denote new and old weight values. Neighboring weights have the slightly different update expression

$$W_i^{(j)*} = W_i^{(j)} + \lambda (\epsilon_{ji} - W_j^{(j)}) \tag{6.8}$$

where $j \neq p$.

The shape of the neighborhood may for example be characterized by a square or a diamond. A refinement of this basic method involves a 'conscience' mechanism, whereby nodes which have been selected frequently are discouraged. As noted by

Mulier and Cherkassy (1995), the above equations allow us to note that there is an implied iterative non-linear transformation which is being implemented.

An interesting presentation of this learning rule is given by Kohonen (1995) and Ritter et al., (1992), who make an analogy with data compression techniques, in which the primary aim is subsequent reconstruction of the data with minimal error. They show that the SOM has a similar interpretation, whereby the learning procedure amounts to a search for a set of weights to minimize the expected reconstruction error. The learning rule embodies the principle of gradient descent and there is therefore an element of similarity with backpropagation. Also, as well as being an independent statistical procedure in its own right, the SOM may be used as a pre-filter to other forms of NN, for instance to a standard multiplayer Perceptron using backpropagation.

6.1.6 Potential benefits of the approach

The SOM technique can be used as a method of clustering questionnaire responses in order to categorize respondents into segments. It differs from traditional clustering techniques in that it uses a 2-dimensional grid within the dataspace, and therefore the clusters represented by adjacent points on the grid are spatially linked to each other. Traditional clustering methods (see e.g. Everitt, 1993) may involve a variety of algorithms but share the property of building distinct self-contained clusters in the same space as the data. In contrast, an SOM market map shows neighboring segments which have many similar characteristics. This is potentially a fuller representation of a market space – if marketers are trying to segment the market for a particular product using a few characteristics, often only a core of consumer or companies in any one segment will actually have all the characteristics of the segment, while others will be closer to that segment than any other, but may differ on one or more attributes. If these attributes are, for instance, used in developing a promotional message, the message may be irrelevant (or worse) to those on the edge of the segment who differ on those attributes. A market map produced using an SOM will be able to show this 'fuzziness' between segments – for instance, two clusters obtained may be found to be very similar yet differ on one attribute (e.g. some are young singles, others are young couples with children). It is then open to marketers either to treat these two as separate segments, or to treat them as one segment but ensure that the marketing mix is suitable for both, perhaps in this example by ensuring that promotion shows usage of the product in a setting which could be equally relevant to both types of people.

6.1.7 Business applications

SOMs have been shown to be useful in different types of business applications. Mazanec (1995) analyzed positioning issues related to luxury hotels, using SOMs based on the discrete-value neighborhood technique. Using data on perceptions of hotels and customer satisfaction, he showed that the non-parametric nature of this analysis allowed for compression of binary profile data.

Cottrell et al. (1998) applied the SOM in a forecasting context, with the nodes in the Kohonen layer used to store profiles describing the shapes of various trends, as opposed to relying solely on traditional parameters such as mean and standard deviation.

Serrano Cimca (1998) examined strategic groupings among Spanish savings banks, using a combination of SOMs and CA. The idea of the strategic group is often used to explain relationships between firms in the same sector, but here the groups were identified using only data from published financial information, thus giving groups of firms that followed similar financial strategies, with similar levels of profitability, cost structures, etc. The methodology allowed the visualization of similarities between firms in an intuitive manner, and showed up profound regional differences between Spanish savings banks.

The Kohonen SOM is a form of NN, which shares with other networks an origin in models of neural processing. As with other NNs, applications of such methods tend to take us into the realm of statistics, with the SOM operating as a new and interesting variant on CA. The aim is to provide a 'topology preserving' data transformation onto a 2-dimensional grid, in which the location of the nodes vis-à-vis each other is important.

The SOM has some similarities with CA, in the sense that both involve 'unsupervised learning', where there is no dependent variable. Most clustering techniques involve attempts to find non-overlapping groups, so that each data point belongs uniquely. In the SOM, however, each data point is associated with the nearest prototype, but this does not exclude an association with others. Indeed, the fact that Kohonen nodes are spatially related in defined 'neighborhoods' is an important feature of the approach. Clustering and SOMs tend to show us different aspects of the data. Clustering, by its concentration on differences, points out the observations that do not conform, while SOMs concentrate on similarities and gradual changes in the data. The relationships between prototypes are a key part of the model. One may navigate between them, and important attributes of the data set may be found in groups of prototypes.

It is also possible to employ the SOM in a predictive format, involving supervised learning. It can be used in this way as a pre-filter to a predictive NN, using methods such as backpropagation. The model first of all derives a Kohonen map, and then applies supervised learning as a second step.

6.2 Example-Applications

6.2.1 The research model

For this study, data were collected from 445 consumers, 220 male and 225 female, and analysed using the neural network software NEUROSHELL from Ward Systems, Inc. This is a backpropagation neural network with one hidden layer. The network had 6 input nodes, corresponding to the 6 explanatory variables (expectation of car, functional ability of car, respondent's own self-image, desire to impress others, price of car, and age of respondent). A hidden layer of 4 hidden nodes was used; this was thought to be a reasonable number of intermediate variables that could be identified and labeled, and the network did not give significantly better results by increasing the number. The 2 output nodes corresponded to satisfaction with car purchased, and

Example-Applications 169

loyalty (likelihood of repurchase). It was believed that responses were likely to vary with gender, and thus the male and female subsamples were analyzed separately. Figure 6.4 shows the network.

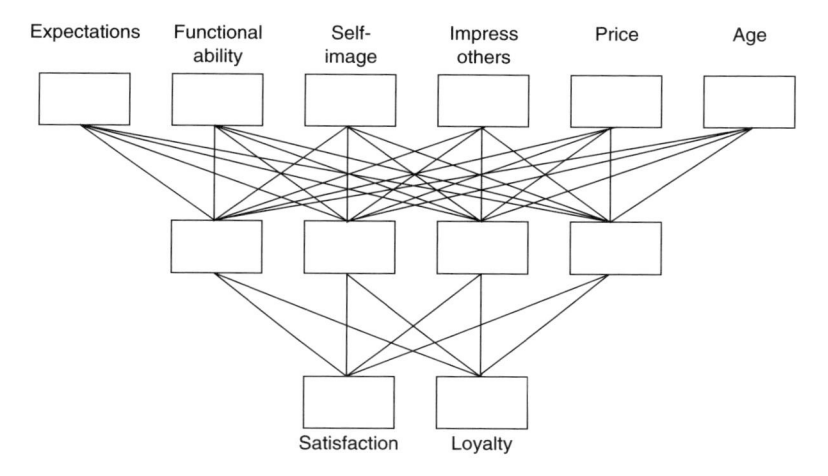

Figure 6.4 *Neural network used in car buyer analysis*

- Measurement of variables. All variables were measured on a 5-point scale.

- Expectations was operationalized as a belief above the future (at the time of purchase), and evaluation of that belief (as Oliver, 1980). Respondents were asked to consider comfort, safety, fuel economy, transportation and performance.

- Functional ability was a measure of the respondents' certainty that their car would function as it should, considering specifically brakes, engine, safety and reliability.

- Self-image was a measure of how well respondents felt their car fitted their own image.

- Impress others: this question asked how much the respondent would like the car to impress family, friends and colleagues.

- Price measured the importance of price to the far purchase decision. A high importance placed on price would generally indicate that the respondent had a limited budget and did not wish to pay a high price for a car, but might in some cases indicate a reluctance to consider cars priced too low, owing to a belief that this indicates poor quality or high risk (e.g. a stolen or rebuilt car).

- Age was measured using the following 5 categories: under 18 (20% of sample); 19–24 (29% of sample); 25–34 (33% of sample); 35–44 (8% of sample); and over 45 (9% of sample). For the male subsample the proportions in each age group were 19%, 27%, 35%, 11% and 7%, while for the female subsample they were 22%, 31%, 32%, 4% and 12%.

- Satisfaction: respondents were asked to rate their overall satisfaction with the ownership of their car.
- Loyalty: respondents were asked how likely they would be to purchase the same make of car again.

6.2.2 Analysis of the data

For each subsample, the neural network was run several times, varying parameters such as learning rate and momentum slightly each time. In no case could the network be made to converge at any error level less than 0.15, and so it was allowed to run (attempting convergence of 0.0001) until it appeared that no further improvement could be made to the quality of its predictions. At this stage, for the optimum configuration for each subsample, R^2 values for the make subsample and 0.43 and 0.35 for the female subsample.

Tables 6.1 and 6.2 show, for male and female data respectively, the weights of the network connections between the nodes and the contributions made by the different variables. It can be seen that these differ considerably between male and female results.

Table 6.1 *Network weights for male buyers*

a) From input node

To hidden node	Expectation	Functional ability	Self-image	Impress others	Price	Age
1	−9.36	2.02	−2.60	−9.22	23.00	−12.7
2	−3.03	−1.92	4.60	−2.96	−7.69	−2.25
3	−3.16	−14.00	1.01	−4.55	2.24	−2.51
4	0.50	−2.33	−2.58	0.62	0.43	−0.11
Total contribution of input mode	16.00	20.30	10.80	17.30	33.30	17.60

a) From input node

To output node	1	2	3	4	Bias of output node
Satisfaction	−7.42	−3.38	4.00	−2.36	2.15
Loyalty	−10.20	−2.32	4.46	−2.22	1.64
Bias of hidden mode	−17.80	1.88	3.03	2.66	

The values and signs (+ or −) of the network connection weights between the input nodes and the 4 hidden nodes were used to deduce suitable intermediate attributes with which to label the hidden nodes. It is appreciated that this labeling must have some

Example-Applications

Table 6.2 *Network weights for female buyers*

a) From input node

To hidden node	Expectation	Functional ability	Self-image	Impress others	Price	Age
1	−0.86	−2.75	−10.40	3.96	0.49	0.03
2	−0.56	1.61	2.78	3.06	−1.26	2.01
3	0.80	0.85	2.68	−4.40	−0.80	−3.60
4	−1.05	−4.90	−3.27	−1.68	3.54	−1.69
Total contribution of input mode	3.30	10.10	19.20	12.80	6.10	7.30

a) From input node

To output node	1	2	3	4	Bias of output node
Satisfaction	−0.97	−0.03	0.39	−1.97	1.30
Loyalty	−2.36	−2.07	−1.84	−2.24	3.78
Bias of hidden mode	−7.44	−3.21	0.85	0.98	

element of subjectivity, but this is true of many causation models that attempt to explain attitudes or behavior in terms of latent variables: for instance, LISREL (Long, 1983a, 1983b). Similarly, in factor analysis, the interpretation and labeling of factors is subjective. After labeling, both networks were analyzed in terms of the relationships between the variables on each layer.

6.2.3 Labeling of hidden nodes: male buyers

Hidden node 1 had a very high positive value was 'functional ability'. This was thought to show an attitude of high cost-consciousness, with some concern for functional ability – getting the best possible for the money paid. Financial constraints necessitated lower expectations, and lack of concern for the car fitting the buyer's own image or impressing others, while the fairly high negative connection with age showed buyers to be relatively young and thus likely to be less affluent. The node was thus labeled 'Price consciousness'.

For hidden node 2, the only positive input was from 'self-image'. There was a fairly high negative connection from 'price', indicating a lack of importance, and the other connections were, although negative, all small in value. Thus the overriding attitude here was a desire to have a car that reflected the buyer's self-image, and thus the node was labeled 'Individuality'.

By far the highest value connection to hidden node 3 was the negative connection from functional ability, showing a high level of uncertainty that the car would function correctly. Other connections being much smaller in value, this node was labeled 'Low confidence'.

Finally, for hidden node 4, all connections, whether positive or negative, were small in value. There appeared to be no overriding influencing factor on this node, which was therefore labelled 'Equity/balance/desires congruence'.

6.2.4 Labeling of hidden nodes: female buyers

Hidden node 1 showed a high negative connection from 'self-image'. The highest positive connection was from 'impress others'. The connection from 'functional ability' was also negative, and the other connections very small in value. This was interpreted as an attitude of concern with impressing others at the expense both of the buyer's own self-image and being sure of correct functioning, and the hidden node was thus labeled 'Status-seeking'.

Hidden node 2 also showed concern with impressing others, but this time the connection from 'self-image' was also positive. This node also showed a positive link with age and functional ability. It was thought, although still showing concern with status, to indicate a more mature and confident attitude than hidden node 1, and was thus labeled 'Social confidence'.

Hidden node 3 had a negative connection from 'impress others', a positive connection from 'self-image', and very small connections from 'expectations' and 'functional ability' (positive) and 'price' (negative). This seemed to indicate a balanced and 'down to earth' attitude, with little concern for others' opinions, and so was labeled 'Rationality'.

The only positive connection to hidden node 4 was from 'price', indicating a concern for price above all else, so the node was labeled 'Price consciousness'.

Table 6.3 summarizes the labels given to the hidden nodes.

Table 6.3 *Labels given to the hidden nodes*

Hidden node	Male	Female
1	Price consciousness	Status seeking
2	Individuality	Social confidence
3	Low confidence	Rationality
4	Equity/balance/desires congruence	Price consciousness

6.2.5 Findings: male car buyers

Links between input and hidden nodes show that:

- Price consciousness is negatively linked with both expectations and a desire to impress others. Buyers who are heavily constrained by price in their choice of car have lower expectations, and believe that a cheaper car is unlikely to impress others. Conversely, buyers with high expectations and/or a high desire to impress others have a low degree of price consciousness.

Example-Applications 173

- Younger buyers are the most price conscious.

- Individuality is negatively linked with price importance. Buyers for whom it is important to find a car that fits their own self-image believe that they will need to pay more for this. This may be because they want a model, such as a sports car or off-road vehicle, that immediately gives off a particular image, or they want a more basic model customized to their taste.

- A high level of distrust in the car's functional ability is correlated with low expectations, low desire to impress others, and a small degree of price importance (links to hidden node 3). However, looking back at hidden node 1, a high degree of price importance is linked with some degree of confidence in functional ability. This suggests that a low level of confidence in a car is not the result of having to buy a cheap car, but is a more fundamental buyer attitude of lack of confidence, either in his own decision-making or in cars in general. This may of course be rooted in past experience of his current car or a previous one.

- A sense of equity, balance and desires congruency on the part of the male buyer is most affected by uncertainty regarding the functioning of the car, and lack of fit between his own self-image and the car.

Links between hidden and output nodes show that:

- The expected link between satisfaction and loyalty is in evidence: connections from each of the 4 hidden nodes are either both positive or both negative.

- The most price-conscious buyers are the least likely to be satisfied, and the least likely to be loyal. This seems intuitively correct, as price-conscious buyers could be tempted to try a different make owing to availability of a cheaper model, dealer discounts or special finance deals. The converse of this finding is that the least price-conscious buyers are more likely to be loyal to a particular make, which confirms previous findings (Diem, 1994) of a high degree of loyalty among owners of upmarket models such as Lincoln and Cadillac.

- Rather surprisingly, low confidence was a predictor of satisfaction and loyalty. This may indicate that the doubts of such buyers about the functioning of their cars are as yet unconfirmed, or that their lack of confidence extends to all cars, and therefore they prefer to stay with a model they know. This finding, however, could be seen to agree with that of Srinivasan and Ratchford (1991), that subjective knowledge leads to less perceived risk but increases search. If the lack of confidence, i.e. greater perceived risk, is caused by a lack of subjective knowledge, then the search is decreased, and therefore the probability of buying the same model again is higher.

- Overall satisfaction and loyalty are not greatly affected either by degree of individuality or by need for equity, balance and desires congruency.

6.2.6 Findings: female car buyers

Owing to the resulting interconnections of contribution weights from input factors to hidden nodes in the neural network pertaining to female buyers, 3 of the 4 hidden nodes were labeled differently from their male counterparts. The only hidden node that applied to both male and female car owners was the degree of price consciousness.

Links between input and hidden nodes show that:

- Female consumers' perceived status as delivered by the ownership of a particular type of car does not seem to be influenced by product expectations, perceived performance or even by their perceived self-image. The price of the car has a slight influence on perceived status.

- Perceived product performance, the consumer's self-image and her desire to impress others are all factors that have an effect on the degree of social confidence felt by female car owners. Older female buyers are more likely to feel socially confident.

- As would be expected, the degree of rationality felt by female car owners is positively related to product expectations and perceived performance. It is interesting that this hidden node also shows a positive connection from self-image, and the highest negative correlation with age of the 4 hidden nodes. This could indicate the existence of a segment of young female buyers who make their car purchase decisions independently, and feel they have the ability to make a rational and sensible choice of a car that will function correctly and also fit their own image. These buyers do not find it necessary to impress others with their choice. This finding ties in with the increasing proportion of women among buyers under 25 (Candler, 1991).

- As with the male buyers, a high degree of price consciousness is associated with low expectations, and lack of concern for the car to fit the buyer's self-image or to impress others. Unlike the male buyers, however, highly price-conscious female buyers have low confidence that their car will function correctly. Conversely, for female buyers, perceived performance, and to a lesser extent the desire to have a car fitting their own self-image, were the main factors tending to lower price consciousness, while for male buyers the main factors doing so were high expectations and desire to impress others.

- Price consciousness showed a negative link with age, though not nearly such a strong link as for male buyers.

Links between hidden and output nodes show that:

- The formation of overall satisfaction felt by female car owners is mainly instrumental, being positively impacted by the degree of rationality, while all other hidden nodes show a small negative impact.

- Correlation between satisfaction and loyalty is not as strong as for male buyers. Each hidden node has a significantly lower impact on loyalty than on satisfaction.

- None of the 4 hidden nodes seems to have a great deal of impact on car brand loyalty with regard to female consumers. This may indicate that there are other factors, not considered in this study, which are more likely to affect loyalty in female car buyers.

6.2.7 Conclusions and implications

The study showed clear difference in the attitudes of male and female consumers. The price of a car was shown to be important for both male and female buyers, but for different reasons. For male buyers, paying a higher price for a car meant that they could have higher expectations and impress others more, whereas for female buyers a higher price was more important in assuring them that their car would perform as it should. A high level of price consciousness tended to reduce satisfaction and loyalty for both male and female buyers, but to a much large extent for male buyers.

The major influence on satisfaction for female buyers was their degree of rationality, positively related to expectations, product performance and fit with self-image. Satisfaction for male buyers was most highly linked with low price consciousness, but was also positively linked with the hidden node labeled 'Low confidence', which was correlated with a low level of certainty about the car's performance. Some ideas on this finding were given above. Loyalty for male buyers was highly correlated with satisfaction, while for female buyers this was less apparent.

The positive link between age and both satisfaction and loyalty, found by Peterson and Wilson (1992) and Diem (1994), is borne out to some extent in the finding, in the male contingent, that younger buyers were most price conscious and hence least likely to be satisfied or loyal. The findings for female buyers are inconclusive on this aspect. However, the sample used was heavily weighted towards younger buyers, with only 17% of the whole sample being over 35, and only 9% over 45. A further study, with a sample including a higher proportion of respondents between 45 and 55, and also over 55, would be likely to give a more balanced picture.

The generally smaller contribution weights at both levels of the female network, compared with the male network, tend to suggest that the factors considered in this study are less important to female buyers than to male buyers. In addition, several aspects of car choice that have been previously shown to impact upon satisfaction and loyalty have not been examined, such as search behavior, satisfaction with car dealer, overall life satisfaction.

With regard to the methods used, this study shows the applicability of a neural network approach in bringing together psychometric and econometric approaches to the measurement of attitudes and emotions. The latent constructs that may be represented by hidden nodes can be particularly useful in the early stages of model development, when investigating the determinants of consumer responses. The fact that neural networks attempt to mimic the workings of the brain means that the model developed may be a realistic, albeit extremely simplified, representation of what is actually going on in a consumer's mind.

Further research in this area could include the comparison of the foregoing analysis with analysis of the same data by other methods, such as the LISREL model or pure linear regression models. The results achieved by each method could be compared, and the method's accuracy as a predictor of consumer responses tested with new data, in order to discover the advantages and disadvantages of each method and the situations to which each would be most applicable.

CHAPTER 7

Approximate Algorithms for Management Problems

NOTE: This chapter is based on a previously published research paper by Hurley, S. and Moutinho, L. (1996).

Optimization methods have been widely used in marketing. These have traditionally involved linear programming, integer and mixed-integer programming, and non-linear programming (Lilien et al., 1992). As with the general integer programming methods, general non-linear programming is inherently a difficult problem. Until recently it has been the prevailing wisdom that general solution techniques are not always successful, and that special insight into the structure of the problem is often required. However, a new breed of general optimization methods are currently in use in areas such as operations research, which we believe will be able to solve important industry-based marketing problems more successfully than traditional methods (assuming such methods exist for a particular problem). Successful in this context means first and foremost the quality of solution found, but also ease of extendibility to different formulations of the same problem.

7.1 Genetic Algorithms

Genetic algorithms were invented by Holland (1975) to mimic some of the processes of natural evolution and selection. They attempt to simulate natural evolution in the following manner.

The first step is to represent a candidate solution to the problem that you are solving by a string of genes that can take on some value from a specified finite range or alphabet. This string of genes, which represents a solution, is known as a chromosome. Then an initial population of legal chromosomes is constructed at random. At each generation, the fitness of each chromosome in the population is measured (a high fitness value would indicate a better solution than would a low fitness value). The selection procedure is biased towards selecting the fitter chromosomes to produce offspring for the next generation, which inherit the best characteristics of both parents. After many generations of selection for the fitter chromosomes, the result is hopefully a population that is substantially fitter than the original.

The theoretical basis for the genetic algorithm is the schemata theorem (Holland, 1975), which states that individual chromosomes with good, short, low-order schemata or building blocks (that is, beneficial parts of the chromosome) receive an exponentially increasing number of trials in successive generations. All genetic algorithms consist of the following components (Goldberg, 1989).

1. Chromosomal representation
   Each chromosome represents a legal solution to the problem, and is composed of a string of genes. The binary alphabet {0,1} is often used to represent these genes, but sometimes, depending on the application, integers or real numbers are used. In fact, almost any representation can be used that enables a solution to be encoded as a finite-length string.

2. Initial population
   Once a suitable representation has been decided upon for the chromosomes, it is necessary to create an initial population to serve as the starting point for the genetic algorithm. This initial population can be created randomly or by using specialized, problem-specific information. From empirical studies, over a wide range of function optimization problems, a population size of between 30 and 100 is usually recommended.

3. Fitness evaluation
   Fitness evaluation involves defining an objective or fitness function against which each chromosome is tested for suitability for the environment under consideration. As the algorithm proceeds we would expect the individual fitness of the best chromosome to increase, as well as the total fitness of the population as a whole.

4. Selection
   We need to select chromosomes from the current population for reproduction. If we have a population of size $2n$, where n is some positive integer value, the selection procedure picks out two parent chromosomes, based on their fitness values, which are then used by the crossover and mutation operators (described below) to produce two offspring for the new population. This selection/crossover/mutation cycle is repeated until the new population contains $2n$ chromosomes: that is, after n cycles. The higher the fitness value, the higher the probability of those chromosomes being selected for reproduction.

5. Crossover and mutation
   Once a pair of chromosomes has been selected, crossover can take place to produce offspring. A crossover probability of 1.0 indicates that all the selected chromosomes are used in reproduction: that is, there are no survivors. However, empirical studies (De Jong, 1975) have shown that better results are achieved by a crossover probability of between 0.65 and 0.85, which implies that the probability of a selected chromosomes surviving to the next generation unchanged

(apart from any changes arising from mutation) ranges from 0.35 (1 0.65) to 0.15 (1 0.85). One-point crossover involves taking the two selected parents and crossing them at a randomly chosen point. For example, if we have the following parents (with x and y representing individual values within the chromosome):

$$\begin{array}{lcccccccc} \text{parent 1} & x_1 & x_2 & x_3 & x_4 & x_5 & x_6 & x_7 & x_8 \\ \text{parent 2} & y_1 & y_2 & y_3 & y_4 & y_5 & y_6 & y_7 & y_8 \end{array}$$

and we cross at point 3 say, the following offspring would be produced:

$$\begin{array}{lcccccccc} \text{child 1} & x_1 & x_2 & x_3 & x_4 & x_5 & x_6 & x_7 & x_8 \\ \text{child 2} & y_1 & y_2 & y_3 & y_4 & y_5 & y_6 & y_7 & y_8 \end{array}$$

If we use only the crossover operator to produce offspring, one potential problem that may arise is that if all the chromosomes in the initial population have the same value at a particular position then all future offspring will have this same value at this position. For example, if all the chromosomes have a 0 in position two then all future offspring will have a 0 at position two. To combat this undesirable situation a mutation operator is used. This attempts to introduce some random alteration of the genes: for example, 0 becomes 1 and vice versa. Typically this occurs infrequently, so mutation is of the order of about one bit changed in a thousand tested. Each bit in each chromosome is checked for possible mutation by generating a random number between 0 and 1, and if this number is less than or equal to the given mutation probability, e.g. 0.001, then the bit value is changed.

This completes one cycle of the simple genetic algorithm. The fitness of each chromosome in the new population is evaluated and the whole procedure repeated:

   Generate random population
   REPEAT
      evaluate fitness of current population
      select chromosomes, based on fitness, for reproduction
      perform crossover and mutation to give new improved population
   UNTIL *finished*

where *finished* indicates that either an optimal or suitable suboptimal has been found, or the maximum number of generations has been exceeded.

7.1.1 Site location analysis using genetic algorithms

Site acquisition and retail location is an important consideration in the enhancement of corporate profitability. For many types of market, a multi-unit company will find that individual optimum locations do not necessarily result in a generally optimum network in a market area (Achabal et al., 1982). In the situation where a number of sites already exist, say 50 or more, and there is a choice of several proposed sites, the problem of finding the optimal network is difficult. We shall consider the following proposed sites to use, to augment and improve the existing network in terms of profitability, attractiveness to potential customers, or any other suitable metric. The existing network is assumed to be dynamic: that is, existing sites may be removed from the network if this gives an improvement in overall network performance.

7.1.2 Chromosome representation

Each chromosome represents a possible network consisting of existing sites and possible new sites. If there are S_e existing sites and S_p possible new sites, the length of chromosome will be $S_e + S_p$. The individual genes within each chromosome are represented by a binary alphabet: 0 indicates that a particular site is not used in the network, whereas a 1 would indicate that a site is used. The position within the chromosome is important, as this indicates the site under consideration. For example, bit position 4 (from left to right) represents site 4. To illustrate, if we have 4 existing outlets and 3 possible new sites, then the chromosome {1 1 1 1 0 1 0} represents a network where sites 1, 2, 3 and 4 are used (the existing network) and site 6 is used; sites 5 and 7 remain unused.

7.1.3 Fitness function

The most important problem-dependent aspect in applying genetic algorithms is finding a suitable function to determine the fitness or goodness of a chromosome in the genetic population. One possible fitness function involves a slight modification of the Penny and Broom spatial interaction model (Penny and Broom, 1988), and is given by

$$\sum_i \sum_j EXP_{ij} = \sum_i \sum_j \left[\beta_0 \left(\sum_k E_k H_{ik} \right) \cdot \frac{W_j e^{-\beta_1 T_{ij}}}{\sum_m W_m e^{-\beta_1 T_{im}}} \right] \quad (7.1)$$

where EXP_{ij} is the expenditure from zone i to site j; β_0 and β_1 are parameters; E_k is the mean expenditure on the product/service category by household category k; H_{ik} is the number of households of category k located in zone i; W_j is a subjective measure of attraction of the proposed store/outlet; T_{ij} is the travel time from zone i to the site at j; W_m is a subjective measure of attractiveness of competitor m or outlets from the same company (i.e. inter-company competition); and T_{im} is the travel time from zone i to competitor m.

In the original Penny and Broom model, W_m considered only competitors, but here we consider outlets from the same company as well. The genetic algorithm will then attempt to maximize this expression: that is, find a network of sites that maximizes customer expenditure.

Genetic Algorithms

7.1.4 Genetic operators

Each chromosome is represented by a binary string with an associated fitness. If 2 chromosomes are selected for reproduction by the selection procedure, the various crossover operators (Goldberg, 1989) can be used to generate offspring. For example, if the two chromosomes

$$\begin{array}{ccccccc} 1 & 1 & 1 & 1 & 0 & 1 & 0 \\ 1 & 0 & 1 & 1 & 0 & 0 & 1 \end{array} \quad \begin{array}{l} \text{(sites 5 and 7 unused)} \\ \text{(sites 2, 5 and 6 unused)} \end{array}$$

are selected for reproduction, and one-point crossover is used (e.g. at position 3), then the following offspring are produced:

$$\begin{array}{ccccccc} 1 & 1 & 1 & 1 & 0 & 0 & 1 \\ 1 & 0 & 1 & 1 & 0 & 1 & 0 \end{array} \quad \begin{array}{l} \text{(sites 5 and 6 unused)} \\ \text{(sites 2, 5 and 7 used)} \end{array}$$

Similarly, the standard mutation operator can be used: that is, a bit is changed with a low probability, e.g. 0.001.

7.1.5 Simple illustration

Given 4 existing sites and 3 possible new sites, consider a population of 5 chromosomes, consisting of the following:

$$\begin{array}{lccccccccl} C_1 & 1 & 0 & 1 & 1 & 0 & 1 & 1 & \text{fitness} = 1562 \\ C_2 & 0 & 1 & 1 & 1 & 1 & 1 & 0 & \text{fitness} = 3511 \\ C_3 & 1 & 0 & 1 & 0 & 0 & 0 & 1 & \text{fitness} = 4756 \\ C_4 & 1 & 1 & 1 & 1 & 0 & 1 & 1 & \text{fitness} = 1929 \\ C_5 & 1 & 0 & 0 & 1 & 1 & 1 & 1 & \text{fitness} = 756 \end{array}$$

In this illustration the fitness values for each chromosome were randomly selected, whereas in actual site analysis using genetic algorithms the fitness would be calculated using Equation 7.1. Chromosomes C_2 and C_3 are the most fit, so they would be more likely to be selected for crossover and mutation. If one-point crossover was used at a randomly chosen position, say position 2, the following offspring would be produced:

$$\begin{array}{lccccccc} C_2 & 1 & 0 & 1 & 1 & 1 & 1 & 0 \\ C_3 & 0 & 1 & 1 & 0 & 0 & 0 & 1 \end{array}$$

If their respective fitness values, calculated using Equation 7.1, were 4212 and 5681, then we have found a network of sites, represented by chromosome C_3, which is theoretically better than any network in the previous population.

The advantages in using GAs are as follows:

- They find an optimal or near-optimal site location in reasonable time.
- The goodness of alternative site networks can be easily accessed.
- Poor networks can be identified, and therefore avoided.
- It is relatively easy to solve different formulations of the site location problem.

7.2 Tabu Search

Tabu search is an iterative procedure for solving discrete combinatorial optimization problems. The basic idea, described by Glover et al. (1993), is to explore the *search space* of all feasible solutions by a sequence of moves. A move from one solution to another is the best available. However, for each iteration, to escape from locally optimal but not globally optimal solutions and to prevent cycling, some moves are classified as forbidden or *tabu* (or *taboo*). Tabu moves are based on the short-term and long-term history of the sequence of moves. Sometimes a tabu move can be overridden; such *aspiration criteria* might include the case that, by forgetting that a move is tabu, leads to a solution that is the best obtained so far.

Suppose f is the real-valued objective function on a search space S, and it is required to find a $c \in S$ such that $f(c)$ has maximal or near-maximal value. A characterization of the search space S is that there is a set of k moves $M(s) = \{m_1, K, m_k\}$, and the application of the moves to a feasible solution $s \in S$ leads to k solutions $M(s) = \{m_1(s), K, m_k(s)\}$. The subset $N(s) \subseteq M(s)$ of *feasible* solutions is known as the *neighborhood* of s.

The method commences with a (possibly random) solution $s_0 \in S$, and determines a sequence of solutions $s_0, s_1, K, s_n \in S$. For each j, $N'(s_j)$ is the set of those solutions in $N(s_j)$ that are either tabu, but satisfy the aspiration criteria, or non-tabu. A solution in $N'(s_j)$ that maximizes f is selected. Note that it is possible, and even desirable, to avoid convergence at a local maximum, that $f(s_{j+1}) < f(s_j)$.

The following procedure describes the tabu search method more formally:

    k = 1

    generate initial solution s

    WHILE *not finished*

        Identify $N(s) \subset S$ (neighborhood set)

        Identify $T(s) \subseteq N(s)$ (tabu set)

        Identify $A(s) \subseteq T(s)$ (aspirant set)

        Choose $s' \in (N(s) - T(s)) Y A(s)$, for which $F(s')$ is maximal

        $s = s'$

        $k = k + 1$

    END WHILE

The procedure continues until either a maximum number of iterations have been completed or an acceptable suboptimal solution has been found. The conditions for a neighbor to be tabu or an aspirant will be problem specific. For example, a move m_r may be tabu if it could lead to a solution that has already been considered in the last q iterations (recency or short-term condition) or which has been repeated many times before (*frequency* or long-term condition). A tabu move satisfies that aspiration criteria if, for example, the value of $f(s')$ with $s' \in T(s_j)$ satisfies $f(s') > f(s_i)$ for all $i, 0 \leq i \leq j$.

7.2.1 Example

In this example, the search space S is the set of all rooted binary trees with n terminal nodes and therefore $n1$ internal nodes. The objective function f associates with each tree a real value, and might, for example, involve the height of and the weighted distance between terminal nodes. The search commences with an initial tree, whose nodes are labeled arbitrarily from 1 to $2n - 1$. A move m_{ij} consists in taking 2 nodes i and j and swapping the subtrees whose roots are at nodes i and j. Such a swap is only valid if i is not an ancestor or descendant of j. Figure 7.1 illustrates the move m_{26} applied to a tree with 5 terminal nodes. Note that the set of terminal nodes is left invariant by such a move.

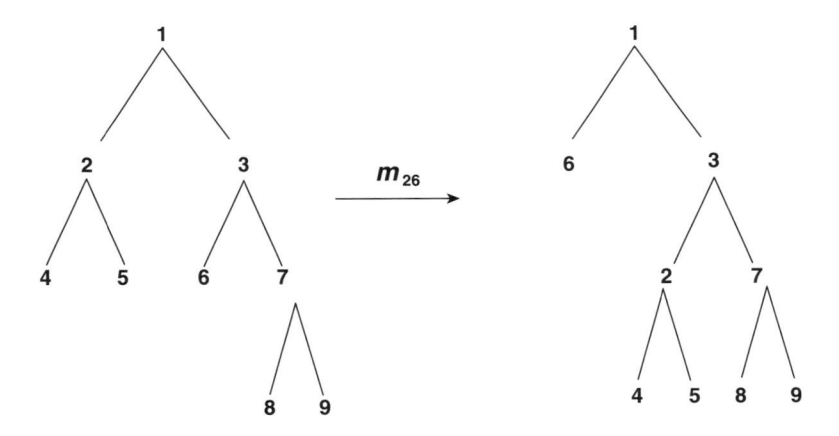

Figure 7.1 *Example of a move applied to a tree with 5 terminal nodes*

In this example, a move m_{ij} is tabu if one of i, j is the index of a recent move. This representation allows the exploration of the whole search space form any initial tree. It has similarities with a successful implementation of tabu search for traveling salesperson problem in Glover (1991).

7.2.2 Application of tabu search to segmentation

Ramaswany and DeSarbo (1990) have proposed a new methodology for deriving hierarchical product-market structures from disaggregate purchase data. A hierarchical product-market tree was estimated from scanner panel purchase data in a maximum likelihood framework. The derived product-market representation portrays both products and market segments as terminal nodes in a hierarchical tree where the closer a product is to a particular segment the higher is the revealed preference of that product. The hierarchical representation of products and segments and the composition of the market segments are derived simultaneously. Ramaswany and DeSarbo's new methodology, called SCULPTURE (Stochastic Ultrametric Purchase Tree), has been developed by formulating a stochastic choice model.

Given only scanner panel purchase data, we also consider the problem of deriving product-market structures by determining a hierarchical tree representation where terminal nodes are used for both products and segments. A segment's preference for a product is inversely related to d_{sj}, the length of the unique path between the terminal nodes corresponding to the segment s and product j.

The raw data are the values x_{hj} that represent the number of choices of product j for household h. The objective is to determine the tree and values of a_s, which are the proportion of households in the sample belonging to the segment s, by maximizing the expression

$$L(\mathbf{a}, \mathbf{x}, \mathbf{d}) = \prod_h \sum_s a_s \prod_j \left(\frac{exp(-d_{sj})}{\sum_k exp(-d_{sk})} \right)^{x_{hj}}$$

which measures the likelihood of the sample having this product-market structure. In the application of tabu search to this multi-modal optimization problem, a move will be either to change the vector $\mathbf{a}$ or to change the tree. These moves, and the notion of tabu, will be along the lines of the example in a previous section. Thus a solution of the search space t is represented by

- a set of integer values y_s, one for each segment, with $\sum_s y_s = N$, for some fixed N; and

- a binary tree, each of whose terminal nodes corresponds either to a segment or to a product.

Such a solution is evaluated from the expression $L(\mathbf{a}, \mathbf{x}, \mathbf{d})$ by calculating the values of $a_s = y_s/N$ and d_{sj}, the length of the path between the terminal nodes representing the segment s and the product j. A move is either

- to increment y_u and decrement y_v for two segments u, v; or

- to swap the subtrees whose roots are at nodes i, j.

Precise definition of a tabu move will be found by experimentation. One of the advantages of this method of solving the optimization problem is that the tabu search acts directly on the hierarchical tree rather than, as in Ramaswany and DeSarbo (1990), the distances that are constrained to correspond to a tree. A second advantage is that the optimization of the vector $\mathbf{a}$ and the tree are considered in parallel rather than as individual optimization problems to be solved sequentially for each iteration.

7.3 Simulated Annealing

Simulated annealing (SA) is a stochastic computational technique derived from statistical mechanics for finding near-globally minimum-cost solutions to large optimization problems. The method has a direct analogy with thermodynamics, specifically with the way that liquids freeze and crystallize, or metals cool and anneal. At high temperatures, the molecules of a liquid move freely with respect to one another. If the liquid is cooled slowly, thermal mobility is restricted. The atoms are often able to line themselves up and form a pure crystal that is completely regular. This crystal is the state of minimum energy for the system, which would correspond to the optimal solution in a mathematical optimization problem. In order to make use of this analogy with thermodynamical systems for solving mathematical optimization problems, one must first provide the following elements:

- A description of possible system configurations: that is, some way of representing a solution to the minimization (maximization) problem. Usually this involves some *configuration* of parameters $\mathbf{X} = (x_1, x_2, \ldots, x_N)$ that represents a solution.

- A generator of random changes, known as *moves*, in a configuration. These changes are typically solutions in the *neighborhood* of the current configuration: for example, a change in one of the parameters x_i.

- An objective or cost function $E(\mathbf{X})$ (analogue of energy), whose minimization is the goal of the procedure.

- A control parameter T (analogue of temperature) and an *annealing schedule*, which indicates how T is lowered from high values to low values: for example, after how many random changes in configuration is T reduced and by how much?

7.3.1 Sales territory design using simulated annealing

In this section we indicate how the technique of simulated annealing can be applied to the problem of designing the territories for an organization that wishes to deploy a salesforce over a large geographical area. In the first subsection, we determine a mathematical model of the problem. This has been chosen to be simplistic for the purpose of the descriptive ease, yet it incorporates many of the criteria relevant to the design. In the second subsection we describe how such a model may be optimized.

We shall assume that the geographical area is presented as a number of small sales coverage units (SCUs), and that, for each unit, relevant statistical or factual information is available. For example, the SCUs might be zipcodes (USA) or postcodes (UK), and the information might consist of volume sales in a previous time period, the average time in contact with each customer per call, the contiguous SCUs, and the traveling time between contiguous SCUs. The required properties of the territory design are:

- *contiguity:* the SCUs in a territory form a connected cohesive block;
- *equality of workload:* each territory has equal sales workload;
- *equality of sales potential:* each territory has equal sales potential.

The problem of dividing the region into territories is seen as assigning each SCU to a single territory in such a way that, first, the constraints of contiguity, equal workload, equal sales potential are satisfied; and, second, the profit differs from those of Zoltners and Sinha (1983) and others by adding explicitly the maximization of profit, and allows extensions to models where profit is measured by a more complex formula. We have also added the constraint of equal sales potential as a desirable feature, to ensure, for example, that commission potential is balanced among the SCUs. In the notion of Howick and Pidd (1990), the model we have chosen can be classified as multiple criteria using a travel measure and centre-seeking alignment.

We shall suppose that the size of the salesforce (that is, the number of territories required) is fixed, and also that the number of calls to each customer in a time period has been predetermined. A package based on the algorithm to solve the sales territory design could be used on a what if ... basis if these variables are unknown quantities.

7.3.2 Information about a single SCU

In a single SCU the salesforce will divide its time between maintaining existing customers, prospecting for new customers, and administering the SCU. We shall assume that the administration time is subsumed in the variables representing the contact time with the customer. For customer c, the workload w_c, measured in hours, will depend on n_c, the number of calls; on t_c, the average time spent in contact with the customer; and on s_c, the average time spent in traveling to make a call:

$$w_c = n_c t_c + n_c s_c$$

Summing over all customers in the SCU we get a total workload W given by

$$W = \sum_c w_c = \sum_c n_c t_c + \sum_c n_c s_c$$

For a salesforce centered at a distance d from the centre of this SCU, the values s_c will all be approximately equal to $s = 2d/u$, where u is the average traveling speed. This assumes that separate calls require separate journeys from the center of the territory.

For a particular SCU, let the workload for customer contact be $a = \sum_c n_c t_c$, and let $n = \sum_c n_c$ be the total number of calls. Then the total workload for the SCU is $W = a + ns$. The sales potential depends on whether a customer is an existing or prospective one. For an existing customer, the sales potential q_c is measured using the sales q'_c for the previous time period and the holding rate h_c:

$$q_c = q'_c h_c$$

For a prospective customer, the sales potential is measured by r_c, the estimated volume of sales if the customer is converted, and the probability v_c of the conversion:

$$q_c = r_c v_c$$

Note that both h_c and v_c are influenced by the values of n_c, the number of calls that the customer receives, and t_c, the average contact time. Summing over all customers in a SCU, we obtain a sales potential of $b = \sum_c q_c$. The profit p_c associated with each customer is measured by the margin m on the sales and the average cost of x_c of servicing the customer:

$$p_c = mq_c - z_c$$

For a customer c, the two components of x_c are the cost of the time spent in contact with the customer and the cost of the sales calls. If these are the only components, and f is the rate per hour for customer contact and g is the cost per unit distance for traveling, then

$$z_c = fw_c + gn_c s_c$$

Summing over all customers, we obtain a profit for the SCU of given by

$$p = \sum_c p_c = m \sum_c q_c - f \sum_c w_c - g \sum_c n_c s_c$$
$$= mb - f(a + ns) - 2ngd/u$$

7.3.3 The model

Suppose there are J SCUs numbered from 1 to J, and that for the jth SCU, $1 \leq j \leq J$, we have the following values derived in the last subsection:

- a_j denotes the workload for customer contact;
- b_j denotes the sales potential;
- n_j denotes the total number of calls required;
- s_j denotes the traveling distance from the center of the SCU to the designated center of the territory in which it lies;
- p_j denotes the profit.

In addition we suppose that, for each pair j and k of the contiguous SCUs, the distance between their centers is the number d_{jk}. These values could be placed in a 2-dimensional array array $J \times J$ array H, where a zero entry indicates that the corresponding SCUs are not contiguous. Now suppose that I territories are required, which are numbered from 1 to I. The value I will be significantly smaller than J. The problem of determining a territory design can be considered as the determination of an assignment function F, which assigns to each SCU j the territory $i = F(j)$. That is, for each j, $1 \leq j \leq J$:

$$F(j) = i \tag{7.2}$$

for some i, $1 \leq i \leq I$. We now consider how the constraints and the maximization of profit are affected by this assignment.

7.3.4 Contiguity

We shall need to be able to ascertain for any design that all the territories are contiguous. For the other constraints we shall also be required to determine a distance between 2 (not necessarily contiguous) SCUs in the same territory. Both can be accomplished by using Floyd's algorithm on subarrays of the array H as the distance matrix of a graph (Sedgewick, 1988). Thus it is possible, using the representation described above, for a new territory design to be efficiently checked for contiguity.

7.3.5 Equal workload

The distance between two SCUs of a territory can be taken to be the shortest path between them using as intermediate junctions any other centers of the territory as are convenient to use. If j, k are the SCUs, then we denote this distance by D_{jk}. As mentioned in the paragraph above, these values can be simultaneously and efficiently determined using Floyd's algorithm. Suppose that the main office of territory i is placed at SCU. From the expression for the workload of the SCU in the previous subsection, we have that the work of the territory is A_i, given by

$$A_i = \sum_{j, F(j)=i} \left(a_j + n_j s_j\right) = \sum_{j, F(j)=i} \left(a_j + n_j D_{j, c_i}\right)$$

The choice of the center c_i of territory i may be chosen, for example, as that SCU in the territory that minimizes the expression for A_i. The constraint that the workload of each territory should be precisely the same will be impossible to achieve in practice. Instead, the objective function, that is, the function that the simulated annealing algorithm maximizes, includes a term, $A_{\max}$, which is the maximum deviation of the workload in any territory from the average workload over all territories:

$$A_{\max} = \max|A_i - A| \qquad (7.3)$$

for $i = 1, 2, K, I$, and where A, the average of the workload taken over all territories, is given by

$$A = (1/I) \sum_{i=1}^{I} A_i$$

The objective function used should attempt to minimize the term $A_{\max}$. This corresponds to designing territories that have a workload that is as equal as possible.

7.3.6 Equality of sales potential

The sales potential for territory is the aggregate of the sales potential for each SCU in that territory. If B_i denotes this total sales then

$$B_i = \sum_{j, F(j)=i} b_j$$

In a similar way for the discussion of the equality of workload, denote by B the average sales potential, so that

$$B = (1/I) \sum_{i=1}^{I} B_i$$

Then the equality of sales potential is catered for in the objective function by including the term

$$B_{\max} = \max|B_i - B| \tag{7.4}$$

for each $i = 1, 2, K, I$.

7.3.7 Profit

The overall profit Q of the organization is given by the aggregate P of the expected profits from sales in each territory less the cost R of administering the salesforce over all the territories. For territory i, the profit P_i is the sums of the profits from the SCUs in that territory. Thus

$$P_i = \sum_{j, F(j)=i} P_j = mB_i - fA_i - (2g/u) \sum_{j, F(j)=i} n_j D_{j,c_i}$$

Assuming R is independent of the territory design, the objective is to maximize P where

$$P = \sum_{i=1}^{I} P_i = mIB - fIA - (2g/u) \sum_{i=1}^{I} \sum_{j, F(j)=i} n_j D_{j,c_i} \tag{7.5}$$

To summarize, the formulation of the territory design problem is to determine an assignment function F, defined by Equation 7.2, that:

1. makes the territories contiguous;
2. minimizes the maximum deviation in the workload of territories;
3. minimizes the maximum deviation in the sales potential of territories;
4. maximizes P given by Equation 7.5.

The objective function, to be maximized, can therefore be written as

$$E = P - A_{\max} - B_{\max} \tag{7.6}$$

Each term in the objective function could be weighted to reflect the relative importance of one term over another: for example, profit over equal sales potential.

7.3.8 Application of simulated annealing

An initial design is found for which the territories are contiguous. The profit P is computed, along with A_{max} and B_{max}. Denote this design by $\mathbf{X_{old}}$. Also initialized is the value of the control parameter, T.

A move from $\mathbf{X_{old}}$ is to select at random an SCU j in territory i, remove it and place it in territory k. The move is valid if territories i, k remain contiguous. If the move is valid then the new design is called $\mathbf{X_{new}}$, and the difference in the objective function values, $\Delta E = E_{old} - E_{new}$ is computed. The new design is accepted when ΔE is negative and with probability $prob = e^{\Delta E/T}$ when it is positive. When accepted, the value of $\mathbf{X_{old}}$ becomes $\mathbf{X_{new}}$. The method now continues to select another move at random, and so on until N_c moves have been tried for the temperature T at which point T is reduced, and the whole process is repeated until T falls below a certain threshold. The full procedure is as follows:

```
Initialize T
Initialize X_old
WHILE T > T_min DO
  FOR u = 1 to N_c DO
    Make a random move by removing SCU j from territory i to k
    Call the new design X_new
    IF territories i, k are contiguous THEN
      compute E_new and ΔE = E_old - E_new
      IF ΔE < 0 or random < prob = e^(Δe/T) THEN
        X_old becomes X_new
      END IF
    END IF
  END FOR
  reduce T
END WHILE
```

where N_c is the number of random changes in configuration at each temperature T, and the variable *random* is a randomly generated number in the range [0,1]. Precise details about the values of T and the annealing schedule will need to be determined by experimentation.

CHAPTER 8
Other Statistical, Mathematical and Co-pattern Modeling Techniques

8.1 Discriminant Analysis

Like regression analysis, discriminant analysis (DA) uses a linear equation to predict the dependent variable (say, sales). However, while in regression analysis the parameters (coefficients) are used to minimize the sum of squares, in discriminant analysis the parameters are selected in such a way as to maximize the ratio:

$$\frac{\text{Variance between group means}}{\text{Variance within groups}}$$

Discriminant analysis is used in marketing for predicting brand loyalty and buying or attempting to predict consumer behavior in general; this classification method could be used when the data (the independent variables) are interval scales.

8.2 Automatic Interaction Detection (AID)

The regression analysis mentioned above attempts to identify association between the dependent and the independent variables, one at a time. In addition, the assumption is that the data are measured on interval scales. In many other marketing research situations we need a method able to handle nominal *or* ordinal data and to identify *all* the significant relationships between the dependent and the independent variables. Automatic interaction detection (AID) is a computer-based method for interactively selecting the independent variables in order to be able to predict the dependent variables. It splits the sample of observations into two groups on a sequential routine, trying to keep the subgroups that emerge as homogenous as possible, relative to the dependent variable. The homogeneity is measured by minimizing the sum-of-square deviations of each subgroup member from its subgroup mean. AID is used in marketing for market segments analysis, analyzing the effect of advertising levels on retail sales, predicting consumption/sales and brand loyalty.

The method is not as powerful as regression analysis and since the minimum subgroup size should be no less than 30, the original sample of objects required must be fairly large (1000 or more).

8.3 Logical Type Discriminant Models: The C5 Algorithm

The C5 algorithm provides the induction of logical type discriminant models, namely classification trees and sets of propositional rules. In addition to the original software implemented by Quinlan (1993), available programs that may be used to run this algorithm are included in some well-known data mining and statistical packages (e.g. the SPSS Clementine version).

Classification trees translate a hierarchical partitioning process that starts with a sample of observations concerning descriptors and segment membership (root node) and successively divides nodes based on the descriptors values. This process attempts to decrease diversity in each new descendent node of the tree, in order to decrease the risk of classification. Thus, in a classification tree each terminal node (leaf) represents a set of relatively homogeneous observations in what concerns segment membership, the class distribution tending to concentrate in one particular segment.

A prepositional rule is represented by a *if* condition *then* class logical type expression where the condition is a conjunctive preposition that allocates specific values to the descriptors. A set of prepositional rules may provide means to classify observations that meet the conditions associated with each class.

The C5 algorithm grows a classification tree based on the Information Gain Ratio measure, an entropy based criterion (14). According to this criterion, the selection of a specific predictor X_j to split a node O is guided by the objective of decreasing diversity (entropy) in the descendent nodes. Diversity in these child nodes should then be inferior to diversity in the parent node O. As a consequence, the frequency distribution in each child node will thus tend to concentrate in specific segments.

In other words, splitting a node O based on a chosen attribute X_j (and on a particular categorization of X_j levels) translates the capacity of the chosen attribute to add information concerning classification of individuals of node O into the segments. If X_j is metric or ordinal, binary partitions will be considered as candidates (thresholds will be the sorted values of X_j). If X_j is categorical, its categories will yield a partition of node O. As an option, C5 provides a heuristic procedure that considers possible combinations of attributes categories in order to optimizse the Information Gain Ratio.

To deal with missing observations concerning a chosen attribute (X_j) to split node O, C5 divides these observations among the descendent nodes of O, according to the empirical distribution of frequencies associated with the correspondent categorization (partition) a_j^*.

Logical Type Discriminant Models: The C5 Algorithm

C5 provides pruning of the initial classification tree to avoid overfitting. A descendent subtree A_O of node O will be pruned if its pessimistic error of classification is greater than the one corresponding to node O (pessimistic error being the upper bound of a confidence interval associated with the proportion of incorrectly classified observations).

The final classification tree may be translated in a set of prepositional rules, each one corresponding to a leaf node. Each initial rules condition (descriptors values) is obtained following the path from the root to each terminal node and the rules class is the modal segment for this leaf.

After deriving the classification tree, C5 provides means to simplify, reduce and rank the initial set of prepositional rules that corresponds to the leaves of the classification tree, yielding a new model of classification.

Simplification of the initial subset of rules obeys the minimum pessimistic error criterion, trying to generalize rules by removing propositions from the rules conditions (pessimistic error is considered to compare precision of alternative rules).

After simplification, a simulated annealing heuristic is applied to each subset, discarding some rules in order to minimize an estimate of the number of bits necessary to encode to encode each subset (Minimum Description Length criterion).

Finally, rules within each subset are sorted by precision and subsets are sorted according to a minimum of false positives criterion. As such, subsets that incorrectly classify the least number of cases are ranked in first place.

Classification of an observation x_j within a class (segment) is finally provided by the first rule that covers it. If it is covered by multiple rules corresponding to different classes, voting takes place, the weight associated with each vote being the precision associated to each rule. When x_j isn't covered by any rule, a default classification is used and x_j is allocated to the segment that contains the most training cases not covered by any rule.

Costs of incorrect classification of an observation that belongs to a class l^* in a class l of the dependent variable ($l, l^* \in \{1 \ldots S\}$) may also be incorporated in the final classification decision. In this case a minimum cost criterion is adopted (instead of maximum precision).

Classification trees and prepositional rules may be associated with the corresponding measures of precision for classification. In particular, hit rates measures (the proportion of correctly classified observations, P_r) returned by estimated models may illustrate model fitting.

As resubstitution errors tend to overestimate precision, discriminant models based on a training sample may be applied to a test (or holdout) sample where the corresponding hit rates prove more realistic estimates of classification precision.

Recently, an analysis of the performance of several classification algorithms (18) suggests that, in what concerns classification precision, there is some empirical evidence that similar performances can be achieved by several discriminant methods, namely linear discriminant analysis, logistic regression, neural networks and classification trees. When choosing an algorithm for profiling a segment structure, additional criteria must, thus, be taken into account. Namely, the need for specific parametric assumptions, the capacity to deal with missing observations, the existence of

Example

AGE ≤ 40 [Mode: regular users] (636.796)
  AGE ≤ 27 [Mode: first time users] (111.869)
    AGE ≤ 18 **[Mode: regular users] (5.378, 0.961)** *then regular users*
    AGE ≤ 18 [Mode: first time users] (106.491)
      EDUCATION L. ≤ 4 **[Mode: first-time users] (40.043, 0.681)** *then first-time users*
      EDUCATION L. > 4 [Mode: regular users] (66.448)
        FEMALE **[Mode: first-time users] (30.174, 0.567)** *then first-time users*
        MALE [Mode: regular users] (36.274)
          AGE ≤ 24 **[Mode: regular users] (4.909, 0.973)** *then regular users*
          AGE > 24 [Mode: regular users] (31.366)
            AGE ≤ 25 **[Mode: first-time users] (5.887, 0.789)** *then first-time users*
            AGE > 25 **[Mode: regular users] (25.478, 0.62)** *then regular users*
  AGE > 27 [Mode: regular users] (524.926)
    EDUCATION L. ≤ 4 [Mode: regular users] (184.832)
      INCOME L. ≤ 1 **[Mode: first-time users] (14.759, 0.773)**
      INCOME L. > 1 [Mode: regular users] (170.073)
        OTHER REGIONS [Mode: regular users] (62.302)
          [SINGLE or DIVORCED] **[Mode: first-time users] (7.59, 0.642)** *then first-time users*
          [MARRIED or WIDOW] **[Mode: regular users] (54.667, 0.606)** *then regular users*
        LISBON **[Mode: regular users] (81.659, 0.611)** *then regular users*
        OPORTO [Mode: regular users] (26.112)
          INCOME L. ≤ 2 [Mode: first-time users] (16.175)
            FEMALE [Mode: first-time users] (12.467)
              AGE ≤ 34 **[Mode: first-time users] (8.447, 0.848)** *then first-time users*
              AGE > **[Mode: regular users] (4.02, 0.959)** *then regular users*
            MALE **[Mode: first-time users] (3.708, 0.662)** *then first-time users*
          INCOME L. > 2 **[Mode: regular users] (9.937, 0.726)** *then regular users*
    EDUCATION L. > 4 **[Mode: regular users] (340.094, 0.704)** *then regular users*
AGE > 40 **[Mode: regular users] (813.204, 0.594)** *then regular users*

Note: the terminal nodes (leafs) of the tree are signed in bold and the number and proportion of correctly classified cases are presented between parenthesis.

estimation problems and the interpretability of results, should be considered. Regarding these criteria some advantages of the proposed discriminant logical type models (based on the C5 algorithm, in particular) may be referred:

1. C5 is a purely nonparametric procedure that requires no assumptions concerning the data, as opposed to other discriminant methods that may be restricted to obey to some assumptions (e.g. normality in linear discriminant analysis).

Logical Type Discriminant Models: The C5 Algorithm

Table 8.1 *5 set of propositional rules (C5 Ra)*

Rules for first-time users:	Rules for regular users:
IF OPORTO and AGE > 27 and AGE ≤ 34 and FEMALE and EDUCATION L. ≤ 4 and INCOME L. ≤ 2 then *first-time users* (7, 0.889) **IF** age ≤ 40 and EDUCATION L. ≤ 4 and INCOME L. ≤ 1 then *first-time users* (26, 0.786) **IF** OTHER REGIONS and AGE > 27 and AGE ≤ 40 and [SINGLE or DIVORCED] and EDUCATION L. ≤ 4 then *first-time users* (7, 0.778) **IF** AGE > 24 and AGE ≤ 25 then *first-time users* (14, 0.75) **IF** AGE > 18 and AGE ≤ 27 and EDUCATION L. ≤ 4 then *first-time users* (36, 0.711) **IF** AGE > 18 and AGE ≤ 27 and FEMALE then *first-time users* (52, 0.611) **IF** AGE ≤ 27 then *first-time users* (104, 0.538)	IF AGE ≤ 18 then *regular users* (5, 0.857) IF AGE ≤ 40 then *regular users* (592, 0.63) IF AGE > 40 then *regular users* (756, 0.604)

Default : Regular users

2. The C5 algorithm has a specific procedure (summarized in this text) to deal with missing values, as opposed to general statistical discriminant approaches that rely on complete observations for allowing parameters estimation. This specific C5 procedures may also be seen as advantageous when compared to similar approaches to deal with missing values, in particular the CARTs surrogates approach.

3. The induction of logical type discriminant models has no estimation problems. Some estimation problems may, however, occur (boundary solutions or non-identified parameters) when trying to derive statistical models (e.g. when trying to maximize complex likelihood functions as those that may be associated with mixture models).

Table 8.2 *5 set of propositional rules (C5 Rb)*

Rules for first-time users	Rules for regular users
IF AGE 24 and AGE $\leq$ 25 then *first-time users* (14, 0.75) IF AGE $>$ 18 and AGE $\leq$ 27 and EDUCATION L. $\leq$ 4 then *first-time users* (36, 0.711) IF AGE $\leq$ 40 and INCOME L. $\leq$ 1 then *first-time users* (38, 0.675) IF AGE $\leq$ 53 and EDUCATION L. $\leq$ 2 then *first-time users* (22, 0.667)	IF AGE $\leq$ 18 then *first-time users* (5, 0.857) IF AGE $>$ 53 and EDUCATION L. $\leq$ 2 then *first-time users* (18, 0.8) IF OTHER REGIONS and AGE $>$ 40 and EDUCATION L. $\leq$ 2 then *first-time users* (14, 0.75) IF AGE $>$ 25 and AGE $\leq$ 27 and MALE and EDUCATION L. $>$ 4 then *first-time users* (24, 0.615) IF EDUCATION L. $>$ 2 then *first-time users* (1324, 0.615)

Rules for heavy users	
IF OTHER REGIONS and AGE $>$ 67 and EDUCATION L. $>$ 2 then *heavy users* (12, 0.786) IF AGE $>$ 51 and AGE $\leq$ 53 and EDUCATION L. $\leq$ 3 and INCOME L. $>$ 3 then *heavy users* (2, 0.75) IF age $>$ 40 and AGE $\leq$ 41 and EDUCATION L. $>$ 3 and INCOME L. $>$ 3 then *heavy users* (6, 0.75) IF OPORTO and AGE $>$ 53 and EDUCATION L. $>$ 4 and INCOME L. $>$ 3 then *heavy users* (5, 0.714) IF AGE $>$ 53 and SINGLE and MALE and INCOME L. $\leq$ 3 then *heavy users* (4, 0.667)	IF OPORTO and AGE $>$ 53 and AGE $\leq$ 62 and EDUCATION L. $\leq$ 3 and INCOME L. $\leq$ 3 then *heavy users* (4, 0.667) IF AGE $>$ 53 and DIVORCED and MALE and INCOME L. $\leq$ 3 then *heavy users* (1, 0.667) IF AGE $>$ 53 and AGE $\leq$ 70 and WIDOW and EDUCATION L. $>$ 2 then *heavy users* (6, 0.625) IF LISBON and AGE $>$ 53 and MALE then *heavy users* (29, 0.548) IF AGE $>$ 64 and MARRIED and EDUCATION L. $>$ 2 and INCOME L. $\leq$ 3 then *heavy users* (81, 0.53)

Default : Regular users

Table 8.3 *Classification precision*

Recursive based partitioning model C5 CT

Actual	Predicted		
	First-time users	Regular users	Heavy users
Training s (hit rate = 63.3%)			
First-time users	71[a]	225	
Regular users	29	847[a]	
Heavy users	0	278	
Test s (hit rate = 62%)			
First-time users	25[a]	121	
Regular users	23	448[a]	
Heavy users	4	142	

Recursive based partitioning model C5 Ra

Actual	Predicted		
	First-time users	Regular users	Heavy users
Training s (hit rate = 63.2%)			
First-time users	67[a]	229	
Regular users	26	850[a]	
Heavy users	0	278	
Test s (hit rate = 62.1%)			
First-time users	25[a]	121	
Regular users	22	449[a]	
Heavy users	4	142	

Recursive based partitioning model C5 Rb

Actual	Predicted		
	First-time users	Regular users	Heavy users
Training s (hit rate = 64%)			
First-time users	52[a]	244	0
Regular users	19	854[a]	3
Heavy users	1	255	22[a]
Test s (hit rate = 61.9%)			
First-time users	26[a]	120	0
Regular users	20	441[a]	10
Heavy users	1	140	5[a]

[a] = the numbers of correctly classified cases

4 In what regards interpretability, a set of propositional rules as well as the corresponding measures of precision) speaks for itself. In fact, the use of natural (logical type) language makes the profiles and the structure of classification easy to interpret thus proving to be very appealing to practitioners.

Some limitations of this approach may also be considered:

1 C5 results do not include measures of the descriptor's relative importance for discrimination (typically provided by statistical approaches).

2 As the C5 results consistency must be based on cross-validation procedures, the quantity of available data is a critical issue for the proposed approach.

In what concerns the first limitation some insight concerning the relative importance of descriptors based on the classification tree construction may be obtained, presuming that descriptors that are first selected for node splitting are more discriminant. This is, naturally, an empirical approach and further research will, thus, be needed to confirm that these results are consistent with those provided by significant tests, for example.

8.4 Multidimensional Scaling

Multidimensional scaling (MS) is a measurement technique concerned mainly with the representation of relationship, differences, dissimilarities (or similarities), substitutability, interaction, etc., among behavioral data such as perceptions, preferences and attitudes. The input data on various objects (variables) which are to be analyzed are collected from the subjects (respondents) by a number of direct or indirect questions. The questions can be either of Likert type (i.e. a 5-point scale questionnaire indicating the level of agreement or disagreement to statements) or, alternatively, asking each of the respondents to rank the variables to be investigated (for example, products, brands, characteristics, etc.). When the number of variables investigated are n, the number of all possible relationships among these variables (along k dimensions) are $n(n1)/2$. In order to visualize and quantify the overall attitudinal data of these respondents with regard to the n variables investigated along (k) dimensions, the data should be input onto one of the available software packages.

The solution (output) of the MS computer program is of a metric nature, consisting of a geometric configuration, usually in 2 or 3 dimensions. The distances between the variables (objects) and/or respondents (subjects) investigated, which are presented as points in the configuration, represent the (dis)similarity, substitutability, relationship, etc. Multidimensional scaling is used particularly in its non-metric version, the non-metric multidimensional scaling (NMS). The advantage of NMS in relation to, say, factor or cluster analyses is the ability to see the entire structure of variables together and to obtain metric output, from attitudinal (non-metric) input data. In addition, NMS enables easy comprehension of the results since the decision maker can visualize and assess the relationships among the variables.

Multidimensional scaling and non-metric multidimensional scaling in particular have been successfully applied in investigating various marketing problems (for example, market research, sales and market share, market segmentation, determination of marketing mix, consumer buyer behavior, brand positioning, branch preference, export marketing, etc.). An introduction to multidimensional scaling is presented by Diamantopoulos and Schlegelmilch (1997). Discussion on when to use NMS techniques in marketing research is offered by Coates et al. (1994).

8.5 Conjoint Analysis

This technique is concerned with the joint effects of two or more independent variables on the ordering of a dependent variable. Conjoint analysis, like multidimensional scaling, is concerned with the measurement of psychological judgments, such as consumer preferences. Products are essentially bundles of attributes, such as price and color. For example, conjoint analysis software generates a deck of cards, each of which combines levels of these product attributes. Respondents are asked to sort the cards generated into an order of preference. Conjoint analysis then assigns a value to each level and produces a ready-reckoner to calculate the preference for each chosen combination. The preference logic of conjoint analysis is as follows. The respondent had to base his or her overall ranking of the versions on an evaluation of the attributes presented. The values that the individual implicitly assigns each attribute associated with the most preferred brand must, in total, sum to a greater value than those associated with the second most-preferred brand. The same relationship must hold for the second and third most-preferred brands, the third and fourth most-preferred brands and so forth. The computation task then is to find a set of values that will meet these requirements.

Potential areas of application for conjoint analysis include product design, new product concept descriptions and testing, price–value relationships, attitude measurement, promotional congruence testing, the study of functional versus symbolic product characteristic, and to rank a hypothetical product against existing competitors already in the market and suggest modifications to existing products which would help to strengthen a products performance. The limitations of conjoint analysis are quite clear when, for example, we are using this technique to predict trial rate. These include:

1. Utility measurement rather than actual purchase behavior is used as the predictor.

2. The configuration of elements used in the concepts may not be complete.

3. In the case of a new product that differs substantially from its principal competitors, the same elements cannot be used for aggregating utilities.

4. The effects of promotion and distribution effort on competitive reaction are not considered.

5. Perceptions from a concept statement and those from the actual product may differ.

6 New products may take several years to reach the market, during which time customer preferences and competitive products may have undergone substantial changes.

Conjoint analysis has been applied widely on consumer research (Vriens, 1994), in advertising evaluation (Stanton and Reese, 1983) and other commercial uses (Cattin and Wittink, 1982).

8.6 Correspondence Analysis

Correspondence analysis is a visual or graphical technique for representing multi-dimensional tables. It can often be impossible to identify any relationships in a table and very difficult to account for what is happening. Correspondence analysis unravels the table and presents data in an easy-to-understand chart. One approach for generating maps uses cross-classification data (e.g. brands rated as having or not having a set of attributes) as a basis (Hoffman and Franke, 1986). In this approach both brands and attributes are simultaneously portrayed in a single space. This technique is particularly useful to identify market segments, track brand image, position a product against its competition and determine who non-respondents in a survey most closely resemble. Correspondence analysis shows the relationships between rows and columns of a correspondence or a cross-tabulation table. This method can be used for analyzing binary, discrete or/and continuous data. CA belongs to the family of multidimensional scaling techniques and could be employed to scale a matrix of non-negative data to represent points (described by rows or columns) in a lower dimensional space. It facilitates both within- and between-set squared distance comparisons (Carroll et al., 1986) and the results could be represented graphically and used as such in marketing investigations.

Figure 8.1 shows the different stages of correspondence analysis. The results of a cross-tabulation is used as raw data in a correspondence analysis. The specific mathematics involved in correspondence analysis can be found in Greenacre (1984).

Figure 8.2 presents the output of a study that maps out how bank branch personnel in various roles see themselves (internal perceptions) and what are their colleagues' (external) perceptions with regard to the 27 selling bank branch functions identified (Meidan and Lim, 1993). The figures represent the output of a study where respondents were asked who they felt were mainly responsible for the selling function of identifying customers' needs in a bank. The responses of various function holders are indicated by the triangular signs on the map (e.g. counselor, manager, business development officer, etc.). The respondents themselves were grouped into three categories indicated by the circles (e.g. lower grades (cashier, statements clerk), middle grades (counselors, officers), managerial grades (branch managers, etc.)).

The interpretation of data output is fairly straightforward, although not all dimensions could be labeled. The closer two points are on the map, the closer the relationship. For example:

1 Lower grades tend to believe that the enquiries clerk and receptionist are mainly responsible for identifying customer needs.

Latent Analysis

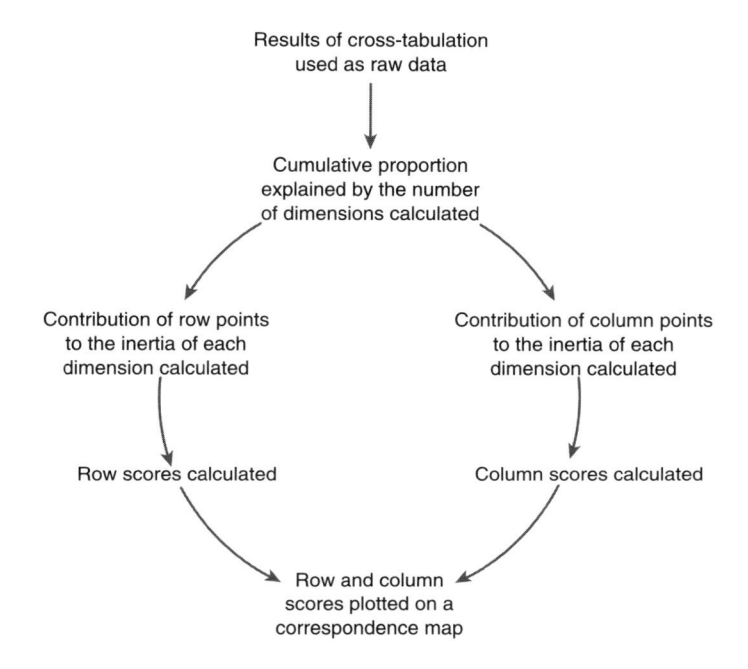

```
                    Results of cross-tabulation
                         used as raw data
                                │
                                ▼
                    Cumulative proportion
                    explained by the number
                    of dimensions calculated
                       ╱              ╲
                      ▼                ▼
        Contribution of row points    Contribution of column points
           to the inertia of each        to the inertia of each
           dimension calculated          dimension calculated
                   │                          │
                   ▼                          ▼
         Row scores calculated       Column scores calculated
                       ╲              ╱
                        ▼            ▼
                       Row and column
                       scores plotted on a
                       correspondence map
```

Figure 8.1 *Procedural steps for correspondence analysis*

2 Middle grades, however, are more inclined to see this as mainly the counselors' responsibility. Some middle grades also tend to consider it the responsibility of cashiers, investment officers or everyone (all).

3 Managerial grades believe that this function is mainly their own responsibility. These beliefs of various role players within the branch are, of course, of paramount importance, as it might lead to under-training for certain function(s) at grade levels, where customer contact is higher. Therefore, this kind of study could focus the training efforts and needs for specific selling functions and certain grade levels/roles.

8.7 Latent Analysis

Latent structure analysis (LA) is a statistical technique somewhat related to factor analysis, which can be used as a framework for investigating causal systems involving both manifest variables and latent factors having discrete components. Latent structure analysis shares the objective of factor analysis, i.e. first, to extract important factors and express relationships of variables with these factors, and second, to classify respondents into typologies.

The latent class model treats the manifest categorical variables as imperfect indicators of underlying traits, which are themselves inherently unobservable. The latent class model treats the observable (manifest) categorical variables as imperfect

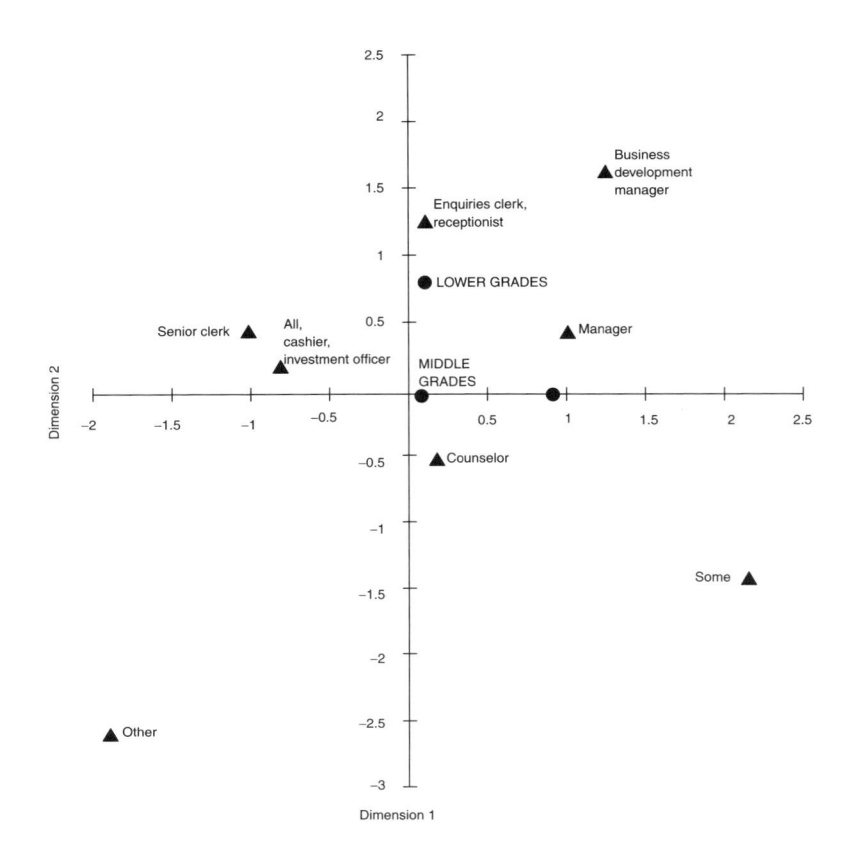

Figure 8.2 *Success and the experience of the sales staff*
Source: Meidan and Lim, 1993.

indicators of underlying traits, which are themselves inherently unobservable (latent). This technique is appropriate for the analysis of data with discrete components.

Essentially, LA attempts to explain the observed association between the manifest variables by introducing one (or more) other variables. Thus, the basic motivation behind latent analysis is the belief that the observed association between two or more manifest categorical variables is due to the mixing of heterogeneous groups. In this sense, latent analysis can be viewed as a data-unmixing procedure. This assumption of conditional independence is directly analogous to the assumption in the factor-analytic model.

The main advantage of latent analysis is that it could be used for investigating causal systems involving latent variables. A very flexible computer program for maximum likelihood latent structure analysis, called MLLSA, is available to marketing researchers. Latent class models have great potential and no doubt will be used more frequently in marketing investigations in the future.

One of the major limitations related to LA concerns the estimation problem, which previously made this class of models largely inaccessible to most marketing researchers. This problem was later solved by formulating latent class models in the same way as in the general framework of log-linear models. Latent structure analysis models have been used in segmentation research, consumer behavior analysis, advertising research and market structure analysis.

One of the best papers in this field is by Dillon and Mulani (1989). A number of latent structure models have been developed (DeSarbo, 1993) for problems associated with traditional customer response modeling (for example, for more regression, conjoint analysis, structural equation models, multidimensional scaling, limited dependent variables, etc.). Such latent structure models simultaneously estimate market segment membership and respective model coefficients by market segment, to optimize a common objective function.

8.8 Fuzzy Sets

The fuzzy set theory is a relatively new approach that has been growing steadily since its inception in the mid-1960s. In the fuzzy set theory, an abstract concept such as a sunny day can be considered as a fuzzy set and defined mathematically by assigning to each individual in the universe of discourse, a value representing its grade of membership in the fuzzy set. This grade corresponds to the degree to which that individual is similar or compatible with the concept represented by the fuzzy set. Thus, individuals may belong in the fuzzy set to a greater or lesser degree as indicated by a larger or smaller membership grade. These membership grades are very often represented by real member values ranging in the closed interval between 0 and 1. Thus, a fuzzy set representing our concept of sunniness might assign a degree of membership 1 to a cloud cover of 0%, 0.8 to a cloud cover of 20%, 0.4 to a cloud cover of 30% and 0 to a cloud cover of 75%. These grades signify the degree to which each percentage of cloud cover approximates our subjective concept of sunniness, and the set itself models the semantic flexibility inherent in such a common linguistic term. Vagueness in describing many consumer behavior constructs is intrinsic, not the result of a lack of knowledge about the available rating. That is why a great variety of definitions in marketing exist and most of them cannot describe the fuzzy concepts completely. So long as the semantic assessment facets in the construct can be quantified and explicitly defined by corresponding membership functions, the initial steps of the mathematical definition of marketing constructs are achieved. Recognizing the difficulty of accurate quantification of the semantic assessment facets like product interest, hedonic value and others, some researchers utilize the fuzzy mathematical method (Klir and Yuan, 1995; Zimmerman, 1991) to quantify the assessment facets by membership functions so that the results obtained are more accurate than the traditional statistical methods and more suitable for the semantically modified assessment facets.

The benefits of using fuzzy sets are:

1. The membership function is deliberately designed in fuzzy set theory to treat the vagueness caused by natural language. Therefore, using membership functions to assess the semantically defined measuring facets is more reliable

and accurate than using the traditional statistical methods to score points or scatterplot.

2 The membership function standardizes the semantic meaning of assessment facets so that we can compare the degree of the definition of marketing constructs regardless of the differences of timing, situation, consumer and so on.

3 The membership functions are continuous functions which are more accurate in measuring the assessment facets than the traditional discrete methods.

4 The fuzzy mathematical method is easier to perform than the traditional method, once the membership of assessment facets are defined.

Some of the main characteristics, advantages, limitations and applications of simulation and fuzzy sets in marketing are presented in Table 8.4 below:

Table 8.4 *Fuzzy set theory*

BASED ON	MARKETING APPLICATIONS
Vagueness concerning the description of the semantics of the terms. It is essentially a factual modeling process that attempts to fine-tune the expression of knowledge. It does this via using a linguistic scale describing the characteristics under each of the main dimensions of the model to form fuzzy sets; a hierarchical aggregation of information based on fuzzy aggregation operators; and a conceptual hypercube to determine the rank and ranking size of the outcomes. Includes the concept of membership function (between 0 and 1).	Modeling consumer behavior. Marketing planning (Diagnosis and Prognosis). New product testing. Perceived price testing. Marketing communication effects research.
MAIN ADVANTAGE	**MAIN LIMITATIONS**
Flexibility which accommodates a degree of uncertainty or fuzziness, in diagnosis. This fuzziness is indeed lauded as realistic in expressing human judgment.	Difficult measurement scaling and estimation of the bipolar descriptors. Linguistic scale for characteristics description. Description of the values for the parameters of the model.

8.9 Fuzzy Decision Trees

Inductive decision trees were first introduced in 1963 with the Concept Learning System Framework. Since then they have continued to be developed and applied. The structure of a decision tree starts with a root decision node, from which all branches originate. A branch is a series of nodes where decisions are made at each node enabling progression through (down) the tree. A progression stops at a leaf node, where a decision classification is given.

As with many data analysis techniques (e.g. traditional regression models), decision trees have been developed within a fuzzy environment. For example, the well-known decision tree method ID3 was developed to include fuzzy entropy measures. The fuzzy decision tree method was introduced by Yuan and Shaw (1995) to take account of cognitive uncertainty, i.e. vagueness and ambiguity.

Central to any method within a fuzzy environment is the defining of the required membership functions. Incorporating a fuzzy aspect (using membership functions) enables the judgments to be made with linguistic scales.

Summary of fuzzy decision tree method: In this section a brief description of the functions used in the fuzzy decision tree method are exposited. A fuzzy set A in a universe of discourse U is characterized by a membership function μ_A which take values in the interval [0, 1]. For all $\mu \in U$, the intersection $A \cap B$ of two fuzzy sets is given by $\mu_{A \cap B} = \min(\mu_A(u), \mu_A(u))$.

A membership function $\mu(x)$ of a fuzzy variable Y defined on X, can be viewed as a possibility distribution of Y on X, i.e. $\pi(x) = \mu(x)$, for all $x \in X$. The possibilistic measure $- E_\alpha(Y)$ of ambiguity is defined as:

$$E_\alpha(Y) = g(\pi) = \sum_{i=1}^{n}(\pi^* - \pi^*_{i+1})\ln[i],$$

where $\pi^* = \{\pi_1^*, \pi_2^*, \ldots, \pi_n^*\}$ is the permutation of the possibility distribution $\pi = \{\pi(x_1), \pi(x_2), \ldots, \pi(x_n)\}$, sorted so that $\pi_i^* \geq \pi_{i+1}^*$ for $i = 1, \ldots, n$, and $\pi_{i+1}^* = 0$.

The ambiguity of attribute A is then:

$$E_\alpha(A) = \frac{1}{m}\sum_{i=1}^{m} E \propto (A(u_i)),$$

where $E \propto (A(u_i)) = g(\mu_{Ts}(u_i)/\max_{1 \leq j \leq s}(\mu_{Tj}(u_i)))$, with T the linguistic scales used within an attribute.

The fuzzy subsethood $S(A, B)$ measures the degree to which A is a subset of B (see Kosko, 1986) and is given by:

$$S(A, B) = \frac{\sum_{u \in U} \min(\mu_A(u), \mu_B(u))}{\sum_{u \in U} \mu_A(u)}$$

Given fuzzy evidence E, the possibility of classifying an object to Class C can be defined as:

$$\mu = (C_i \backslash E) = \frac{S(E, C_i)}{\max_j S(E, C_j)}$$

where $S(E, C)$ represents the degree of truth for the classification rule.

Knowing a single piece of evidence (i.e. a fuzzy value from an attribute) the classification ambiguity based on this fuzzy evidence is defined as:

$$G(E) = g(\pi(C \backslash E))$$

The classification ambiguity with fuzzy partitioning $P = \{E_1, \ldots, E_k\}$ on the fuzzy evidence F, denoted as $G(P \backslash F)$, is the weighted average of classification ambiguity with each subset of partition:

$$G(P \backslash F) = \sum_{i=1}^{k} w(E_i \backslash F) G(E_i \cap F),$$

Where $G(E_i \cap F)$ is the classification ambiguity with fuzzy evidence $E_i \cap F$, $w(E_i \backslash F)$ is the weight which represents the relative size of subset $E_i \cap F$ in F.

$$w(E_i|F) = \frac{\sum_{u \in U} min(\mu_{Ei}(u), \mu_F(u))}{\sum_{j=1}^{k} \left[\sum_{u \in U} min(\mu_{Ei}(u), \mu_F(u)) \right]}$$

The fuzzy decision tree method considered here utilizes these functions. In summary, attributes are assigned to nodes based on the lowest level of ambiguity. A node becomes a leaf node if the level of subsethood (based on the conjunction (intersection) of the branches from the root) is higher than some truth value β assigned to the whole of the decision tree. The classification from the leaf node is to the decision class with the largest subsethood value.

The results of the decision tree, are classification rules each with an associated degree of truth in their classification. These rules are relatively simple to read and apply.

8.10 Artificial Intelligence

Artificial intelligence (AI) models have emerged in the last few years as a follow-up to simulation, attempting to portray, comprehend and analyze the reasoning in a range of situations. Although the two methods of artificial intelligence (expert systems and neural networks) are, in a certain sense, simulations, because of the importance and the potential of these methods, we have introduced them under a separate stand-alone heading.

8.11 Expert Systems

Simply defined, an expert system is a computer program which contains human knowledge or expertise which it can use to generate reasoned advice or instructions.

8.11.1 Method based on marketing main advantages main limitations applications

The knowledge base is usually represented internally in the machine as a set of IF ... THEN rules and the inference engine of the expert system matches together appropriate combinations of rules in order to generate conclusions.

In determining whether a particular marketing domain is suited for this methodology the following checklist is useful:

- Are the key relationships in the domain logical rather than computational? In practical terms, the answer requires an assessment of whether the decision area is knowledge-intensive (e.g. generating new product areas) or data-intensive (e.g. allocating an advertising budget across media).

- Is the problem domain semi-structured rather than structured or unstructured? If the problem is well structured, a traditional approach using sequential procedures will be more efficient than an expert system approach. This would be true, for example, when the entire problem-solving sequence can be enumerated in advance.

- Is knowledge in the domain structured? If the problem is well structured, a traditional approach using sequential procedures will be more efficient than an expert system approach. This would be true, for example, when the entire problem-solving sequence can be enumerated in advance. Moreover, for highly unstructured domains, expert system performance may be disappointing because the available problem-solving strategies may be inadequate.

- Is knowledge in the domain incomplete? In other words, is it difficult to identify all the important variables or to specify fully their interrelationships? Expert systems are particularly applicable in domains with incomplete knowledge.

- Will problem solving in the domain require a direct interface between the manager and the computer system? A direct interface may be necessary in situations calling for online decision support. Such situations generally are characterized by a high level of decision urgency (e.g. buying and selling stocks) or complexity (e.g. retail site selection). Expert systems are particularly useful in these contexts because of their flexible and friendly user–interaction facilities coupled with their ability to explain their reasoning (Rangaswamy et al., 1989). A number of expert systems in marketing have been developed over the years, in particular focusing on the following domains: marketing research, test marketing, pricing, generation of advertising appeals, choice of promotional technique, selection of effective sales techniques, negotiation strategies, site selection, allocation of marketing budget, promotion evaluation, strategic positioning, strategic marketing, assessment of sales territories, brand management, marketing planning, international marketing, bank marketing, tourism marketing and industrial marketing (see Curry and Moutinho, 1991).

The greatest single problem with regard to the effectiveness and applicability of expert system models in the management and marketing context concerns the construction and validation of the knowledge base.

8.12 Fuzzy Logic and Fuzzy Expert Systems

The domain expert's reasoning processes are already structured in a manner developed over the years, different from any other individual in the world. The precise way in which a part of his knowledge and skill are made available to others through a computer program has to be worked out on a highly individual basis through the domain expert – knowledge engineer interaction.

Fortunately, the tools of fuzzy systems theory make it possible for this interaction to take place mainly in terms of words, many of which are already familiar to both. The concepts of fuzzy logic are already a part of every individual's knowledge; what is new is the development of theory to formalize everyday non-formal thinking concepts, and use them in computer programming.

Most of us have had some contact with conventional logic at some point in our lives. In conventional logic, a statement is either true or false, with nothing in between. This principle of true or false was formulated by Aristotle some 2000 years ago as the law of the excluded middle, and has dominated Western logic ever since.

Of course, the idea that things must be either true or false is in many cases nonsense. Is the statement 'I am good' completely true or completely false? Probably neither. How about 'I am rich'? This can be true (Donald Trump) or false (Skid Row), but how about most of us? The idea of gradations of truth is familiar to everyone.

Fuzzy logic offers a better way of representing reality. In fuzzy logic, a statement is true to various degrees, ranging from completely true through half-truth to completely false.

Topics covered by Fuzzy expert systems include general purpose fuzzy expert systems, processing imperfect information using structured frameworks, fuzzy linguistic inference network generator, fuzzy associative memories, the role of approximate reasoning in medical expert systems, MILORD (a fuzzy expert systems shell), COMAX (which is an autonomous fuzzy expert system for tactical communications networks (...). Fuzzy expert systems provide an invaluable reference resource for researchers and students in artificial intelligence (AI) and approximate reasoning (AR), as well as for other researchers looking for methods to apply similar tools in their own designs of intelligent systems.

8.13 Rough Set Theory

Rough set theory (RST) is a fairly new approach to decision making in the presence of uncertainty and vagueness (Pawlak, 1997). Rough set theory was first introduced by Zdzislaw Pawlak in the early 1980s, as a new mathematical tool to deal with vagueness and uncertainty. This approach seems to be of fundamental importance to artificial intelligence (AI) and cognitive sciences, especially in the areas of machine learning, knowledge discovery from databases, expert systems, decision support systems, inductive reasoning and pattern recognition. One of the main advantages of RST is that it does not need any preliminary of additional information about data, such as probability distributions or basic probability assignments. This means that RST has numerous real-world applications (Pawlak et al., 1995).

The main concept of RST is an indiscernabilty relation normally associated with a set of attributes. The key problem in this description is the informal term 'normally associated'. In real life, such an association does not exist until additional assumptions are made. The subjectivity issue is more complicated than in other methods for managing uncertainty, therefore RST is potentially an important tool in the analysis of data with important applications in data mining and knowledge discovery. However, claims of its superiority (objectivity) over other approaches remains to be substantiated by scientific evidence (Koczkodaj et al., 1988). The results of RST are a set of 'if ... then ...' rules which enable prediction of classification of objects.

The critical issues of data mining were examined by Lingras and Yao (1998) who used the theory of rough sets, which is a recent proposal for generalizing classical set theory the Pawlak rough set model is based on the concept of an equivalence relation. Research has shown that a generalized rough set model need not be based on equivalence relations axioms. Lingras and Yao (1998) demonstrated that a generalized rough set model could be used for generating rules from incomplete databases. These rules are based on plausibility functions. These authors also emphasized the importance of rule extraction from incomplete databases in data mining.

A RST approach was used by Dimitras et al. (1999) to provide a set of rules able to discriminate between healthy and failing firms in order to predict business failure. The evaluation of its prediction ability was the main objective of the study. The results were very encouraging, compared with those from discriminate and logit analyses, and proved the usefulness of the method. The rough set approach discovers relevant subsets of characteristics and represents in these terms all important relationships between the key constructs. The method analyzes only facts hidden in the input data and communicates with the decision maker in the material language of rules derived from his or her experience.

A recent development on RST is the variable precision rough set model (VPRS), by Ziarko (1993a, 1993b). Unlike RST which constructs deterministic rules (i.e. 100% in correct classification by a rule) VPRS enables a level of confidence in correct classification by a rule. That is, they are probabilistic rules.

Dissatisfied customers pose numerous potential problems for any organization, for example, negative word of mouth, reduced change of repeat lower brand loyalty. All of these problems will negatively affect the measurements of any business, e.g. profits and market shares. Therefore, assessing customer satisfaction level and more importantly why they are dissatisfied has great benefits to any company. This is particularly true in highly competitive globalized markets, where search costs are low and the cost of switching supplier negligible.

8.14 Variable Precision Rough Sets (VPRS)

A further RST innovation has been the development by Ziarko (1993b) of a variable precision rough sets (VPRS) model, which incorporates probabilistic decision rules. This is an important extension, since as noted by Kattan and Cooper (1998), when discussing computer-based decision techniques in a corporate failure setting. In real-world decision making, the patterns of classes often overlap, suggesting that predictor information may be incomplete ... This lack of information results in probabilistic decision making, where perfect prediction accuracy is not expected. An et al. (1996) applied VPRS (which they termed Enhanced RST) to generating probabilistic rules to predict the demand for water. Relative to the traditional rough set approach, VPRS has the additional desirable property of allowing for partial classification compared to the complete classification required by RST. More specifically, when an object is classified using RST it is assumed that there is complete certainty that it is a correct classification. In contrast, VPRS facilitates a degree of confidence in classification, invoking a more informed analysis of the data, which is achieved through the use of a majority inclusion relation. This chapter extends previous work by providing an empirical exposition of VPRS, where we present the results of an experiment which applies VPRS rules to the corporate failure decision. In addition, we mitigate the impact of using the subjective views of an expert (as employed in previous studies) to discretize the data, by utilizing the sophisticated FUSINTER discretization technique which is applied to a selection of attributes (variables) relating to companies' financial and non-financial characteristics. The discretized data, in conjunction with other nominal attributes, are then used in this new VPRS framework to identify rules to classify companies in a failure setting. To facilitate a comparison of our experimental VPRS results with those of existing techniques, we present the predictive ability of classical statistical methods logit analysis and MDA together with 2 more closely related non-parametric decision-tree methods, RPA and the Elysée method, which utilizes ordinal discriminant analysis.

8.14.1 An overview of VPRS

VPRS (as with RST) operates on what may be described as a decision table or information system. As is illustrated in Table 8.5, a set of objects $U(o_1, \ldots, o_7)$ are contained in the rows of the table. The columns denote condition attributes $C(c_1, \ldots, c_6)$ of these objects and a relate *decision attribute* $D(d)$. A value denoting the nature of an attribute to an object is called a descriptor. As noted above, a VPRS data requirement is that it must be in discrete or categorical form.

Table 8.5 shows that, with this particular example, the condition attribute descriptors comprise 0s and 1s (for example, denoting yes and no answers), and the decision attribute values are L and H (for example, denoting low and high). The table shows that the objects have been classified into one of these decision values, which are also referred to as *concepts*. For the condition attributes in this example, all of the objects (U) can be placed in five groups: $X_1 = \{o_1, o_4, o_6\}$, $X_2 = \{o_2\}$, $X_3 = \{o_3\}$, $X_4 = \{o_5\}$ and $X_5 = \{o_7\}$. The objects within a group are indiscernible to each other so that,

Variable Precision Rough Sets (VPRS)

Table 8.5 *Example of a decision table*

Objects	Condition attributes (c)						Decision attribute (d)
	c_1	c_2	c_3	c_4	c_5	c_6	d
o_1	1	0	1	1	0	1	L
o_2	1	0	0	0	0	0	L
o_3	0	0	1	0	0	0	L
o_4	1	0	1	1	0	1	H
o_5	0	0	0	0	1	1	H
o_6	1	0	1	1	0	1	H
o_7	0	0	0	0	1	0	H

objects o_1, o_4 and o_6 in X_1 have the same descriptor values for each of the condition attributes. These groups of objects are referred to as *equivalence classes* or *conditional classes*, for the specific attributes. The equivalence classes for the decision attribute are: $Y_L = \{o_1, o_2, o_3\}$ and $Y_H = \{o_4, o_5, o_6, o_7\}$. The abbreviation of the set of equivalence classes for the conditional attributes C, is denoted by $E(C) = \{X_1, X_2, X_3, X_4, X_5\}$ and for the decision attribute, it is defined $E(D) = \{Y_L, Y_H\}$. VPRS measurement is based on ratios of elements contained in various sets. A case in point is the conditional probability of a concept given a particular set of objects (a condition class). For example:

$$Pr(Y_L|X_1) = Pr(\{o_1, o_2, o_3\}|\{o_1, o_4, o_6\})$$
$$= \frac{|\{o_1, o_2, o_3\} \cap \{o_1, o_4, o_6\}|}{|\{o_1, o_4, o_6\}|}$$
$$= 0.333$$

It follows that this measures the accuracy of the allocation of the conditional class X_1 to the decision class Y_L. Hence for a given probability value β, the β-positive region corresponding to a concept is delineated as the set of objects with conditional probabilities of allocation at least equal to β. More formally:

$$\beta\text{-positive region of the set } Z \subseteq U : POS_P^\beta(Z)$$
$$= \bigcup_{Pr(Z|X_i) \geq \beta} \{X_i \in E(P)\} \text{ with } P \subseteq C.$$

Following An et al. (1996), β is defined to lie between 0.5 and 1.0. Hence for the current example, the condition equivalence class $X_1 = \{o_1, o_4, o_6\}$ have a majority inclusion (with at least 60% majority needed, i.e. $\beta = 0.6$) in Y_H, in that most objects (2 out of 3) in X_1 belong in Y_H. Hence X_1 is in $POS_C^{0.6}(Y_H)$. It follows $POS_C^{0.6}(Y_H) = \{o_1, o_4, o_5, o_6, o_7\}$. Corresponding expressions for the β-boundary and β-negative regions are given by Ziarko (1993c) as follows:

β-boundary region of the set $Z \subseteq U : BND_P^\beta(Z)$

$$= \bigcup_{1-\beta \langle Pr(Z|X_i)\rangle \geq \beta} \{X_i \in E(P)\} \text{ with } P \subseteq C,$$

β-negative region of the set $Z \subseteq U : NEG_P^\beta(Z)$

$$= \bigcup_{Pr(Z|X_i) \leq 1-\beta} \{X_i \in E(P)\} \text{ with } P \subseteq C.$$

Using P and Z from the previous example, with $\beta = 0.6$, then $BND_C^{0.6}(Y_H) = 0$ (empty set) and $NEG_C^{0.6}(Y_H) = \{o_2, o_3\}$. Similarly for the decision class Y_L it follows $POS_C^{0.6}(Y_L)\{o_2, o_3\}$, $BND_C^{0.6}(Y_L) = 0$ and $NEG_C^{0.6}(Y_L) = \{o_1, o_4, o_5, o_6, o_7\}$.

VPRS applies these concepts by first seeking subsets of the attributes, which are capable (via construction of decision rules) of explaining allocations given by the whole set of condition attributes. These subsets of attributes are termed *β-reducts* or *approximate reducts*. Ziarko (1993c) states that a *β-reduct*, a subset P of the set of conditional attributes C with respect to a set of decision attributes D, must satisfy the following conditions: (i) that the subset P offers the same quality of classification (subject to the same β value) as the whole set of condition attributes C; and (ii) that no attribute can be eliminated from the subset P without affecting the quality of the classification (subject to the same β value).

The quality of the classification is defined as the proportion of the objects made up of the union of the β-positive regions of all the decision equivalence classes based on the condition equivalence classes for a subset P of the condition attributes C.

As with decision tree techniques, ceteris paribus, a clear benefit to users of VPRS is the ability to interpret individual rules in a decision-making context (as opposed to interpreting coefficients in conventional statistical models). Hence VPRS-generated rules are relatively simple, comprehensible and are directly interpretable with reference to the decision domain. For example, users are not required to possess the technical knowledge and expertise associated with interpreting classical models. These VPRS characteristics are particularly useful to decision makers, who are interested in interpreting the rules (based on factual cases) with direct reference to the outcomes they are familiar with.

8.15 Dempster-Shafer Theory

The Dempster-Shafer Theory (DST) of evidence originated in the work of Dempster (1967) on the theory of probabilities with upper and lower bounds. It has since been extended by numerous authors and popularized, but only to a degree, in the literature on Artificial Intelligence (AI) and Expert Systems, as a technique for modeling reasoning under uncertainty. In this respect it can be seen to offer numerous advantages over the more traditional methods of statistics and Bayesian decision theory. Hajek (1994) remarked that real, practical applications of DST methods have been rare, but subsequent to these remarks there has been a marked increase in the applications incorporating the use of DST. Although DST is not in widespread use, it has been applied with some success to such topics as face recognition (Ip and Ng, 1994), statistical classification (Denoeux, 1995) and target identification (Buede and Girardi, 1997). Additional applications centered around multi-source information, including plan recognition (Bauer, 1996).

Applications in the general areas of business decision making are in fact quite rare. An exception is the paper by Cortes-Rello and Golshani (1990), which although written for a computing science/AI readership does deal with the knowledge domain of forecasting and marketing planning. The DST approach is as yet very largely unexploited.

Decision analysis relies on a subjectivist view of the use of probability, whereby the probability of an event indicates the degree to which someone believes it, rather than the alternative frequentist approach. The latter approach is based only on the number of times an event is observed to occur. Bayesian statisticians may agree that their goal is to estimate objective probabilities from frequency data, but they advocate using subjective prior probabilities to improve the estimates.

Shafer and Pearl (1990) noted that the three defining attributes of the Bayesian approach are:

1 Reliance on a complete probabilistic model of the domain or frame of discernment.

2 Willingness to accept subjective judgments as an expedient substitute for empirical data.

3 The use of Bayes theorem (conditionality) as the primary mechanism for updating beliefs in light of new information.

However, the Bayesian technique is not without its critics, including among others Walley (1987), as well as Caselton and Luo (1992) who discussed the difficulty arising when conventional Bayesian analysis is presented only with weak information sources. In such cases we have the Bayesian dogma of precision, whereby the information concerning uncertain statistical parameters, no matter how vague, must be represented by conventional, exactly specified, probability distributions.

Some of the difficulties can be understood through the Principle of Insufficient Reason, as illustrated by Wilson (1992). Suppose we are given a random device that randomly generates integer numbers between 1 and 6 (its frame of discernment), but with unknown chances. What is our belief in 1 being the next number? A Bayesian will use a symmetry argument, or the principle of insufficient reason to say that the Bayesian belief in a 1 being the next number, say P(1) should be 1/6. In general in a situation of ignorance a Bayesian is forced to use this principle to evenly allocate subjective (additive) probabilities over the frame of discernment.

To further understand the Bayesian approach, especially with the regard to representation of ignorance, consider the following example, similar to that in Wilson (1992). Let a be a proposition that;

> I live in Byres Road, Glasgow.

How could one construct $P(a)$, a Bayesian belief in a? Firstly we must choose a frame of discernment, denoted by Θ and a subset A of Θ representing the proposition

a; then would need to use the Principle of Insufficient Reason to arrive at a Bayesian belief. The problem is there are a number of possible frames of discernment Θ that we could choose, depending effectively on how many Glasgow roads can be enumerated. If only two such streets are identifiable, then $\Theta = \{x_1, x_2\}$, $A = \{x_1\}$. The principle of insufficient reason then gives $P(A)$, to be 0.5, through evenly allocating subjective probabilities over the frame of discernment. If it is estimated that there are about 1,000 roads in Glasgow, then $\Theta = \{x_1, x_2, \ldots, x_{1000}\}$ with again $A = \{x_1\}$ and the other xs representing the other roads. In this case the theory of insufficient reason gives $P(A) = 0.001$.

Either of these frames may be reasonable, but the probability assigned to A is crucially dependent upon the frame chosen. Hence one's Bayesian belief is a function not only of the information given and one's background knowledge, but also of a sometimes arbitrary choice of frame of discernment. To put the point another way, we need to distinguish between uncertainty and ignorance. Similar arguments hold where we are discussing not probabilities per se but weights which measure subjective assessments of relative importance. This issue arises in decision support models such as the analytic hierarchy process (AHP), which requires that certain weights on a given level of the decision tree sum to unity, see Saaty (1980).

The origins of Dempster-Shafer theory go back to the work by A.P. Dempster (1967, 1968) who developed a system of upper and lower probabilities. Following this, his student G. Shafer, in his 1976 book *A Mathematical Theory of Evidence*, added to Dempster's work, including a more thorough explanation of belief functions. Even though DST was not created specifically in relation to AI, the name Dempster-Shafer Theory was coined by J.A. Barnett (1981) in an article which marked the entry of the belief functions into the AI literature. In summary, it is a numerical method for evidential reasoning (a term often used to denote the body of techniques specifically designed for manipulation of reasoning from evidence, based upon the DST of belief functions; see Lowrance et al. (1986).

Following on from the example concerning Glasgow roads in the previous section, one of the primary features of the DST model is that we are relieved of the need to force our probability or belief measures to sum to unity. There is no requirement that belief not committed to a given proposition should be committed to its negation. The total allocation of belief can vary to suit the extent of our knowledge. The second basic idea of DST is that numerical measures of uncertainty may be assigned to overlapping sets and subsets of hypotheses, events or propositions as well as to individual hypotheses. To illustrate, consider the following expression of knowledge concerning murderer identification adapted from Parsons (1994).

Mr Jones has been murdered, and we know that the murderer was one of 3 notorious assassins, Peter, Paul and Mary, so we have a set of hypotheses, i.e. frame of discernment, $\Theta = \{Peter, Paul, Mary\}$. The only evidence we have is that the person who saw the killer leaving is 80% sure that it was a man, i.e. $P(\text{man}) = 0.8$. The measures of uncertainty, taken collectively are known in DST terminology as a basic probability assignment (*bpa*). Hence we have a *bpa*, say m_1 of 0.8 given to the focal element {Peter, Paul}, i.e. $m_1(\{Peter, Paul\}) = 0.8$; since we know nothing about the remaining probability it is allocated to the whole of the frame of the discernment, i.e. $m_1(\{Peter, Paul, Mary\}) = 0.2$.

The key point to note is that assignments to singleton sets may operate at the same time as assignments to sets made up of a number of propositions. Such a situation is simply not permitted in a conventional Bayesian framework, although it is possible to have a Bayesian assignment of prior probabilities for groups of propositions (since conventional probability theory can cope with joint probabilities). As pointed out by Schubert (1994), DST is in this sense a generalization of the Bayesian Theory. It avoids the problem of having to assign non-available prior probabilities and makes no assumptions about non-available probabilities.

The DS/AHP method allows opinions on sets of decision alternatives and addresses some of the concerns inherent within the standard AHP:

- The number of comparison and opinions are at the decision maker's discretion.
- There is no need for consistency checks at the decision alternative level.
- The allowance for ignorance/uncertainty in our judgments.

We remind the reader that the direction of this method is not necessarily towards obtaining the highest ranked decision alternative, but towards reducing the number of serious contenders.

8.16 Chaos Theory

Chaos theory has the potential to contribute valuable insights into the nature of complex systems in the business world. As is often the case with the introduction of a new management metaphor, chaos is now being discovered at all levels of managerial activity (Stacey, 1993).

What is chaos theory?: Chaos theory can be compactly defined as the qualitative study of unstable aperiodic behavior in deterministic non-linear dynamical systems (Kellert, 1993: 2). A researcher can often define a system of interest by representing its important variables and their interrelationships by a set of equations. A system (or, more technically, its equations) is dynamical when the equations are capable of describing changes in the values of system variables from one point in time to another. Non-linear terms involve complicated functions of the system variables such as: $y_t + 1 = x_t y_t$.

Chaos theorists have discovered that even simple non-linear sets of equations can produce complex aperiodic behavior. The most familiar example being the logistic equation of the form: $x_{t+1} = rx_t(1 - x_t)$ where x lies between zero and one. This system is deterministic in the sense that no stochastic or chance elements are involved. Figure 1 depicts the behavior of this system for varying levels of r.

At values of $r < 2$, iterating over the logistic equation will result in the system stabilizing at $x = 0$ (Figure 8.3(a)). Between $r = 2$ and $r = 3$ the system reaches equilibrium at progressively higher and higher values of x (Figure 8.3(b)). At around

$r = 3$ the system is seen to bifurcate into two values. The steady state value of x alternates periodically between two values (Figure 8.3(c)). As r continues to increase it continues to increase in periodicity, alternating between 2, then 4, 8 and 16 points. When r is approximately 3.7 another qualitative change occurs the system becomes chaotic. The output ranges over a seemingly infinite (non-repeating) range of x values (Figure 8.3(d)).

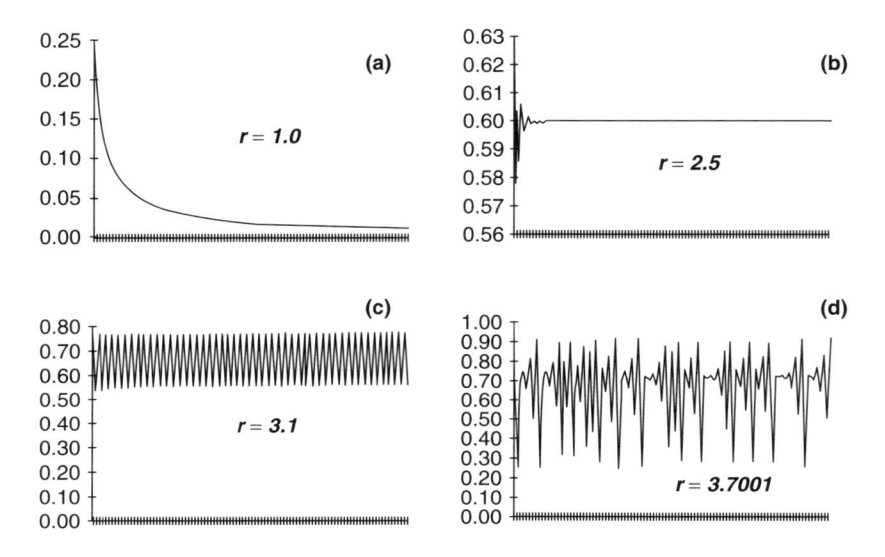

Figure 8.3 *Output of logistic equation for varying r*

Chaotic systems are also unstable, exhibiting a sensitive dependence on initial conditions. The Lyapunov exponent is a mathematically precise measure of the degree of sensitive dependence on initial conditions. The Lyapunov exponent takes the one-dimensional form $e^{\lambda t}$. If $\lambda < 0$ then the initial differences will converge exponentially. If $\lambda = 0$ then the displacements will remain constant over time, while if $\lambda > 0$ small differences will magnify over time. All chaotic systems have a λ value that is greater than zero.

Initially, the system of interest would have to be specified in terms of non-linear dynamical equations. Few researchers in the social sciences have attempted to identify non-linear deterministic behaviors in their systems of interest. In the main, quantitative research in the social sciences has tended to be both statistical and linear in nature. Of course, it is possible that the appeal of chaos theory may excite an interest in developing non-linear models.

The researcher would also need to demonstrate that the system was capable of chaotic behavior over some valid region of its parameters. By running digital simulations of the non-linear systems, researchers would hope to discover regions of chaos in the models that could be linked with phenomena in the observed world. Ideally, the Lyapunov exponent could then by calculated and found to be greater than zero.

8.17 Data Mining

Data mining (DM), or knowledge discovery, is the computer-assisted process of digging through and analyzing enormous sets of data and then extracting the meaning of the data nuggets. DM is being used both to describe past trends and to predict future trends.

8.17.1 Mining and refining data

Experts involved in significant DM efforts agree that the DM process must begin with the business problem. Since DM is really providing a platform or workbench for the analyst, understanding the job of the analyst logically comes first. Once the DM system developer understands the analyst's job, the next step is to understand those data sources that the analyst uses and the experience and knowledge the analyst brings to the evaluation.

The DM process generally starts with collecting and cleaning information, then storing it, typically in some type of data warehouse or datamart. But in some of the more advanced DM work, advanced knowledge representation tools can logically describe the contents of databases themselves, then use this mapping as a meta-layer to the data. Data sources are typically flat files of point-of-sale transactions and databases of all flavors.

DM tools search for patterns in data. This search can be performed automatically by the system (a bottom-up dredging of raw facts to discover connections) or interactively with the analyst asking questions (a top-down search to test hypotheses). A range of computer tools such as neural networks, rule-based systems, case-based reasoning, machine learning, and statistical programs either alone or in combination can be applied to a problem.

Typically with DM, the search process is interactive, so that as analysts review the output, they form a new set of questions to refine the search or elaborate on some aspect of the findings. Once the interactive search process is complete, the data-mining system generates report findings. It is then the job of humans to interpret the results of the mining process and to take action based on those findings.

AT&T, A.C. Nielsen, and American Express are among the growing ranks of companies implementing DM techniques for sales and marketing. These systems are crunching through terabytes of point-of-sale data to aid analysts in understanding consumer behavior and promotional strategies. Why? To increase profitability, of course.

Many marketers believe one of the most powerful competitive weapons is understanding and targeting each customer's individual needs. To this end, more companies are harnessing DM techniques to shed light on customer preferences and buying patterns. With this information, companies can better target customers with products and promotional offerings.

A.C. Nielsen's Spotlight is a good example of a DM tool. Nielsen clients use Spotlight to mine point-of-sale databases. These terabyte-size databases contain facts (e.g. quantities sold, dates of sale, prices) about thousands of products, tracked across hundreds of geographic areas for at least 125 weeks. Spotlight transforms tasks that would take a human from weeks to months to do into which a computer can do in minutes to hours. Nielsen says it has sold about 100 copies of Spotlight (DOS and Windows) to U.S. clients, who have in turn deployed it to field-sales representatives in multiple regional centers. The software frees analysts to work on higher-level projects instead of being swamped by routine, laborious chores.

In the past two years, a global group at Nielsen has changed the U.S. version of Spotlight for use in other countries. Spotlight is the most widely distributed application in the consumer packaged-goods industry, claims Mark Ahrens, director of custom software sales at Nielsen.

American Express is analyzing the shopping patterns of its card holders and using the information to offer targeted promotions.

8.17.2 Siftware

Hardware and software vendors are extolling the DM capabilities of their products whether they have true DM capabilities or not. This hype cloud is creating much confusion about data mining. In reality, data mining is the process of sifting through vast amounts of information in order to extract meaning and discover knowledge.

It sounds simple, but the task of data mining has quickly overwhelmed traditional query-and-report methods of data analysis, creating the need for new tools to analyze databases and date warehouses intelligently. The products now offered for DM range from online analytical processing (OLAP) tools.

8.17.3 Invasion of the data snatchers

The need for DM tools is growing as fast as data stores swell. More-sophisticated DM products are beginning to appear that perform bottom-up as well as top-down mining. The day is probably not too far off when intelligent agent technology will be harnessed for the mining of vast public online sources, traversing the Internet, searching for information and presenting it to the human user.

Data mining is evolving from answering questions about what has happened and why it happened.

A handful of DM tools are sometimes lumped together under the rubric information discovery or knowledge discovery. They often have a resemblance algorithmically speaking to expert systems or AI. Most of these autonomous tools are low-touch but high-tech.

DM can also be defined as discovery tools, which take large amounts of detailed transaction-level data and apply mathematical techniques against it, finding or discovering insights into consumer behavior.

Most humans are better at detecting anomalies than inferring relationships from large data sets, and that's why information discovery can be so useful. Rather than relying on a human to come up with hypotheses that can be confirmed or rejected based on the evidence (i.e. data), good discovery tools will look at the data and essentially generate the hypotheses.

Data Mining

Others have described DM as an intensive search for new information and new combinations pursuing defined paths of inquiry and allowing unexpected results to generate new lines of analysis and further exploration. They are clearly thinking of iterative exploratory techniques of data surfing using MDA or OLAP tools. MDA represents data as n-dimensional matrices called hypercubes. OLAP and related hypercubes let users iteratively calculate metrics such as sales, revenue, market share, or inventory over a subset of available data, by exploring combinations of one or more dimensions of data.

The idea is to load a multidimensional server with data that is likely to be combined. Imagine all the possible ways of analyzing clothing sales: by brand name, size, color, location, advertising, and so on. If you fill a multidimensional hypercube with this data, viewing it from any 2-D perspective (n-dimensional hypercubes have $n*(n-1)$) sides, or views will be easy and fast.

Most businesses need more than a single DM tool. Multidimensional databases, OLAP products, DM, and traditional decision-support tools all belong in your toolbox right alongside standard relational databases.

For example, rather than use an OLAP or hypercube tool, you are better off creating a warehouse using a relational database if you have lots of data or are facing complex loading and consolidation from multiple data sources. Why? Because there's a mature utility market to support those activities. However, don't expect mining operations that represent joins across many multi-row tables to be fast. That's where OLAP servers shine, providing blindingly fast results to queries along predefined dimensions.

8.17.4 Mining with query tools

Most of these tools come with graphing components. Some even support a degree of multidimensionality, such as pivoting, intelligent drilling, crosstab reporting, and time-series analysis. A few are beginning to offer easy-to-use intelligent support (versus alerts that can be established programmatically). If you need to select a new query-and-reporting tool and need to support a mixed environment of PCs and Macs, be sure to make that a feature on your checklist.

You should think of query-and-reporting tools as generic mining tools. They generally support direct access to source data and may offer cross-database joins, but their unbridled use can wreak havoc with production systems. And, given the challenges of performing joins across systems, it may be hard for end users to know if the answer they are getting is accurate.

Because information-discovery tools have only recently gained widespread attention as DM tools, they still tend to be rather technical and best suited for analysts with strong mathematical backgrounds. Look for explosive growth in this area of DM tools as better user interfaces make them easier for end users to harness. As for intelligent agents, especially agents such as Internet gofers and email filters, within a year, you'll wonder how you ever lived without them.

The popularity of DM shows that businesses are looking for new ways to let end users find the data they need to make decisions, serve customers, and gain a competitive advantage. If your workers aren't asking for better mining tools, you'd better ask why.

8.18 Data Mining (knowledge discovery in databases)

Data are a valuable resource. As such, perhaps one can mine the resource for its nuggets of gold. In part, the interest in data mining has been driven by individuals and organizations who find themselves with large data holdings, which they feel ought to be sources of valuable information. They may have little idea what to do with them. Computer hardware and software vendors, hoping to increase their sales, have fanned the interest.

There is no firm distinction between data mining and statistics. Much commercial data mining activity uses relatively conventional statistical methods. A difference is that data miners may be working with quite huge data sets. A data set with values of 20 or 30 variables for each of several hundred thousand records is, in the context of commercial data mining, small.

This more exploratory form of data mining applies a search process to a data set, often a very large data set, and looks for interesting associations. While the data may initially have been collected to answer some primary question or questions, the expectation is that there will be other interesting and potentially useful information in the data. Most experienced statisticians have at some time encountered unexpected and interesting results when, as a prelude to the main analysis, they have set out to do a careful exploratory analysis. Is it possible to set up automatic processes that may bring such results to attention?

Much of the focus of data-mining research has been on ways to find views of data that highlight interesting or unusual features, a search for what statisticians would call outliers. Research on data visualization is in this same tradition.

Some data-mining approaches are fairly specific to individual research areas, such as astrophysics at one extreme or business data processing at the other. There is a need for courses which compare and contrast a variety of statistical methodologies, including decision-tree methods, classical statistical methods and modern regression methods as described.

Perhaps the best way to understand data mining is that it puts a new spin on statistical analysis. The name has been effective, far more than conventional terminology, in selling to business the idea that data can be a valuable resource. Extracting the information requires effort. The sheer size of many of the data sets raises huge computing problems. There has been an inevitable attention to the heavy computing demands. There has not always been a matching attention to statistical issues.

Data miners may come to their task with a database management perspective, with a computing systems perspective, with a statistical perspective, or with a numerical algorithms perspective. Different parts of the data mining literature reflect the different perspectives of those who come to data mining from these different backgrounds. All too often, the technical difficulty of the data management and other computing tasks distracts attention form statistical inference from data issues.

Data Mining

8.18.1 A computing perspective on data mining

Fayyad argues that there may be a misunderstanding of the aims of data mining. Data mining is not about automating data analysis. Data mining is about making analysis more convenient, scaling analysis algorithms to large databases, and providing data owners with easy-to-use tools to help them navigate, visualize, summarize, and model data.

I personally look forward to the proper balance that will emerge from the mixing of computational algorithm-oriented approaches characterizing the database and computer science communities with the powerful mathematical theories and methods for estimation developed in statistics (Fayyad 1998).

Data mining is a set of methods used in the knowledge discovery process to distinguish previously unknown relationships and patterns within data.

Data mining, like all forms of exploratory analysis, is open to abuse. Under torture, the data may yield false confessions. Data mining readily becomes data dredging, a practice that well deserves its bad reputation. Classical inferential procedures may require substantial adaptation, or have little relevance, for data-mining applications with large data sets.

8.18.2 Data-mining tools

Tree-based regression and neural nets have been widely promoted as data-mining tools. Both these methods are beginning to attract interest from the statistical community. The commonest application is discrimination, e.g. a bank may want to distinguish good from bad lending risks. Fayyad et al., (1996) distinguish knowledge discovery in databases (KDD) from data mining. KDD, it is said, refers to the overall process of discovering useful knowledge from data, while data mining refers to the initial step of extracting patterns, without the additional steps designed to check whether these patterns are meaningful.

Decision trees and neural nets seem most effective with very large data sets, with at least some tens of thousands of records. For smaller data sets, parametric methods which build in more structure may be preferable. In the trade-off between sampling variance and model bias, sampling variance may be more serious in data sets with some hundreds of records, while model bias may be more important in data sets with tens of thousands of records. Biases that are inherent in the data themselves are unaffected by sample size.

8.18.3 Try New Data-mining Techniques – they can overcome, augment traditional stat analysis

Data-mining techniques have recently gained popularity with researchers in part because they overcome many of the limitations of traditional statistics and can handle complex data sets. New data-mining applications which are appearing at an explosive rate, offer a powerful complement though not a replacement to statistical techniques, and have useful customer satisfaction research applications.

Researchers typically must try to answer a set of common customer satisfaction questions. For example, companies that are evaluating their continuous improvement programs often study the importance that customers place on different product and service attributes. Some research directly asks respondents to rate the importance of different attributes, but most researchers use statistically inferred ratings of importance. That is, using statistical methods (typically multiple regression), the researchers regress ratings of customer satisfaction with different attributes (independent variables) against overall satisfaction (dependent variable).

But multiple regression and related techniques make numerous assumptions that researchers often violate in practice. For example, a typical problem in customer satisfaction research is high levels of correlation between attributes, which can dramatically affect the statistical value that determines the relative importance of those attributes. If the research shows high levels of correlation between attributes, then that statistical value that determines their relative importance probably will be biased, and the importance ratings are likely to be inaccurate.

Another assumption of statistical analysis that can skew results is that the ratings follow a normal distribution essentially, that the scores will resemble a normal bell curve which isn't the case with customer satisfaction. Past research has shown that data about customer satisfaction is often positively skewed, and that most satisfaction scores fall at the upper end of the scale (for example, in the 8- to 10-point range on a 10-point scale).

Finally, these statistical techniques also assume that the relationships between the independent and dependent variables are linear, even though research has clearly demonstrated that those relationships are often far from a straight line. In many industries, statistical assumptions don't hold and can result in biased and misleading results (Garver 2002).

References

Achabal, D. D., Gorr, W. L. and Mahajan, V. (1982) 'MULTILOC: a multiple store location decision model', *Journal of Retailing*, 58(2): 5–25.
Agresti, A. (1989) 'Tutorial on modelling ordinal categorical response data', *Psychological Bulletin*, 105: 290–301.
Agresti, A. (1990) *Categorical Data Analysis*. New York: John Wiley and Sons, Inc.
Agresti, A. (1996) *An Introduction to Categorical Data Analysis*. New York: John Wiley and Sons, Inc.
Agresti, A. and Finlay, B. (1997) *Statistical Methods for the Social Sciences* (Third edition). Prentice-Hall.
An, A., Shan, N., Chan, C., Cercone, N. and Ziarko, W. (1996) 'Discovering rules for water demand prediction: An Enhanced Rough-Set Approach', *Engineering Applications in Artificial Intelligence*, 9(6): 645–53.
Anderson, E. B. (1997) *Introduction to the Statistical Analysis of Categorical Data*. New York: Springer.
Barford, N. C. (1985) *Experimental Measurements: Precision, Error and Truth* (Second edition). New York: John Wiley and Sons.
Barnett, J. A. (1981) 'Computational methods for a mathematical theory of evidence', *Proceedings 7th International Joint Conference on Artificial Intelligence (IJCAI), Vancouver* Vol II, 868–75.
Barrett, J. P. (1974) 'The coefficient of determination – limitations', *The American Statistician*, 28: 19–20.
Bauer, M. (1996) 'A Dempster-Shafer Approach to Modeling Agent Preferences for Plan Recognition', *User Modeling and User-Adapted Interaction*, 5, 317–48.
Bearden, W. O., Netemeyer, R. G. and Mobley, M. F. (1993) *Handbook of Marketing Scales: Multi-item Measures for Marketing and Consumer Behaviour Research*. London: Sage Publications.
Berndt, E. R. (1991) *The Practice of Econometrics*. London: Addison-Wesley.
Buede, D. M. and Girardi, P. (1997) 'A target identification comparison of Bayesian and Dempster-Shafer multisensor fusion', *IEEE Transaction on Systems, Man and Cybernetics Part A: Systems and Humans*, 27(5), 569–77.
Candler, J. (1991) 'Woman car buyer do not call her a niche anymore', *Advertising Age*, January 21: S8.
Carroll, J., Green, E. and Schaffer, M. (1986) 'Interpoint distance comparisons in correspondence analysis', *Journal of Marketing Research*, 23, August: 271–90.
Caselton, W. F. and Luo, W. (1992) 'Decision making with imprecise probabilities: Dempster-Shafer theory and applications', *Water Resources Research*, 28(12): 3071–83.
Cattin, P. and Wittink, D. R. (1982) 'Commercial use of conjoint analysis: a survey', *Journal of Marketing*, Summer: 44-53.

Chance (1991) in D. J. Hand et al. (1994) *A Handbook of Small Data Sets*. London: Chapman and Hall.

Childers, T. L., Houston, M. J. and Heckler, S. (1985) 'Measurement of individual differences in visual versus verbal information processing', *Journal of Consumer Research,* 12: 125–34.

Chonko, L. B., Howell, R. D. and Bellenger, D. (1986) 'Congruence in sales force evaluations: relation to sales force perception of conflict and ambiguity', *Journal of Personal Selling and Sales Management,* 6: 35–48.

Christensen, R. (1997) *Log-Linear Models and Logistic Regression* (Second edition). New York: Springer.

Clogg, C. C. and Shihadeh, E. S. (1994) *Statistical Models for Ordinal Variables (Advanced Quantitative Techniques in the Social Sciences).* London: Sage Publications, Inc.

Coates, D., Doherty, N. and French, A. (1994) 'The new multivariate jungle', in G. J. Hooley and M. K. Hussey (eds), *Quantitative Methods in Marketing*. New York: Academic Press.

Cohen, A. (1980) 'On the graphical display of the significant components in a two-way contingency table', *Communications in Statistics – Theory and Methods,* A9: 1025-41.

Collett, D. (1991) *Modelling Binary Data*. London: Chapman and Hall.

Collett, D. (2003) *Modelling Binary Data* (Second edition). London: Chapman and Hall.

Cortes-Rello, E. and Golshani, F. (1990) 'Uncertain reasoning using the Dempster-Shafer method: an application in forecasting and marketing management', *Expert Systems,* 7(1): 9–17.

Cottrell, M., Girard, B. and Rousset, P. (1998) 'Forecasting of curves using a Kohonen classification', *Journal of Forecasting,* 17: 429–39.

Cox, D. R. and Snell, E. J. (1989) *Analysis of Binary Data* (Second edition). London: Chapman and Hall.

Cox, D. R. and Wermuth, N. (1992) 'A comment on the coefficient of determination for binary responses', *The American Statistician,* 46: 1.

Crawley, M. J. (2005) *Statistics: An Introduction Using R*. Chichester: Wiley.

Curry, B. and Moutinho, L. (1991) 'Expert systems and marketing strategy: an application to site location decisions', *Journal of Marketing Channels,* 1(1): 23–7.

Dalgaard, P. (2002) *Introductory Statistics with R*. New York: Springer.

De Jong, K. A. (1975) 'An analysis of the behaviour of a class of genetic adaptive systems. PhD dissertation', *Dissertation Abstracts International,* 36.

Dempster, A. P. (1967) 'Upper and lower probabilities induced by a multi-valued mapping', *Annals of Mathematical Statistics,* 38: 325–39.

Dempster, A. P. (1968) 'A Generalization of Bayesian Inference (with discussion)', *Journal of the Royal Statistical Society Series B,* 30(2): 205–47.

Denoeux, T. (1995) 'A k-nearest neighbour classification rule based on Dempster-Shafer theory', *IEEE Transactions on Systems, Man and Cybernetics,* 25(5): 804–13.

DeSarbo, W. S. (1993) 'A lesson in customer response modelling', *Marketing News,* 27(12): H24–H25.

Diamantopoulos, A. and Schlegelmilch, B. B. (1997) *Taking the Fear out of Data Analysis*. London: Dryden Press.

Diem, W. R. (1994) 'Bond stronger with age', *Advertising Age*, 65: 5–6.

Dillon, W. R. and Mulani, N. (1989) 'LADI: a latent discriminant model for analyzing marketing research data', *Journal of Marketing,* 26, February: 15–29.

Dimitras, A. I., Slowinski, R., Susmaga, R. and Zopounidis, C. (1999) 'Business failure prediction using rough sets', *European Journal of Operational Research,* 11(4): 263–80.

REFERENCES

Dobson, A. (2002) *An Introduction to Generalized Linear Models* (Second edition). London: Chapman and Hall/CRC.
Draper, N. and Smith, H. (1981) *Applied Regression Analysis*, (Second edition). New York: John Wiley and Sons.
Draper, N. R. and Smith, H. (1998) *Applied Regression Analysis* (Third edition). Chichester: Wiley.
Everitt, B. S. (1993) *Cluster Analysis*. London: Edward Arnold.
Everitt, B. S. and Hothorn, T. (2006) *A Handbook of Statistical Analyses Using R*. London: Chapman and Hall/CRC.
Fahrmeir, L. and Tutz, G. (2001) *Multivariate Statistical Modelling Based on Generalized Linear Models* (second edition). New York: Springer.
Faraway, J. J. (2005) *Linear Models with R*. London: Chapman and Hall/CRC.
Faraway, J. J. (2006) *Extending the Linear Model with R*. London: Chapman and Hall/CRC.
Fayyad, U. (1998) 'Editorial', *Data Mining and Knowledge Discovery*, 2, 5–7.
Fayyad, U. M., Piatetsky-Shapiro, G. and Smyth, P. (1996) 'From data mining to knowledge discovery: An overview', in U. Fayyad, G. Piatetsky-Shapiro, P. Smyth and R. Uthurusamy, *Advances in Knowledge Discovery and Data Mining*, 1–34. Cambridge, MA: AAAI Press/MIT Press.
Ford, N. M., Walker, O. C. Jr. and Churchill, G. A. Jr. (1975) 'Expectation-specific measures of the inter-sender conflict and role ambiguity experienced by industrial salesmen', *Journal of Business Research*, 3: 95–112.
Fox, J. (2002) *An R and S-Plus Companion to Applied Regression*. London: Sage Publications.
Fox, J. (2005) 'The R Commander: a basic statistics graphical user interface to R', *Journal of Statistical Software*, 14(9).
Franses, P. H. and Paap, R. (2001) *Quantitative Models in Marketing Research*. Cambridge: Cambridge University Press.
Friendly, M. (1992) 'Graphical methods for categorical data', *SAS User Group International Conference Proceedings*, 17: 190–200.
Garver, M. (2002) 'Try new data-mining techniques: they can overcome and augment traditional stat analysis', *Marketing News*, September 16: 31–3.
Gill, J. (2001) *Generalized Linear Models: A Unified Approach*. London: Sage Publications.
Glover, F. (1991) *Multilevel Tabu Search and Embedded Search Neighborhoods for the Travelling Salesman Problem*. Boulder, CO: Graduate School of Business, University of Colorado at Boulder.
Glover, F., Taillard, E. and de Werra, D. (1993) 'A user's guide to tabu search', *Annals of Operations Research*, 41: 3–28.
Goldberg, D. E. (1989) *Genetic Algorithms in Search, Optimization and Machine Learning*. London: Addison-Wesley.
Grätzer, G. (2000) *Math into LaTeX* (third edition). Boston, MA: Birkhäuser.
Greenacre, M. J. (1984) *Theory and Applications of Correspondence Analysis*. New York: Academic Press.
Greene, J. and D'Oliveira, M. (2005) *Learning to Use Statistical Tests in Psychology* (third edition). Milton Keynes: Open University Press.
Hajek, P. (1994) 'Systems of conditional beliefs in Dempster-Shafer theory and expert systems', *Int. J. General Systems*, 22: 113–24.
Hand, D. J., Daly, F., Lunn, A. D., McConway, K. J. and Ostrowski, E. (1994) *A Handbook of Small Data Sets*. London: Chapman and Hall.
Hardy, J. P. (1993) *Regression with Dummy Variables*. London: Sage.

Hoffmann, J. P. (2004) *Generlized Linear Models: An Applied Approach.* Harlow: Pearson Education.
Hoffman, L. and Franke, R. (1986) 'Corresondence analysis: graphical representation of categorical data in marketing research', *Marketing Research,* 23, August: 213–27.
Holland, J. H. (1975) *Adaption in Natural and Artificial Systems.* Ann Arbor, MI: University of Michigan Press.
Howick, R. S. and Pidd, M. (1990) 'Sales force deployment models', *European Journal of Operational Research*, 48(3): 295–310.
Hurley, S. and Moutinho, L. (1996) 'Approximate algorithms in marketing management', *Journal of Consumer Services and Retailing,* 3(3): 145–54.
Hutcheson, G. D. and Sofroniou, N. (1999) *The Multivariate Social Scientist: Introductory Statistics using Generalized Linear Models.* London: Sage Publications.
Ip, H. H. S. and Ng, J. M. C. (1994) 'Human face recognition using Dempster-Shafer theory', *ICIP. 1st International Conference on Image Processing,* 2: 292–5.
Kanji, G. K. (1999) *100 Statistical Tests.* London: Sage Publications.
Kattan, M. W. and Cooper, R. B. (1998) The predictive accuracy of computer-based classification decision techniques, a review and research directions', *OMEGA,* 26(4): 467–82.
Kellert, S. H. (1993) *In the Wake of Chaos: Unpredictable Order in Dynamical Systems.* Chicago, IL: University of Chicago Press.
Klir, J. G. and Yuan, B. (1995) *Fuzzy Sets and Fuzzy Logic: Theory and Application.* Englewood Cliffs, NJ: Prentice-Hall.
Knuth, D. E. (1984) *The T_EX Book.* New York: Addison-Wesley and the American Mathematical Society.
Koczkodaj, W. W., Orlowski, M. and Marek, V. W. (1998) 'Myths about rough set theory', *Communications of the ACM,* 41(11): 102–3.
Kohonen, T. (1995) *Self Organisation and Associative Memory* (second edition). New York: Springer.
Kopka, H. and Daly, P. W. (2003) *Guide to LAT_EX* (Fourth edition). New York: Addison-Wesley.
Kosko, B. (1986) 'Fuzzy entropy and conditioning', *Information Science,* 30: 165–74.
Koteswara, R. K. (1970) 'Testing for the independence of regression disturbances', *Econometrica,* 38: 97–117.
Kotler, P. and Schultz, R. L. (1970) 'Marketing simulations: review and prospects', *Journal of Marketing,* July: 237–95.
Lamport, L. (1994) *LAT_EX: A Document Preparation System* (Second edition). New York: Addison-Wesley.
Leavitt, C. (1970) 'A multi-dimensional set of rating scales for television commercials', *Journal of Applied Psychology,* 54: 427–9.
Lilien, G. L., Kotler, P. and Moorthy, K. S. (1992) *Marketing Models.* Englewood Cliffs, NJ: Prentice-Hall.
Lindsey, J. K. (1995) *Introductory Statistics: A Modelling Approach.* Oxford: Oxford University Press.
Lindsey, J. K. (1997) *Applying Generalized Linear Models.* New York: Springer-Verlag.
Lingras, P. J. and Yao, Y. Y. (1998) 'Data mining using extensions of the rough set model', *Journal of the American Society for Information Science,* 49(5): 415–22.
Lipkin, B. S. (1999) *LAT_EX for LINUX.* New York: Springer-Verlag.
Loewenthal, K. M. (2001) *An Introduction to Psychological Tests and Scales.* New York: Psychology Press.

Long, S. J. (1983a) 'Confirmatory factor analysis', *Quantitative Applications in the Social Sciences Series. Sage University Paper 33*. London: Sage Publications.
Long, S. J. (1983b) 'Covariance structure models. an introduction to LISREL', *Quantitative Applications in the Social Sciences Series. Sage University Paper 34*. London: Sage Publications.
Lowrance, J. D., Garvey, T. D. and Strat, T. M. (1986) 'A Framework for Evidential-Reasoning Systems', *Proceedings of the 5th National Conference on Artificial Intelligence (AAAI-86), Philadelphia*: 896–901. London: Sage Publications.
McCullagh, P. and Nelder, J. A. (1983) *Generalized Linear Models*. London: Chapman and Hall.
McCullagh, P. and Nelder, J. A. (1989) *Generalized Linear Models* (Second edition). London: Chapman and Hall.
McCulloch, W. and Searle, S. (2001) *Generalized, Linear and Mixed Models*. Chichester: Wiley.
Maindonald, J. and Braun, J. (2003) *Data Analysis and Graphics Using R. An Example-based Approach*. Cambridge Series in Statistical and Probabilistic Mathematics. Cambridge: Cambridge University Press.
Mazanec, J. A. (1995) 'Positioning analysis with self-organising maps: an exploratory study on luxury hotels', *Cornell Hotel and Restaurant Administration Quarterly,* 36: 80–95.
Meidan, A. and Lim, I. (1993) 'The role of bank branch personnel in the sales process: an investigation of internal and external perceptions within the branch', *Proceedings of the 1993 MEG Conference: Emerging Issues in Marketing, Loughborough Business School* 2, July: 660–70.
Menard, S. (1995) *Applied Logistic Regression Analysis. Quantitative Applications in the Social Sciences*, 106. London: Sage Publications.
Meyer, D., Zeileis, A., Hornik, K. (2003) 'Visualizing independence using extended association plots', in Hornik, K., Leisch, F. and Zeileis, A. (eds.) *Proceedings of the 3rd International Workshop on Distributed Statistical Computing*.
Meyer, D., Zeileis, A., Hornik, K. (2006) 'The strucplot framework: visualizing multi-way contingency tables with VCD', in Hornik, K., Leisch, F. and Zeileis, A. (eds.) *Journal of Statistical Software,* 17(3).
Miles, J. and Shevlin, M. (2001) *Applying Regression and Correlation: A Guide for Students and Researchers*. London: Sage Publications.
Mitchell, A. (1983) *The Nine American Lifestyles: Who We Are and Where We're Going*. Basingstoke: Macmillan.
Mittelbach, F., Goossens, M., Braams, J., Carlisle, D. and Rowley, C. (2004) *The LaTeX Companion* (second edition). New York: Addison-Wesley.
Moutinho, L. (2008) 'Quantitative methods in marketing', in M. J. Baker and S. J. Hart (eds) *The Marketing Book*, 6th edition. Oxford: Butterworth–Heinemann, Elsevier.
Moutinho, L. A. and Hutcheson, G. D. (2007) 'Store choice and patronage: a predictive modelling approach', *International Journal of Business Innovation and Research*. 1(3): 233–52.
Moutinho, L. A., Goode, M. H. and Davies, F. (1998) *Quantitative Analysis in Marketing Management*. Chichester: Wiley.
Moutinho, L., Davies, F. and Curry, B. (1996) 'The impact of gender on car buyer satisfaction and loyalty – A neural network analysis', *Journal of Retailing and Consumer Services*, 3(3): 135–44.
Mulier, R. and Cherkassy, V. (1995) 'Self-organisation as an iterative kernel smoothing process', *Neural Computation,* 8: 164–77.

Murrell, P. (2006) *R Graphics*. London: Chapman and Hall/CRC.
Nagelkerk, E. (1991) 'A note on a general definition of the coefficient of determination', *Biomelrika* 78(3): 691–2.
Nelder, J. and Wedderburn, R. W. M. (1972) 'Generalized linear models', *Journal of the Royal Statistical Society, A,* 135: 370–84.
Ohanian, R. (1990) 'Construction and validation of a scale to measure celebrity endorsers' perceived expertise, trustworthiness and attractiveness', *Journal of Advertising,* 19: 39–52.
Oliver, R. L. (1980) 'A cognitive model of the antecedent and consequences of satisfaction decisions', *Journal of Marketing Research* 17 (November): 466–9.
Open University (1984) MDST242 *Statistics in Society, Unit A5: Review* (Second edition). Milton Keynes: The Open University, Figure 2.13.
Parsons, S. (1994) 'Some qualitative approaches to applying the Dempster-Shafer theory', *Information and Decision Technologies,* 19: 321–37.
Pawlak, Z., Grzymala-Busse, J., Slowinski, R. and Ziarko, W. (1995) 'Rough Sets', *Communications of the ACM,* 38(11): 88–95.
Pawlak, Z. (1997) 'Rough set approach to knowledge-based decision support', *European Journal of Operational Research,* 99(1): 48–57.
Penny, N. J. and Broom, D. (1988) 'The Tesco approach to store location', in N. Wrigley (ed.), *Store Choice, Store Location and Market Analysis.* Routledge.
Peterson, R. A. and Wilson, W. R. (1992) 'Measuring customer satisfaction: fact and artifact', *Journal of the Academy of Marketing Science,* 20(1): 61–71.
Powers, D. A. and Xie, Y. (1999) MDST242 *Statistical Methods for Categorical Data Analysis.* New York: Academic Press.
Quinlan, J. (1993) MDST242 *C4.5: Programs for Machine Learning.* San Francisco, CA: Morgan Kaufmann Publishers.
Ramaswany, V. and DeSarbo, W. S. (1990) 'SCULPTURE: a new methodology for deriving and analyzing hierarchical product-market structures from panel data', *Journal of Marketing Research*, 27: 418–27.
Rangaswamy, A., Eliahberg, J. B., Raymond, R. and Wind, J. (1989) 'Developing marketing expert systems: an application to international negotiations', *Journal of Marketing*, 53: 24–39.
Raudenbush, S. W. and Bryk, A. S. (2002) *Hierarchical Linear Models: Applications and Data Analysis Methods (Advanced Quantitative Techniques in the Social Sciences*, Second edition). London: Sage Publications, Inc.
R Development Core Team (2007) *R: A Language and Environment for Statistical Computing.* Vienna, Austria: R Foundation for Statistic Computing http://www.R-project.org.
Ritter, H., Martinetz, T. and Schulten, K. (1992) *Neural Computation and Self-Organising Maps.* New York: Addison-Wesley.
Rose, D. and Sullivan, O. (1993) *Introducing Data Analysis for Social Scientists.* Milton Keynes: Open University Press.
Rosenblatt, F. (1958) 'The perceptron: a probability model for information storage and organisation in the brain', *Psychological Review,* 65(6).
Rumerlhart, D. E., McClelland, J. L., and the PDP Research Group (1986) *Parallel Distributed Processing: Explorations in the Microstructure of Cognition, Volumes 1 and 2.* Cambridge, MA: MIT Press.
Rutherford, A. (2001) *Introducing ANOVA and ANCOVA: a GLM approach.* London: Sage Publications.
Ryan, T. P. (1997) *Modern Regression Methods.* Chichester: John Wiley and Sons.

REFERENCES

Saaty, T. L. (1980) *The Analytic Hierarchy Process: Planning, Priority Setting, Resource Allocation.* New York: McGraw-Hill.
Sarle, W. S. (1995) *Measurement Theory: Frequently Asked Questions. Dissemination of the International Statistical Applications Institute* (Fourth editon). AQ ACG Press.
Schubert, J. (1994) *Cluster-Based Specification Techniques in Dempster-Shafer Theory for an Evidential Intelligence Analysis of Multiple Target Tracks.* Department of Numerical Analysis and Computer Science, Royal Institute of Technology, S-100 44 Stockholm, Sweden.
Scott, S. C., Goldberg, M. S. and Mayo, N. E. (1997) 'Statistical assessment of ordinal outcomes in comparative studies', *Journal of Clinical Epidemiology*, 50(1): 45–55.
Sedgewick, R. (1988) *Algorithms in C.* New York: Addison-Wesley.
Serrano Cimca, C. (1998) 'From financial information to strategic groups: a self-organising neural network approach', *Journal of Forecasting*, 17(5–6): 415–28.
Shafer, G. (1976) *A Mathematical Theory of Evidence.* Princeton: Princeton University Press.
Shafer, G. and Pearl, J. (1990) *Readings in Uncertain Reasoning.* San Francisco, CA: Morgan Kaufmann Publishers Inc.
Siegel, S. and Castellan Jr, N. J. (1988) *Nonparametric Statistics for the Behavioral Sciences* (Second edition). New York: McGraw-Hill.
Simonoff, J. (2003) *Analyzing Categorical Data.* New York: Springer.
Sofroniou, N. and Hutcheson, G. D. (2002) 'Confidence intervals for the predictions of logistic regression in the presence and absence of a variance-covariance matrix', *Understanding Statistics: Statistical Issues in Psychology, Education and the Social Sciences*, 1(1): 3–18.
Srinivasan, N. and Ratchford, B. T. (1991) 'An empirical test of a model of external search for automobiles', *Journal of Consumer Research.*, 18(2): 233–42.
Stacey, R. D. (1993) *Strategic Management and Organisational Dynamics.* London: Pitman Publishing.
Stanton, W. W. and Reese, R. M. (1983) 'Three conjoint segmentation approaches to the evaluation of advertising theme creation', *Journal of Business Research.*, June: 201–16.
Venables, W. N. and Ripley, B. D. (2002) *Modern Applied Statistics with S* (Fourth edition). New York: Springer.
Venables, W. N., Smith, D. M. and the R Development Core Team (2002) *An Introduction to R.* Bristol: Network Theory Ltd.
Verzani, J. (2005) *Using R for Introductory Statistics.* London: Chapman and Hall/CRC.
Vriens, M. (1994) 'Solving marketing problems with conjoint analysis', in G. J. Hooley and M. K. Hussey (eds.) *Quantitative Methods in Marketing.* New York: Academic Press.
Walley, P. (1987) 'Belief-function representations of statistical evidence', *Annals of Statistics*, 10: 741–61.
Wells, W. D., Leavitt, C. and McConville, M. (1971) 'A reaction profile for TV commercials', *Journal of Advertising Research*, 11: 11–17.
White, H. (1989) 'Learning in artificial neural networks: a statistical perspective', *Neural Computation,* 1.
Wilson, P. N. (1992) 'Some Theoretical Aspects of the Dempster-Shafer Theory', PhD Thesis, Oxford Polytechnic.
Yuan, Y. and Shaw, M. J. (1995) 'Induction of fuzzy decision trees', *Fuzzy Sets and Systems*: 125–39.
Zaichkowsky, J. L. (1985) 'Measuring the involvement construct', *Journal of Consumer Research,* 12: 341–52.
Zelterman, D. (2006) *Models for Discrete Data.* Oxford: Oxford University Press.

Ziarko, W. (1993a) 'Variable precision rough set model', *Journal of Computer and System Sciences,* 46: 39–59.
Ziarko, W. (1993b) 'Analysis of uncertain information in the framework of variable precision rough sets', *Foundations of Computing and Decision Sciences,* 18: 381–96.
Ziarko, W. (1993c) 'A variable precision rough set model', *Journal of Computer and System Sciences,* 46: 39–59.
Zimmerman, H. J. (1991) *Fuzzy Set Theory and its Applications* (Second edition). Amsterdam: Kluwer Academic.
Zoltners, A. A. and Sinha, P. (1983) 'Sales territory alignment: a review and model', *Management Science*, 29(11): 1237–56.

Index

adaptation 162-3
adjusted R^2 statistic 29, 70–1
advertising method 85–6, 100–6
age factor 168–70, 171, 172, 174
algorithms 221–2
   approximate 177–90
   back propagation 157, 158–64, 167–8
   genetic 177–81
analytic hierarchy process 214, 215
annealing schedule 185, 190
ANOVA 36, 47, 55, 149, 150
approximate reasoning 208
approximate reducts 212
artificial intelligence (AI) 154, 206, 209, 213, 214, 219
aspiration criteria 182–3
association plot 141
attitudes 1, 9, 192
attributes 1, 2, 15, 200, 209, 211–13, 222
automatic interaction detection 191–2

backpropagation algorithm 157–64, 167–8
basic probability assignment 215–16
Bayesian decision theory 213–14
beliefs 1, 9, 214–15
binary comparisons 84, 86, 122
binary data 57–8, 61
binary tree 183, 184
binomial distribution 19
boxplots 93–4, 112–13, 115, 123, 125, 131
brain 153–4, 156
brands 191, 192, 200, 209

C5 algorithm 192–8
CARTs 195
case-based reasoning 217–18
categorical explanatory variables 35–6, 76–82, 100–6
categorized continual data 3–5
category identifier 133, 138, 140, 146
central tendency 6, 12
chaos theory 215–16

chromosome representation 178, 180
classification trees 192–3, 198, 206
cluster analysis 155, 157, 164–5, 167–8
clustered bar chart 131
cognitive theory 153–68
COMAX 208
computing technology 154–5, 208, 221–2
concepts 205, 211
conditionality 211–12, 213
confidence 171, 172, 173, 174, 175
confidence intervals 193
   continuous data 22–3, 30–1, 38–9, 43–4, 50
   dichotomous data 64–6, 72
   ordered data 89, 95–6, 102–4, 109–10, 115–17
   unordered data 126, 133–4, 141–2, 148
conjoint analysis 199–200
connectionism 153, 154
conscience mechanism 166–7
consumers 199, 203, 218, 219
   see also customers
consumption 19–35, 100–4, 191, 192
contiguity 185–6, 188
continuation ratio logits 83
continuous data 1, 2–6, 17–55
continuous distribution 8–11
correspondence analysis 200–1
cross-classification data 200
cross-tabulation 200, 201
cross-validation procedures 198
crossover (genetic algorithms) 178–9
customers 203, 210, 222–3
   female buyers 170, 171, 172, 174–5
   male buyers 170, 171–3, 175
   see also consumers; consumption

data
   measurement scales 1–15
   mental manipulation of 153–68
   recording 3–5, 7–11, 13–14

data *cont.*
    snatchers (invasion of) 218–19
    see also continuous data; dichotomous data; ordered data; unordered data
data compression techniques 167
data mariner 155
data-mining 192, 209, 217–22
decision-making 205, 209–15, 221–2
decision trees 205, 210, 212, 214, 221–2
delta rule 158, 161
Dempster-Shafer Theory (DST) 213–16
dependent groups 47–55, 113–19, 145–52
dependent variables 191–2, 199, 222
descendent nodes 192–3
descriptors 193, 211–12
deviance
    continuous data 23–8, 31–3, 40–1, 44–6, 51–2, 54
    dichotomous data 66–8, 73–5, 80–1
    measure ($-2LL$) 66–8
    ordered data 90–2, 94, 97–9, 101–2, 104–5, 108, 110–11, 115–16, 118
    unordered data 127–8, 134–6, 141–3, 149
deviation coding 36, 38, 76, 77–8
deviation plot 141
dichotomous data 13, 38, 57–82
discretization 210
discriminant analysis 154, 161, 163, 191, 193, 210
discriminant models 192–8
distance matrix 188
dummy codes 37–9, 42–3, 76

Elysée method 210
Enhanced RST 210
entropy 192, 205
equal-distance codes 4, 5
equal sales potential 185–6, 188–9
equal workload 185–6, 188
equity/balance/desires congruence 172–3
equivalence 209, 211, 212
estimation problems 195
Euclidean distance 164, 165, 166
expectations 168–75
experimental designs, simple
    continuous data 36–55
    dichotomous data 82
    ordered data 106–19
    unordered data 137–52
expert systems 154, 206–9, 213, 219
explanatory variables 18
extended association plots 139

F-statistic 27–8, 32–4, 40–1, 45–7, 51–2, 54–5
factor analysis 4, 156, 171, 201–2
false statements 208
feedforward logistic network 163
fitness function/evaluation 178, 180–1
frequency 14, 15, 182, 213
Friedman test 118, 120
functional ability 168–73
FUSINTER discretization technique 210
fuzzy decision trees 205–6
fuzzy logic/expert systems 208–9
fuzzy sets 203–4

Gaussian decay function 166
generalized linear model (GLM) 2
    continuous data 17–19, 55
    dichotomous data 57–62, 82
    ordered data 83, 107, 120–1
    unordered data 121–2, 137
    see also OLS regression
genetic algorithms 177–81
goodness-of-fit statistics
    continuous data 17, 22–9, 31–5, 40, 44–6
    dichotomous data 66–9, 73–5, 80–2
    ordered data 90–3, 97–100
    unordered data 127–30, 134–7
gradient descent 167
greater-than relationship 11–12, 15

hidden layer nodes 156–63, 168, 171–5
hierarchical tree 183–4
hypercubes 219
hypothesis testing 17, 36, 55, 120, 152

identified category 133, 138, 140, 146
ignorance 213, 214, 215
impress others, desire to 168–75
independent variables 191, 199, 222
indicator coding 36, 42–3, 76, 77, 109
individuality 171, 172, 173
inductive reasoning 209
information-discovery tools 219–20
Information Gain Ratio 192
initial population 178
input neurons 153–4, 157
insufficient reason, principle of 214
integer programming 177, 178
intelligent drilling 219–20
interaction term 165
interval data/scale 3, 4, 6
iteration 182, 184, 219

Jonckheere trend test 120

INDEX

kernel methods 164
knowledge 155, 157, 213, 214–15
   discovery (data mining) 209, 217–22
   expert systems 154, 207–9
Kruskal-Wallis test 112, 120

L-trend test 120
latent analysis (LA) 201–3
latent variables 153, 156, 171
learning 165–7
   algorithm 157, 158–64, 168
   machine 154, 155, 209, 218
   process 154–6
   rate 162, 170
   supervised 157, 158, 163, 168
   unsupervised 157, 163, 164, 168
least-squares technique 21
less-than relationship 11–12, 15
likelihood-ratio test 87, 129
line of best-fit 21
linear discriminant analysis 193, 194
linear models 83, 159
linear programming 177
linear regression 176
linguistic scale 203, 204
link function (of GLM) 18–19
links (cognitive theory) 153–68
LISREL 171, 176
log-likelihood statistic 66, 67
log-linear model 121, 203
log odds (logit) 19
logical type discriminant models 192–8
logistic equation 216–17
logistic regression 17, 57, 62–8, 193
   multi-nomial 15, 122–37
   multiple 69–75, 77, 79–82, 95
logit model 121, 122
loyalty 169, 170–1, 173, 174–5
   brand 191, 192, 210
Lyapunov exponent 216–17

machine learning 154, 155, 209, 217–18
management problems 177–90
Mann-Whitney test 120
market maps 163, 167
marketing 177–90, 202–3, 207–8
matched groups/cases 113, 145–6
mathematical operations 5–6, 11–12, 14–15
matrix scatterplot 93, 95
maximum likelihood latent structure analysis (MLLSA) 202
mean deviation 12, 168

mean values 6, 23, 24
measurement scales 1–15
median values 12
membership functions 203–4, 205
mid-category coding 4, 5
MILORD 208
Minimum Description Length criterion 193
mixed-integer programming 177
model bias 222–3
multi-layer Perceptron model 160, 163, 167
multi-nomial logistic regression model 15, 17, 82, 87–8, 94, 101–2, 108, 121–37
multicollinearity 37, 93
multidimensional scaling 198–9, 200
multiple logistic regression 69–75, 77, 79–82, 95
multiple multi-nomial logistic regression 130–7
multiple OLS regression 29–35, 95
multiple proportional odds 93–100, 105
mutation (genetic algorithms) 178–9

neighborhoods 167, 168, 182, 185
nested model 27
net weight change 162
neural networks 153–76, 193, 206, 218, 221–22
neurons 153, 155, 159
NEUROSHELL 168
nodes 153–68, 171–5
non-linear models 156, 159–61, 163–4
non-linear programming 177
non-metric multidimensional scaling 198
non-parametric tests 106–7, 112, 118–19, 167, 194, 210
null model 26–8
numeric system/code 14–15

objective function 189–90
objectivity 209, 214
odds ratio 72–3
OLS regression
   comparisons 36–46, 48–54
   continuous data 6, 17, 19–46, 48–54
   dichotomous data 57–9, 65, 67–8, 70, 76
   multiple 29–35, 95
   ordered data 12, 83, 85, 89, 98–100
   simple 19–29
online analytical processing 219–20
opinions 9
optimization problems 182, 184–5
ordered data 1, 6–12, 36, 83–120
ordinal discriminant analysis 210
output neurons 153–4, 157

P-value
  continuous data 27, 28, 32–5, 41–2, 45–7, 53–5
  dichotomous data 68–9, 75, 80–1
  ordered data 88, 92–4, 98–9, 105–6, 108, 111–12, 115, 118–19
  unordered data 128–30, 136, 143, 149–51
parallel lines test 86, 93
parameter values 158, 161
parametric methods 221–22
pattern matching 153
pattern recognition 154, 158, 209
perceptions (external/internal) 200
Perceptron model 154, 158, 160, 163, 167
pessimistic error criterion 193
pivoting 219–20
polytomous data 13
precision, classification 193, 197–8
predicted probabilities
  dichotomous data 65–6, 73–4, 78–9
  ordered data 89–90, 96–7, 104, 110, 118, 126–7, 133–4, 141–2, 148–9
prediction 19–37, 42, 44, 48, 50, 57, 210
preferences 199, 218
price 168–73, 175
price consciousness 171, 172–3, 174–5
probabilistic rules 210–11
probability 19
  Dempster-Shafer theory 213–16
  of success 58–62
problem solving 207
product-market structures 183–4
profit 180, 186, 189, 218
proportional odds model 12, 15, 17, 83–120
propositional rules 192, 193, 195–6, 198
prototypes 164, 165, 168
pseudo R2 statistic 68–9, 75, 92–3, 99

R statistical package xvii, xviii, 23, 31, 63, 66, 73, 88
R^2 statistic 28–9, 34–5, 68
random component (of GLM) 18–19
ratio data/scale 3, 4, 5, 6
rationality 172, 174, 175
reasoning 209, 213–15, 218–19
recency 182
recursive based partioning model 197
reference category 38
reference vector 164
regression
  analysis 36, 154, 163, 191–2, 220–21

regression cont.
  parameters 107, 109, 115, 116, 125, 132, 139–40, 141
  see also logistic regression; OLS regression
related-groups design 47–55, 113–19, 145–52
repeated measures 113, 145–6
residual sum of squares (RSS) 23–4
response variable 18
revealed preference 183
root mean square (RMS) error 161
root nodes 192, 205
rough set theory (RST) 208–13
rules 193, 210–11, 212, 218

sales coverage units (SCUs) 185–90
sales potential 185–6, 188–9
sampling variance 221–22
satisfaction
  customer 210, 222–3
  neural networks 168, 170–1, 173–5
scaling/scales 1–15, 198–9, 200
scanner panel purchase data 183–4
scatterplots 20–1, 57–8, 63–4, 70, 93, 95
schemata theorem 178
SCULPTURE 184
search space 182, 183, 184
segmentation, tabu search and 183–4
selection (genetic algorithms) 178
self-image 168, 169, 170–5
self-organizing map (SOM) 156, 162–8
siftware/sifting 218–19
Sigmoid function 159–60, 161, 162, 163
significance level 28, 34, 127–30, 134–5, 149–52
simple logistic regression 62–9
simple multi-nomial logistic regression 128–30
simple OLS regression 19–29
simple proportional odds 85–93
simulated annealing (SA) 184–90, 193
simulation 206
site location analysis 179–80, 181
social confidence 172, 174
spatial interaction model 180
Spotlight 218–19
spread 6, 12
squared residuals 23–5
standard deviation 6, 12, 168
standard error 27, 28
statistics
  data mining and 218, 221, 222–3
  methods 192, 203–4, 213
  modeling see modeling
status/status-seeking 172, 174

INDEX

stereotypes 1, 9
stochastic choice model 184
straight-line regression model 21
strategic groups/grouping 168
structural equation models 153, 156
'sub-symbolic' computation 157
subjectivity 209, 214
sum-of-square deviations 192
sum contrasts/comparison 76, 81
supervised training/learning 157, 158, 163, 168
synapses 153
systematic component (of GLM) 18–19

t-statistic
   continuous data 27–8, 34–5, 41–2, 46–7, 52–5
   ordered data 90, 92–3, 97–9, 105–6, 110–12, 116–17, 119
t-test 46–7, 54–5
tabu search 182–4
terminal nodes 183–4, 192, 193
territory design 185–6, 187, 188–90
threshold effect 159–60, 161
time-series analysis 219–20
topology 164, 166, 168
training 157–65, 168

treatment coding method 133
treatment contrasts 38, 43, 76, 109
truth/true statements 208

uncertainty 205, 209–10, 213–16
'universal approximation' 163
unordered data 1, 8, 11, 13–15, 36, 121–52
unrelated groups design 36–47, 107–13, 137–45
unsupervised training/learning 157, 163, 164, 168

variable precision rough sets 210–13

Wald statistics 110, 127–30, 134, 136, 142–4, 149–51
weight adjustment process 166
Wilcoxon test 120
winning node 165–6
workload 185–6, 188

z-statistics
   dichotomous data 66–9, 75, 80–1
   ordered data 110
   unordered data 129–30, 134, 136, 142–4, 149–51